RESEARCH RESULTS

The Descriptive Expressions of Zane Grey

Western Adventure Writer

by

Robert C. Brenner

Print Edition

ISBN 978-1-930199-69-9

Warning

DON'T PLAGIARIZE!

We worked hard to capture the expressions shown in this book to provide useful information from the works of Zane Grey. Our collection of descriptive expressions grows monthly and each of the authors in this series deserves your respect and acknowledgement for their efforts. Don't insult them or our industry by copying their prose. Enjoy what they've written, learn their writing style, but create your own descriptive expressions. Several authors have stolen some of this author's expressions. They were prosecuted and lost, and they are less for it because of their dishonesty. But we are all affected by the poor decisions of these plagiarizers.

We studied successful writers in detail to understand why their works are so good and have lasted through the years. We provide our research results here, not so you can copy them, but so you could understand why these authors are the best in the business and you can adopt their winning formulas. Respect this book. Respect them. Don't plagiarize. Thanks for reading.

INTRODUCTION

How to Use This Book

The best way to use the content of this book is to read the expressions to stimulate your own mind. Then conceive descriptions to make your own writing or speaking create colorful mental images for your readers and listeners.

Profile of Zane Grey

Zane Grey is an American writer of western adventures. He was one of the ten most descriptive authors in our research, He wrote three books that I studied in detail—*Riders of the Purple Sage, West of the Pecos,* and *Sunset Pass*. In *Riders of the Purple Sage,* I found 728 descriptive expressions. *West of the Pecos* has 262 expressions, and *Sunset Pass* was found to contain 197 expressions. (Any book containing over 180 descriptions exceeds the average for all books in print.)

Zane Grey was born in Zanesville, Ohio on January 31, 1872. He died October 23, 1939 in Altadena, California at age 67. He graduated from the University of Pennsylvania and worked with his dad as a dentist until his desire to write took over his interest. He was intrigued by history and loved the West. Grey became a prolific writer of western fiction. His personal life was complicated and, although he remained married to his wife, Dolly, all his life, he was not faithful to one woman. He and Dolly had three children including Romer, Betty and Loren. Grey suffered with bouts of anger, depression and mood swings all his life.

He studied the style and structure of Owen Wister's work and developed his own way of creating vivid descriptions. This became the strongest aspect of his writing. When he traveled, he took a camera, a pen and a notebook so he could take photos and write copious descriptions of the scenery, activities and dialogue. His efforts were highly successful. Through his style of research and writing, Zane Grey made action convincing and colorful.

He wrote to live and lived to write. In this research results document, I focus on three of his novels. In 1910 he wrote *The Heritage of the Desert* in four months. It had breakthrough success. Grey typically completed at least one book every year. His best known book, *Riders of the Purple Sage* (1912) became his most successful Western novel. It tells the story of a gunslinger, who saves a Utah woman from an arranged marriage in a Mormon community. In 1916, he sold movie rights to this book for $2,500.

His books sold well and he was a major force in shaping the myths of the Old West. He became one of the first millionaire authors and John Ford successfully used the settings in Grey's novels to film western scenes, especially those in Arizona and Utah.

Zane Grey was successful because he had a unique style of writing. I choose not to analyze the individual, only his descriptive writing. And in that, he excelled.

Zane Grey wrote 85 adventure books. His most popular and successful book was *Riders of the Purple Sage*, written in 1912. This book had a retail price of $1.30. Reprints of this book today retail for $10 to $26 (hardback is advertised at $17.60 each). At the 10% typical royalty rate back then, he earned 13 cents on each copy sold. Over 1 million hardback copies were sold providing Grey with $130,000 royalty for just this one book—173.3 times the 1912 average annual wage in the U.S. of $750.

Including paperback copies, *Riders of the Purple Sage* sold over 2 million copies in 20 languages. And when one factors in movie rights, we see why he became a very wealthy author.

Of the 85 books that he wrote, here are some that are considered his best:

The Spirit of the Border (1906)
The Last Trail (1909)
The Heritage of the Desert (1910)
Riders of the Purple Sage (1912)
The Lone Star Ranger (1914)
The Rainbow Trail (1915)
Sunset Pass (1930)
West of the Pecos (1936)
Shadow on the Trail (1946)

In this research report, I captured the descriptive expressions found in three of his books: *Riders of the Purple Sage, Sunset Pass*, and *West of the Pecos*.

Here in *The Descriptive Expressions of Zane Grey* you'll find various ways that he created visual images. Reading entries in this book can clear your own "writer's block" and open your right brain to countless ideas to make your own writing efforts interesting, visual, memorable and highly profitable.

Today, our collecting efforts continue. The following information should stimulate your mind to create even better content. Go for it! Like Zane Grey, make your own writing a descriptive and profitable journey.

PERSON / PEOPLE

Descriptive Words, Phrases and Expressions

FEMALE

IN THIS SECTION

Child (6)

CHILD: "I wonder what goes on in {Little} Fay's mind when she sees part of the truth with the wise eyes of a child an', wantin' to know more, meets with strange falseness from you. Fay has taken your pretendin' to care for me, for the thing it looks like on the face. An' her little, formin' mind asks questions. An' the answers she gets are different from the looks of things. (Source: *RIDERS OF THE PURPLE SAGE* by Zane Grey)

CHILD: "Why are children more sincere than grown-up persons?" "Little Fay there ... she sees things as they appear on the face. An Indian does that. So does a dog, an' an Indian an' a dog are most of the time right in what they see. Mebbe a child is always right." (Source: *RIDERS OF THE PURPLE SAGE* by Zane Grey)

CHILD: As Jane entered the unfenced yard, a child saw her, shrieked with joy, and came tearing toward her with curls flying. This child was a little girl of four called Fay. Her name suited er, for she was an elf, a sprite, a creature so fairy-like and beautiful that she seemed unearthly. (Source: *RIDERS OF THE PURPLE SAGE* by Zane Grey)

CHILD: Fay's long lashes fluttered; her eyes opened. At first they seemed glazed over. They looked dazed by pain. Then they quickened, darkened to shine with intelligence—bewilderment—memory—and sudden, wonderful joy. "Muvver," she whispered. "Oh, little Fay! Little Fay!" cried Jane, lifting, clasping the child to her. (Source: *RIDERS OF THE PURPLE SAGE* by Zane Grey)

CHILD: It was a still drowsy afternoon and the three [of them] were sitting in the shade on the wooded knoll that faced the sage slope. Little Fay's brief spell of unhappy longing for her mother—the childish, mystic gloom—had passed, and now where Fay was, there were prattle and laughter and glee. She had emerged from sorrow to be the incarnation of joy and loveliness. She had grown supernaturally sweet and beautiful. For Jane Withersteen the child was an answer to prayer, a blessing, a possession infinitely more precious than all she had lost. For Lassiter, Jane divined, little Fay had become a religion. (Source: *RIDERS OF THE PURPLE SAGE* by Zane Grey)

CHILD: She was a child of the outdoors, of the garden and ditch and field, and she was dirty and ragged. But rags and dirt did not hide her beauty. The one little, thin, bedraggled garment she wore half covered her fine, slim body. Red as cherries were her cheeks and lips; her eyes were violet blue, and the crown of her childish loveliness was the curling golden hair. (Source: *RIDERS OF THE PURPLE SAGE* by Zane Grey)

Girl (15)

GIRL: "... you sweet, wonderful, wild, blue-eyed girl!" (Source: *RIDERS OF THE PURPLE SAGE* by Zane Grey)

GIRL: "Mille was the belle [of the town] them days. I can see her now, a little girl no bigger'n a bird, an' as pretty. She had the finest eyes, dark blue ... black when she was excited, an' beautiful all the time...an' she had light-brown hair with streaks of gold, an' a mouth that every feller wanted to kiss." (Source: *RIDERS OF THE PURPLE SAGE* by Zane Grey)

GIRL: He lifted her and stood her upright beside him, and supported her as she essayed to walk with halting steps. She was like a stripling of a boy; the bright, small head scarcely reached his shoulder. {She] might resemble a boy, but her outline, her little hands and feet, her hair, her big eyes and tremulous lips, and especially something that Venters felt as a subtle essence rather than what he saw proclaimed her sex. (Source: *RIDERS OF THE PURPLE SAGE* by Zane Grey)

GIRL: He slipped his rifle under her, and, lifting her carefully upon it, he began to retrace his steps. The dog trailed in his shadow. The horse that had stood by, drooping, followed without a call. Venters chose the deepest tufts of grass and clumps of sage on his return. His did not rest. His concern was to avoid jarring the [insured] girl and to hid his trail. Gaining the narrow canyon, he turned and held close to the wall till he reached his hiding place. When he entered the dense thicket of oaks, he was hard put to it to force a way through. But he held his burden almost upright, and by slipping sidewise and bending the saplings he got in. Through sage and grass he hurried to the grove of silver spruces. He laid the girl down, almost fearing to look at her. Although marble pale and cold, she was living. Then he sat down to rest. Whitie [the dog] sniffed at the pale girl and whined and crept to Venter's feet. Ring [the other dog] lapped the water in the runway of the spring. (Source: *RIDERS OF THE PURPLE SAGE* by Zane Grey)

GIRL: Little Fay lay in Jane's arms with wide open eyes—eyes that were still shadowed by pain, but no longer fixed, glazed in terror. The golden curls blew across Jane's lips; the little hands feebly clasped her arms; a ghost of a troubled, trustful smile hovered around the sweet lips. Jane awoke to the spirit of a lioness. (Source: *RIDERS OF THE PURPLE SAGE* by Zane Grey)

GIRL: On this day he had found her simple and frank, as natural as any girl he had ever known. About her there was something sweet. Her voice was low and well-modulated. He could not look into her face, meet her steady, unabashed, yet wistful eyes, and think of her as the woman she had confessed herself. The Masked Rider sat before him, a girl dressed as a man. She had been made to ride at the head of infamous forays and drives. She had been imprisoned for many months of her life in an obscure cabin. At times the most vicious of men had been her companions, and the vilest of women, if they had not been permitted to approach her, had, at least, cast their shadows over her. But—in spite of all this—there thundered at Venters some truth that lifted his voice higher than the clamoring facts of dishonor, some truth that was the very life of her beautiful eyes, and it was innocence. (Source: *RIDERS OF THE PURPLE SAGE* by Zane Grey)

GIRL: Seven months in the open had transformed her physically. She was at home in the saddle or on the wagon seat. The long days under the blazing sun, or facing the whispering wind with its dust and sand, rain and chill, the lonely night watch when the wolves mourned and the coyotes wailed, the hard rides over stony ridges to herd old longhorns all grew to be part of her day. (Source: *WEST OF THE PECOS* by Zane Grey)

GIRL: She had changed. To the dark trousers and blouse she had added moccasins of her own make, but she no longer resembled a boy. No eye could have failed to mark the rounded contours of a woman. The change had been to grace and beauty. A glint of warm gold gleamed from her hair and a tint of red shone in the clear, dark grown of cheeks. The haunting sweetness of her lips and eyes, that earlier had been illusive, a promise, had become a living fact. She fitted harmoniously into that wonderful setting; she was like Surprise Valley—wild and beautiful. (Source: *RIDERS OF THE PURPLE SAGE* by Zane Grey)

GIRL: She made a pathetic figure, drooping there, with her sunny hair contrasting so markedly with her white, wasted cheeks and her hands listlessly clasped and her little bare feet propped in the framework of the rude seat. She was the victim of more than accident of fate—a victim to some deep plot the mystery of which burned him. (Source: *RIDERS OF THE PURPLE SAGE* by Zane Grey)

GIRL: Suddenly Venters found her eyes beautiful as he had never seen or felt beauty. They were as dark blue as the sky at night. Then the flashing changed to a long, thoughtful look in which there was wistful, unconscious searching of his face, a look tht trembled on the verge of hope and trust. (Source: *RIDERS OF THE PURPLE SAGE* by Zane Grey)

GIRL: The girl had dawned upon him like a glorious sunrise. (Source: *SUNSET PASS* by Zane Grey)

GIRL: What a slender girl she was! No wonder he had been able to carry her miles and pack her up that slippery ladder of stone. Her boots were of soft, fine leather, reaching clearly to her knees. He recognized the make as one of a boot maker in Sterling. Her spurs, that he had stupidly neglected to remove, consisted of silver frames and gold chins, and the rowels, large as silver dollars, were fancifully engraved. The boots were rather hard to slip off. She wore heavy woolen rider's stockings, half-length, and these were pulled up over the ends of her short trousers. Venters took off the stockings to note her little feet were red and swollen. He bathed them. Then he removed his scarf and bathed her face and hands. (Source: *RIDERS OF THE PURPLE SAGE* by Zane Grey)

Woman (8)

WOMAN: "Why, most every young fellar—an' some older ones—in this country have been struck by lightnin' when they first seen Thiry." (Source: *SUNSET PASS* by Zane Grey)

WOMAN: ... was a high-strung lass. (Source: *SUNSET PASS* by Zane Grey)

WOMAN: Her profile against the black cliff appeared chiseled out of marble, cold, pure, singularly noble, and as sad as her life had been. (Source: *WEST OF THE PECOS* by Zane Grey)

WOMAN: She was a slim, plain, busy woman, with gray hair, kindly eyes, and a motherly manner. (Source: *SUNSET PASS* by Zane Grey)

WOMAN: she was older, fuller of figure, with dark flushed face and roguish eyes. She was richly and fashionably dressed, and that fact, somehow put surprise and confusion far from Rock. (Source: *SUNSET PASS* by Zane Grey)

WOMAN: She was thoroughbred Western, about twenty-one or two, blond, with fair hair more silver than gold. She was not robust-of-build, yet scarcely slender. She wore a faded little blue bonnet not of the latest style, and her plain white dress, though clean and neat. (Source: *SUNSET PASS* by Zane Grey)

WOMAN: Tenderness and sympathy were fast hiding traces of her agitation. He read her mind—felt the reaction of her noble heart—saw the joy she was beginning to feel at the happiness of others. (Source: *RIDERS OF THE PURPLE SAGE* by Zane Grey)

WOMAN: Then her child disappeared. Lost, was the report. The child was stolen. That wrecked Milly Erne. I can see her now, a rail thing, so transparent you could almost look through her—white like ashes—and her eyes! Her eyes have always haunted Venters. She had one real friend—Jane. But Jane couldn't mend a broken heart, and Milly died. (Source: *RIDERS OF THE PURPLE SAGE* by Zane Grey)

MALE

IN THIS SECTION

Bishop (2)

BISHOP: Jane suddenly suffered a paralyzing, horrifying affront to her consciousness of reverence by some strange, irresistible twist of thought wherein she saw his bishop s a man. The train of thought hurdled the rising, crying protests of that other self whose poise she had lost. It was not her bishop who eyed her in curious measurement. It was a man who tramped into her presence without removing his hat, who had no greeting or her, who had no semblance of courtesy. In looks and action he made her think of a bull stamping, cross-grained, into a corral. (Source: *RIDERS OF THE PURPLE SAGE* by Zane Grey)

BISHOP: The bishop was rather tall, of stout build, with iron-gray hair and beard, and eyes of light blue. (Source: *RIDERS OF THE PURPLE SAGE* by Zane Grey)

Boy (2)

BOY: He saw a slender, well-formed youth wearing a ragged gray coat and overalls and top boots, all of which were covered with dirt and grass. His battered black sombrero was pulled well down, shading big, deep eyes of a hue Pecos could not discern, and a tanned, clean-cut face. The sombrero, however, showed a raft of glossy hair through a hole in its crown, and also straggling locks from under the brim on this fine-looking youth.. (Source: *WEST OF THE PECOS* by Zane Grey)

BOY: The boy in his excitement pulled off the old sombrero to crumple it in his hands. He was surprisingly young and his clean, tanned cheeks bore not a vestige of downy beard. Indeed, he looked like a very pretty girl, notwithstanding the strong chin, the sad, almost stern lips. His eyes were large an a very dark blue, almost purple. (Source: *WEST OF THE PECOS* by Zane Grey)

Cattleman (6)

CATTLEMAN: "[Ash Preston] is the oldest son of Gage Preston, a new cattleman to these parts since you rode here. An' Ash is as bad a hombre as ever forked a hoss." (Source: *SUNSET PASS* by Zane Grey)

CATTLEMAN: He was not a great deal changed from the Westerner he had once worked for. The man was a well-preserved man of fifty, scarcely gray, with the lean face, strong chin, thin lips, and yellow-flecked hazel eyes. (Source: *SUNSET PASS* by Zane Grey)

CATTLEMAN: He was probably a man who had never been a cowboy, for he did not show the physical characteristics of the range. He was lean, sallow, hard, with sharp eyes close together and deep under bushy eyebrows. (Source: *SUNSET PASS* by Zane Grey)

CATTLEMAN: Pecos Smith's age must have been between twenty and twenty-five years, which was not very young for a range rider in Texas. He was just above medium height, not so lean and rangy as most horsemen, having wide shoulders and muscular round limbs. All the leather trappings about Smith and his horse were ragged and shiny from use, particularly the gun holster which hung low on his left thigh and the saddle sheath. The ivory handle of his gun was yellow with age. What metal showed, shone with the bright, almost white luster of worn, polished steel. His saddle, bridle, and spurs, also his black sombrero, were of Spanish make, decorated with silver. (Source: *WEST OF THE PECOS* by Zane Grey)

CATTLEMAN: Smith was not an unusual type for a Texan, though he appeared to have Texas characteristics magnified. Many Texans were sandy-haired or tow-headed, and possessed either blue or gray-eyes. This rider had flaxen hair and he wore it so long that it curled from under his sombrero. His face was like a bronze mask, except when he talked or smiled, and then it lightened. In profile it was sharply cut, cold as stone, singularly more handsome than the full face. His eyes assumed dominance over all other features, being a strange-flecked, pale gray, of exceeding power of penetration. His lips, in repose, were sternly chiseled, almost bitter, but as they were mostly open in gay, careless talk or flashing a smile over white teeth, tis last feature was seldom noticed. (Source: *WEST OF THE PECOS* by Zane Grey)

CATTLEMAN: Truman Rock slowly stepped down from the stage-coach with his grip in hand, with an eager and curious expression upon his lean dark face. He wore a lain check suit, rather wrinkled, and a big gray sombrero that had seen service. His step, his lithe shape, proclaimed him to be a rider. A sharp eye might have detected the bulge of a gun worn under his coat, high over his left hip and far back. (Source: *SUNSET PASS* by Zane Grey)

Father

FATHER: "Father was a silent, broken man, killed already on his feet. He had no mind left." (Source: *RIDERS OF THE PURPLE SAGE* by Zane Grey)

Man (28)

MAN: [His} men appeared under the cottonwoods and led a young man out into the line. His ragged clothes were those of an outcast, but he stood tall and straight, his wide shoulders flung back, with the muscles of his bound arms rippling and a blue flame of defiance in the gaze he bent on Tull. (Source: *RIDERS OF THE PURPLE SAGE* by Zane Grey)

MAN: A Mexican man made pretense of work, but the side slant of his beady black eyes told Pecos what he was interested in—behind a counter stood a man in his shirt sleeves. (Source: *WEST OF THE PECOS* by Zane Grey)

MAN: A tall, lithe, belted and booted man stalked out, leisurely, his eagle-like head bare, his yellow hair waving in the wind. (Source: *WEST OF THE PECOS* by Zane Grey)

MAN: Behind a counter stood a man in his shirt sleeves. He was fat and pale, and his dark thin hair fell over his brow, almost to his large, ghoulish eyes. He had a long, sharp nose, a small mouth, and a peaked chin with a dimple in the middle. (Source: *WEST OF THE PECOS* by Zane Grey)

MAN: Blind eyes could have seen what the ragged and half-starved man counted for in the sum of her happiness, yet he looked the gloomy outcast his allegiance had made him. (Source: *RIDERS OF THE PURPLE SAGE* by Zane Grey)

MAN: Every cowhand in the outfit had his sombrero full of bullet homes, proofs of his marksmanship. Pecos was most obliging and he could not resist any kind of a bet. He seldom missed a sombrero tossed into the air, and as often as not he put two bullets through it before it dropped. He would never let anyone handle his gun, which shared with [his horse] Cinco in his affections. Pecos proved to be a round peg fitting snugly into a round hole. (Source: *WEST OF THE PECOS* by Zane Grey)

MAN: He had the look of a man who expected to see someone he knew. There was an easy, careless, yet guarded air about him. (Source: *SUNSET PASS* by Zane Grey)

MAN: He had the lunge, the standing hair, the savageness of a wild animal. (Source: *WEST OF THE PECOS* by Zane Grey)

MAN: He was a bronzed cowman, with bright bold eyes that roved everywhere. (Source: *SUNSET PASS* by Zane Grey)

MAN: He was a craggy faced young rider, dissolute and forceful. (Source: *WEST OF THE PECOS* by Zane Grey)

MAN: He was a heavy, florid Westerner, with clear eyes, breezy manner, smooth of face, and without a gray hair. (Source: *SUNSET PASS* by Zane Grey)

MAN: He was a man of massive build, in the plain garb of an everyday cattleman. He might have been fifty years old and handsome in a bold way. He had a smooth hard face, bulging chin, well-formed large lips, just now stained by tobacco, and great deep gray eyes. (Source: *SUNSET PASS* by Zane Grey)

MAN: He was not an unusual type for a Texan, although he appeared to have Texas characteristics magnified. Many Texans were sandy-haired or tow-headed, and possessed either blue or gray eyes. This rider had flaxen air and he wore it so long that it curled from under his sombrero. His face was like a bronze mask, except when he talked or smiled, and then it lightened. In profile it was sharply but, cold as stone, singularly more handsome hat the full face. His eyes assumed dominance over all other features, being strange-flecked, pale gray, of exceeding power of penetration. His lips, in repose, were sternly chiseled, almost bitter, but as they were mostly open in gay, careless talk or flashing a smile over white teeth, this last feature was seldom noticed. (Source: *WEST OF THE PECOS* by Zane Grey)

MAN: He was thin, hard, burnt, bearded, with the dust and sage thick on him, with his leather wrist bands shining from use, and his boots worn through on the stirrup side, he looked the rider of riders. He wore two guns and carried a Winchester.. (Source: *RIDERS OF THE PURPLE SAGE* by Zane Grey)

MAN: He was what riders in this country call a gunman. He's a man with marvelous quickness and accuracy in the use of a Colt.. (Source: *RIDERS OF THE PURPLE SAGE* by Zane Grey)

MAN: His great, brown hands were skilled in a multiplicity of ways that a woman might have envied. He shared Janes' work.

Lassiter towered above her, and behind or through his black, sinister figure shone something luminous that strangely affected Jane. Good and evil began to seem incomprehensibly blended in her judgement. It was her belief that evil could not come forth from good, yet here was a murderer who dwarfed in gentleness, patience, and love any man she had ever known. (Source: *RIDERS OF THE PURPLE SAGE* by Zane Grey)

MAN: Lassiter released Jane, and like a dizzy man swayed from her, and appeared to be writhing in a kind of convulsion with hoarse, unintelligible, strangled cries. They ceased, and he leaned, shaking against a table where he kept his rider's accoutrements and began fumbling in his saddlebags. His action brought a clinking, metallic sound—the rattling of gun cartridges. His fingers trembled as he slipped cartridges into an extra belt, ut as he buckled it over the one he habitually wore, his hands became steady. This second belt contained two guns, smaller than the black ones swinging low, and he slipped them around so his coat hid them. (Source: *RIDERS OF THE PURPLE SAGE* by Zane Grey)

MAN: Lassiter's father had been dead a year. Frank Erne still lived in the house where Milly had left him. His farm had gone to week, his cattle had strayed or been rustled, his house weathered till it wouldn't keep out rain or wind. An' Frank set on the porch an' whittled sticks, an' day by day wasted away. There was times when he ranted about like a crazy man, but mostly he was always sittin' an' starin' with eyes that made a man curse. I figured Frank had a secret fear that I needed to know. An' when I told him I'd trailed Milly for near three years, an' had got trace of her, an' saw where she'd had a baby, I thought he'd drop dead at my feet. An' when he come 'round more natural-like, he begged me to give up the trail. But he wouldn't explain. So I let him alone, an' watched him day an' night.. (Source: *RIDERS OF THE PURPLE SAGE* by Zane Grey)

MAN: Like rough iron his hard hand crushed Jane's. In it she felt the difference she saw in him. Wild, rugged, unshorn, yet ow splendid—he had gone away a boy—he had returned a man. He appeared taller, wider of shoulder, deeper-chested, more powerfully built. His eyes [were] keener, [and] more flashing. [They] met hers with clear, frank, warm regard in which perplexity was not, nor discontent, nor pain. (Source: *RIDERS OF THE PURPLE SAGE* by Zane Grey)

MAN: Lincoln was a little gray withered cattleman, bright of eye, lean of face, not apparently a day older than Rock had last seen him. He looked like a Texas Ranger, and had been one in his day. (Source: *SUNSET PASS* by Zane Grey)

MAN: On her left sat the black-leather garbed Lassiter, looking like a man in a dream. Hunger was not in him, or composure, or speech, and when he twisted in frequent, unquiet movements, the heavy guns that he had not removed knocked against the table legs. (Source: *RIDERS OF THE PURPLE SAGE* by Zane Grey)

MAN: On his right stalked a short thick individual, ruddy of face and pompous of bearing. (Source: *WEST OF THE PECOS* by Zane Grey)

MAN: Terrill took the Texans to be the rangy, dusty-booted youths, tight-lipped still-faced, gray-eyed young giants, and the older men of loftier stature who surely were the fathers of the boys. (Source: *WEST OF THE PECOS* by Zane Grey)

MAN: The half-breed was dangerous like a snake I the grass was dangerous. (Source: *WEST OF THE PECOS* by Zane Grey)

MAN: The man choked and stammered, and then, as tears welled into his eyes, he found the use of his tongue and cursed. No gentle speech could ever have equaled thE curse in eloquent expression of what he felt for Jane Withersteen. How strangely his look and tone reminded her of Lassiter!. (Source: *RIDERS OF THE PURPLE SAGE* by Zane Grey)

MAN: The Mexican vaquero was a sloe-eyed, swarthy rider no longer young, silent and taciturn, with whom conversation, let alone friendliness was difficult. (Source: *WEST OF THE PECOS* by Zane Grey)

MAN: The Mexicans, the teamsters, the soldiers, the endless hurrying, colorful throng of men, gave Terrill a vague and wonderful impression. These were men of the open, and they had come from everywhere. Buffalo-hunters on their way out to catch the buffalo herds on their spring migration north; horse-dealers and cattlemen in from the ranches; idle, picturesque Mexicans with their serapes, their tight-legged flared-bottom trousers, their high-peaked sombreros; here and there a hard-eyed, watching man whom Lambeth designated as a Texas Ranger; riders on lean, shaggy, wild horses; tall men with guns in their belts; black-coated, black-hatted gamblers, cold-faced and usually handsome; and last, though by far not least, a stream of ragged, broken, often drunken men, long-hired, unshaven, hard and wretched, whose wolfish eyes Terrill did not want to meet. These were the riffraff left of the army, sacrificed to a lost cause. (Source: *WEST OF THE PECOS* by Zane Grey)

MAN: The rider thundered up and almost threw his foam-flecked horse in the sudden stop. He was of giant form, and with fearless eyes. (Source: *RIDERS OF THE PURPLE SAGE* by Zane Grey)

MAN: The white vaquero was a typical Texan who had been reared on the plains. He was tough and uncouth, yet likeable and admirable.. (Source: *WEST OF THE PECOS* by Zane Grey)

Store Owner

STORE OWNER: He looked older, thinner, grayer, and there were deep lines in his face that seemed strange to Rock. Six years was a long time. (Source: *SUNSET PASS* by Zane Grey)

GENDER NOT SPECIFIED

IN THIS SECTION

Children

CHILDREN: Here were sweet-smelling clover, alfalfa, flowers, and vegetables. Like these fresh things were the dozens of babies, tots, toddlers, noisy urchins, laughing girls, a whole multitude of children of one family. For Collier Brandt, the father of all this numerous progeny, was a Mormon with four wives. (Source: *RIDERS OF THE PURPLE SAGE* by Zane Grey)

Rider (2)

RIDER: He dismounted and was partly drunk; that was not the striking thing about him. He looked and breathed the very spirit of the range at its wildest. He was tall, lean and lithe, with a handsome red face, like a devil's eyes, hot as blue flame, and yellow hair that curled scraggily from under a dusty black sombrero. He had just been clean-shaved. Drops of blood and sweat stood out like beads on his lean jowls and curved lips. A gun swung below his hip. (Source: *SUNSET PASS* by Zane Grey)

RIDER: The other rider was a cowboy, young in years, with still gray eyes like Miss Preston's, and [with an] intent, expressionless face, dark from sun and wind. (Source: *SUNSET PASS* by Zane Grey)

PEOPLE IN ACTION

IN THIS SECTION

Bite
Blush
Breathe
Brood
Build (2)
Burn
Buy
Call (3)
Camp (4)
Caress
Carry (5)
Catch
Challenge
Change (5)
Cherish
Chill
Climb (7)
Close
Come
Compliment
Conclude (3)
Confess
Construct (2)
Cool
Cover (2)
Crawl
Creep

Cry (4)
Cut
Dance
Daze
Decide
Depart (4)
Descend (4)
Dim
Disappear
Discover
Divulge
Defy
Depart (3)
Descend
Determined
Disapprove
Drink
Embarrass
Enter (3)
Escape (28)
Examine (2)
Excite
Explore (16)
Faith
Fall (2)
Fear (2)
Fidget (2)

Fight (3)
Fill
Find
Flee
Flick
Flirt
Float
Flush
Free
Gasp (2)
Gaze (5)
Gesture
Give
Glance (2)
Glare
Go (2)
Greet (2)
Handshake
Hang
Happy
Hate
Hear
Help
Hesitate
Hide (4)
Hope
Hug (2)

Humor
Hungry
Hurry
Imagine (2)
Interrupt (2)
Itch
Kill (2)
Kiss (3)
Know
Laugh (5)
Lay (2)
Lead (4)
Lean
Leap
Learn
Lift
Listen (4)
Look (19)
Love (5)
Miss
Moan
Move (14)
Nod
Open
Outline
Pace (2)
Pass

Pause
Penetrate
Perceive
Plan (2)
Point
Proceed
Proud
Push
Perspire
Please
Pursue (31)
Question (3)
Raise (2)
Reach (2)
Realize (2)
Recline (3)
Recognize (3)
Recover (8)
Register
Relieve
Remain
Remember (8)
Reply
Resend
Respect
Restock
Retrace

Return (4)

Ride (11)

Rise

Roll

Rope

Rouse

Rub

Run (2)

Sag

Scan

Seal

Search (7)

Seclude

See (44)

Sense

Shake (4)

Shine

Shame

Shoot (11)

Shootout

Show (5)

Sigh

Sit (3)

Skulk

Sleep (5)

Slip

Smile (8)

Sneak (3)
Snub
Spasm
Speak (48)
Speculate
Stand (2)
Stalk
Stand
Stare (4)
Steady (2)
Steal
Step
Stir
Stop (2)
Strengthen
Stroll
Stubborn
Study (6)
Surmount
Teach
Tease
Tell
Think (27)
Thirsty
Thought
Touch (3)
Track (2)

Trail
Trust
Turn
Twist
Uncertain
Understand
Unfriendly
Uplift
Vanish
Verify
Vibrate
Visit
Vow
Wag
Wait
Walk (24)
Wash
Watch (15)
Wave
Whisper
Whistle
Wipe
Work (2)

Accept

ACTION: ACCEPT: She held out her hand to him—when she gave it—now she stretched it tremblingly forth in acceptance of the decree cruel circumstances had laid upon them. Venters bowed over it – kissed it – pressed it hard—and half stifled a sound very like a sob. Certain it was that, when he raised his head, tears glistened in his eyes. (Source: *RIDERS OF THE PURPLE SAGE* by Zane Grey)

Ache

ACTION: ACHE: He felt only vaguely, as outsider things, the ache and burn and throb of the muscles of his body. (Source: *RIDERS OF THE PURPLE SAGE* by Zane Grey)

Act

ACTION: ACT: Presently Jane began to act her little part, to laugh and play with Fay, to talk of horses and cattle to Lassiter. Then she made deliberate mention of a book in which she kept records of all pertaining to her stock, and she walked slowly toward the table, and when near the door she suddenly whirled and thrust it open. Her sharp action knocked down a woman who had undoubtedly been listening. "Hester," said Jane sternly. "you may go home and you need not come back." (Source: *RIDERS OF THE PURPLE SAGE* by Zane Grey)

Affirm

ACTION: AFFIRM: Venters made a lightening-swift movement. Lassiter smiled, nd then his bronzed eyelids narrowed till his eyes seemed mere gray slits. "You'll kill Tull!" He did not question; he affirmed. (Source: *RIDERS OF THE PURPLE SAGE* by Zane Grey)

Amaze

ACTION: AMAZE: Amazed, he threw up his head so that the ruddy firelight played upon his tanned face. (Source: *WEST OF THE PECOS* by Zane Grey)

Anger

ACTION: ANGER: His massive frame wrestled. Up he sprang, to lift clenched fists, and broke into an ungovernable rage that both astonished and mystified Rock. The rancher's face turned a purple hue; his thick neck bulged almost to bursting. He stamped and cursed and swung his arms, as a man of strength and will baffled and defeated. (Source: *SUNSET PASS* by Zane Grey)

Announce

ACTION: ANNOUNCE: Pecos yelled, "Pole out. The mawnin's broke. We gotta hang today on a peg an' all the days that come after...ridin' the brakes, boy!" (Source: *WEST OF THE PECOS* by Zane Grey)

Annoy

ACTION: ANNOY: "My hands ... are dirty ... my face feels ... so hot and sticky ... my boots hurt." It was her longest speech as yet, and it trailed off in a whisper. It annoyed him that he had never thought of these things. But then awaiting her death and thinking of her comfort were vastly different matters. (Source: *RIDERS OF THE PURPLE SAGE* by Zane Grey)

Answer (3)

ACTION: ANSWER: "My red herd's gone! My horses gone! The white herd will go next. I can stand that. But if I lost Black Star and Night, it would be like parting with my own flesh and blood. Am I in danger of losing my racers?" "A rustler ... or ... or anybody stealin' hosses of yours would most of all want the blacks." Said Lassiter. His evasive rely was affirmation enough. The other rider nodded gloomy acquiescence. (Source: *RIDERS OF THE PURPLE SAGE* by Zane Grey)

ACTION: ANSWER: "When I speak of your purpose, your hate, your guns, I don't believe you've changed." For answer, he unbuckled the heavy cartridge belt, and laid it with the heavy, swinging gun sheaths in her lap. (Source: *RIDERS OF THE PURPLE SAGE* by Zane Grey)

ACTION: ANSWER: Lassiter's answer [to the child's question] was a modest and sincere affirmation. (Source: *RIDERS OF THE PURPLE SAGE* by Zane Grey)

Appear (4)

ACTION: APPEAR: "Well now, I'm glad to hear some of your old self in your vice. Fer when you come up, you looked like the corpse of a dead rider with fire fer eyes." (Source: *RIDERS OF THE PURPLE SAGE* by Zane Grey)

ACTION: APPEAR: Oldring appeared, and Venters had one glimpse of his great breadth and bulk, his gold-buckled belt with hanging guns, his high-top boots with gold spurs. In that moment Venters had a strange, unintelligible curiosity at seeing Oldering alive. The rustler's broad brow, his large black eyes, his sweeping beard, as dark as the wing of a raven, his enormous width of shoulder and depth of chest, his whole splendid presence so wonderfully charged with vitality and force and strength seemed to afford Venters with an unutterable, fiendish joy because fòr that magnificent manhood and life he meant cold and sudden death. (Source: *RIDERS OF THE PURPLE SAGE* by Zane Grey)

ACTION: APPEAR: The appearance of Bishop Dyer startled Jane. He dismounted with his rapid, jerky motion, flung the bridle, and, as he turned toward the inner court, stalked up on the stone flags, his boots rang. In his authoritative front and in the red anger unmistakably flaming in his face he reminded Jane of her father. (Source: *RIDERS OF THE PURPLE SAGE* by Zane Grey)

ACTION: APPEAR: Venters rode on and stopped before Tull's cottage. Women stared at him with white faces, and then flew from the porch. Tull himself appeared at the door, but low, craning his neck. His dark face flashed out of sight; the door banged, a heavy bar dropped with hollow sound. (Source: *RIDERS OF THE PURPLE SAGE* by Zane Grey)

Approach (2)

ACTION: APPROACH: Jane walked down into the outer curt and approached the sorrel. Upstarting, [the horse[laid back his ears, and eyed her. (Source: *RIDERS OF THE PURPLE SAGE* by Zane Grey)

ACTION: APPROACH: The stranger's slow approach might have been a mere leisurely manner of gait or the cramped short steps of a rider unused to walking, yet, as well, it could have been the guarded advance of one who took no chances with men. (Source: *RIDERS OF THE PURPLE SAGE* by Zane Grey)

Approve

ACTION: APPROVE: his gaze approving of her. (Source: *WEST OF THE PECOS* by Zane Grey)

Argue (2)

ACTION: ARGUE: Lassiter's cool argument made Venters waver, not in determination to go, but in hope of success. (Source: *RIDERS OF THE PURPLE SAGE* by Zane Grey)

ACTION: AROUSE: It was the best in her, if the most irritating, that he always aroused. (Source: *RIDERS OF THE PURPLE SAGE* by Zane Grey)

Arrive

ACTION: ARRIVE: At sunset Lambeth rode in, covered with dust and lather. His horse was spent. His hands and face were begrimed. He yelled for water. (Source: *WEST OF THE PECOS* by Zane Grey)

Ask (2)

ACTION: ASK: "Bess, what's wrong with you?" he asked. "Nothing," she answered with averted face. He took hold of her, and gently though masterfully forced her to meet his eye. "You can't look at me and lie," he said. "Now ... what's wrong with you?" (Source: *RIDERS OF THE PURPLE SAGE* by Zane Grey)

ACTION: ASK: Jane took one flashing woman's glance at Bess's scarlet face, at her slender shapely form. "Bern, is this ...?" she questioned in a voice that stung. (Source: *RIDERS OF THE PURPLE SAGE* by Zane Grey)

Assure

ACTION: ASSURE: Little Fay climbed Lassiter's knee. "Does oo love me?" she asked. Lassiter, who was as serious with Fay as he was gentle and loving, assured her in earnest and elaborate speech that he was her devoted subject. (Source: *RIDERS OF THE PURPLE SAGE* by Zane Grey)

Astound

ACTION: ASTOUND: "She was Oldring's Masked Rider!" Venters expected to floor his friend with that statement, but he was not in any way prepared for the shock his words gave. For an instant he was astounded to see Lassiter stunned, then hi own passionate eagerness to unbosom himself, to tell the wonderful story, precluded any other thought. (Source: *RIDERS OF THE PURPLE SAGE* by Zane Grey)

Attract

ACTION: ATTRACT: The West called. Texans impoverished by the war, and the riff-raff left over from the army, were spreading far and wide to the north and west, lured on by something magnetic and compelling. (Source: *WEST OF THE PECOS* by Zane Grey)

Attack

ACTION: ATTACK: he saw the front line of savages spread to left and right. At least six of these, in their thirst for blood charged out of the thicket. Pecos discerned arrows flying like glints of light through the air, some to stick in the carcass of the horse, others in the tree. (Source: *WEST OF THE PECOS* by Zane Grey)

Awaken (9)

ACTION: AWAKEN: A bell awakened him from late slumbers. The sun was up, and as he peeped out over his blanket covering he saw the grass shine gold under the cedars. He had overslept. (Source: *SUNSET PASS* by Zane Grey)

ACTION: AWAKEN: As he laid the girl down in the shallow hollow of the little ridge, with her white face upturned, she opened her eyes. Wide, staring, black, at once like both the night and the stars, they made her face seem still whiter.. (Source: *RIDERS OF THE PURPLE SAGE* by Zane Grey)

ACTION: AWAKEN: He was awakened at dawn by the thump of hoofs. His white horse had come into camp, which was something horses seldom did. (Source: *WEST OF THE PECOS* by Zane Grey)

ACTION: AWAKEN: Sometime in the night she awoke, an unusual thing for her. A noise had disturbed her rest. But the camp was dark and silent. A low rustle of leaves and a tinkle of water could scarcely have been guilty. (Source: *WEST OF THE PECOS* by Zane Grey)

ACTION: AWAKEN: They were stirring long before the red burst of sun glorified the western wall of the canyon. Soon they rode down to the river, in the flush of dawn, and headed up the shore, where they had worn a trail. (Source: *WEST OF THE PECOS* by Zane Grey)

ACTION: AWAKEN: When he awoke, day had dawned and all about him was steel-gray. The air had a cold tang. Arising, he greeted the fawning dogs and stretched his cramped body, and then, gathering together bunches of dead sage sticks, he lighted a fire. Strips of dried beef held to the blaze for a moment served him and the dogs. He drank from a canteen. There was nothing else in his outfit; he had grown used to a scant fare. (Source: *RIDERS OF THE PURPLE SAGE* by Zane Grey)

ACTION: AWAKEN: When his eyes unclosed, day had come again, and he saw the rim of the opposite wall tipped with the gold of sunrise. (Source: *RIDERS OF THE PURPLE SAGE* by Zane Grey)

ACTION: AWAKEN: When the gray dawn came, he rose a gloomy, almost heartbroken man, but victor over evil passions. He could not change the past, and even if he had not loved Bess with all his soul, he had grown into a man who would not change the future he had planned for her. Only, and once for all, he must know the truth, know the worst, stifle all these insistent doubts and subtle hopes and jealous fancies, and kill the past by knowing truly what Bess had been to Oldring. For that matter he knew—he had always known—but he must hear it spoken. Then, when they had safely gotten out of that wild country, to take up a new and an absorbing life, she would forget, she would be happy, and through that, in the years to come, he could not but find life worth living. (Source: *RIDERS OF THE PURPLE SAGE* by Zane Grey)

ACTION: AWAKEN: With the breaking of dawn his eyes opened. The valley lay drenched and bathed, a burnished oval of glittering green. The rain-washed walls glistened in the morning light. Waterfalls of many forms poured over the rims, One, a broad lacy sheet, thin as smoke, slid over the western notch and struck a ledge in its downward fall, to bound into broader leap, to burst far below—into white and gold and rosy mist. (Source: *RIDERS OF THE PURPLE SAGE* by Zane Grey)

Aware (2)

ACTION: AWARE: [She] slipped into utter blackness. When she recovered from faint, she became aware that she was lying on a couch near the window in her sitting room. Her brow felt damp and cold and wet; someone was chafing her hands; she recognized Judkins, and then saw that his lean, hard face wore the hue and look of excessive agitation. (Source: *RIDERS OF THE PURPLE SAGE* by Zane Grey)

ACTION: AWARE: Venters was conscious of an indefinite conflict of change with him. It seemed to be a vague passing of old moods, a dim coalescing of new forces, a moment of inexplicable transition. He was both cast down and uplifted. He wanted to think and think of the meaning, but he resolutely dispelled emotion. His imperative need at present was to find a safe retreat, and this called for action. (Source: *RIDERS OF THE PURPLE SAGE* by Zane Grey)

Bade

ACTION: BADE: Once again, Bess bade Venters farewell under the shadow of Balancing Rock, and this time it was with whispered hope and tenderness and passionate trust. (Source: *RIDERS OF THE PURPLE SAGE* by Zane Grey)

Begin (2)

ACTION: BEGIN: He had postponed his journey to ... until after the passing of the summer rains. The rains were due soon. But until their arrival and the necessity for his trip to the village, he sequestered in a far corner of mind all thought of peril, of his past life, and almost that of the present. (Source: *RIDERS OF THE PURPLE SAGE* by Zane Grey)

ACTION: BEGIN: Jane's passionate, unheeding zeal began to loom darkly. "Lassiter, whatever my intention in the beginning, Fay loves you dearly ... and I ... I've grown to ... to like you." (Source: *RIDERS OF THE PURPLE SAGE* by Zane Grey)

Believe

ACTION: BELIEVE: It there was not an instinct for all three of them in that meeting [with Lassiter], an unreasoning tendency toward a closer intimacy, then Jane believed she had been subject to a queer fancy. She imagined any child would have feared Lassiter, Fay had been a lonely, a solitary elf of the sage, not at all an ordinary child, and exquisitely shy with strangers. She watched Lassiter with great, round, grave eyes, but sowed no fear. As Lassiter took a seat to which Jane invited him, little Fay edged as much as half an inch nearer. The rider's gray, earnest gaze troubled Jane. Then he turned to Fay and smiled in a way that made Jane doubt her sense of the true relation of things. Fay must have found that smile singularly winning for Fay edged closer and closer and then, by way of feminine capitulation, went to Jane from whose side she bent a beautiful, blue glance upon the rider. Lassiter only smiled at her. (Source: *RIDERS OF THE PURPLE SAGE* by Zane Grey)

Bite

ACTION: BITE: Jane bit her tongue to refrain from championing men who at the vry moment were proving to her that they were little and mean compared even with rustlers. (Source: *RIDERS OF THE PURPLE SAGE* by Zane Grey)

Blush

ACTION: BLUSH: The red leaped to Tull's dark cheek. "If you don't go, it means your ruin," he said sharply. (Source: *RIDERS OF THE PURPLE SAGE* by Zane Grey)

Breathe

ACTION: BREATHE: ... he replied, with deep intake of breath. (Source: *RIDERS OF THE PURPLE SAGE* by Zane Grey)

Brood

ACTION: BROOD: Jane had no leisure to brood over the coils that were closing around her. (Source: *RIDERS OF THE PURPLE SAGE* by Zane Grey)

Build (2)

ACTION: BUILD: He cut spruce boughs and made a lean-to for the girl. Then, gently lifting her upon a blanket, he folded the sides over her. The other blanket he wrapped about his shoulders and found a comfortable seat against a spruce tree that upheld the little shack. [The dogs] Ring and Whitie lay near at hand, one asleep, the other watchful. (Source: *RIDERS OF THE PURPLE SAGE* by Zane Grey)

ACTION: BUILD: In the afternoon, he built a gate across a small ravine near camp and here corralled the calves, and he succeeded in completing his task without Bess's being any the wiser. With eight calves in his corral, he concluded that he had enough. (Source: *RIDERS OF THE PURPLE SAGE* by Zane Grey)

Burn

ACTION: BURN: Sambo had put mesquite knots on the fire, as the bright ruddy light and sweet fragrance testified. (Source: *WEST OF THE PECOS* by Zane Grey)

Buy

ACTION: BUY: The savvy ranchers bought him out. They saw a chance and fell on it like a turkey on a grasshopper. (Source: *SUNSET PASS* by Zane Grey)

Call (3)

ACTION: CALL: "Ring ... Whitie ... come," he called softly. Then followed scraping of claws and pattering of feet, and out of the gray gloom below him swiftly climbed the dogs to reach his side and pass beyond. Venters descended, holding to the lasso. (Source: *RIDERS OF THE PURPLE SAGE* by Zane Grey)

ACTION: CALL: her serenity had been disturbed, and now it was broken by open war between her and her ministers. That something within her—a whisper—which she had tried in vain to hush had become a ringing voice, and it called to her. (Source: *RIDERS OF THE PURPLE SAGE* by Zane Grey)

ACTION: CALL: Jane went to the door and softly called for the rider. A faint, musical jingle preceded his step—then his tall form crossed the threshold. (Source: *RIDERS OF THE PURPLE SAGE* by Zane Grey)

Camp (4)

ACTION: CAMP: Despite a downhill pull the wagons did not reach the Colorado [River] until late in the afternoon. The leader of the expedition chose a wooded bend in the river for a camp site, where a cleared spot with pole uprights showed that it had been used before. The leaves on the trees were half grown, the grass was green, flowers on long stems nodded gracefully, and under the bank the river murmured softly. (Source: *WEST OF THE PECOS* by Zane Grey)

ACTION: CAMP: he halted for camp near a rugged little creek, where clear water ran trickling over the stones. (Source: *WEST OF THE PECOS* by Zane Grey)

ACTION: CAMP: He unrolled his tarp under a low-branching cedar, and opened his pack, conscious of pleasurable sensations. It had been years since he had done this sort of thing. When the dead cedar branches burst into a crackling fire, he seemed magically to find his old dexterity at camp tasks. (Source: *WEST OF THE PECOS* by Zane Grey)

ACTION: CAMP: Sometimes when sunset overtook [the] little cavalcade on the march he would camp where they were, usually near grass and water. Otherwise, as days and leagues lengthened between her and the olf home she began keenly to live this adventure. (Source: *WEST OF THE PECOS* by Zane Grey)

Caress

ACTION: CARESS: The heavy money belt lay over her like a caressing arm. (Source: *WEST OF THE PECOS* by Zane Grey)

Carry (5)

ACTION: CARRY: He carried only his rifle, revolver, and a small quantity of bread and meat, and thus lightly burdened he made swift progress down the slope. (Source: *RIDERS OF THE PURPLE SAGE* by Zane Grey)

ACTION: CARRY: He lifted the girl again and pressed on. The valley afforded better traveling than the canyon. Itt was lighter, freer of sage, and there were no rocks. Soon, out of the pale gloom, shone a still paler thing, and that was the low swell of slope. Venters mounted it, and his dogs walked beside him. Once upon the stone he slowed to snail pace, straining his sight to avoid the pockets and holes. Foot by foot he went up. (Source: *RIDERS OF THE PURPLE SAGE* by Zane Grey)

ACTION: CARRY: If he were burdened, he did not feel it. From time to time, when he passed out of the black lines of shade into the wan starlight, he glanced at the white face of the girl, lying in his arms. She had not awakened from her sleep or stupor. He did not rest until he cleared the black gate of the canyon. Then he leaned against a stone breast high to him and gently released the girl from his hold. His brow and hair and the palms of his hands were wet, and there was a kind of nervous contraction of his muscles. They seemed to ripple and string tensely. He had a desire to hurry and no sense of fatigue. (Source: *RIDERS OF THE PURPLE SAGE* by Zane Grey)

ACTION: CARRY: Lifting the girl, he stepped upward, closely attending to the nature of the path under his feet. After a few steps he stopped to mark his line with the crack in the rim. The dogs clung closer to him. While chasing the rabbit, this slope had appeared interminable to him; now, burdened as he was, he did not think of length or height or toil. He remembered only to avoid a misstep and to keep his direction. He climbed on, with frequent stops to watch the rim, and before he dreamed o gaining the bench he bumped his knees into it and saw, in the dim gray light, his rifle and the rabbit. He had come straight up without mishap or swerving off course, and his shut teeth unlocked.. (Source: *RIDERS OF THE PURPLE SAGE* by Zane Grey)

ACTION: CARRY: Venters crossed the belt of cedars, skirted the upper border, and recognized the tree he had marked, even before he saw his waving scarf. Here he knelt and deposited the girl gently, feet first, and slowly laid her out full length. What he feared was to reopen one of her wounds, if he gave her a violent jar, or slipped and fell. But the supreme confidence so strangely felt that night admitted of no such blunders. (Source: *RIDERS OF THE PURPLE SAGE* by Zane Grey)

Catch

ACTION: CATCH: "Well then, just act natural an' talk natural, an' pretty soon ... give them time to hear us ... pretend to go over there to the table, an' then quick-like make a move for the door an' open it." (Source: *RIDERS OF THE PURPLE SAGE* by Zane Grey)

Challenge

ACTION: CHALLENGE: Then Venter's gaze passed to the tables, and swiftly it swept over the hard-featured gamesters, to alight upon the huge shaggy black head of the rustler chief. "Oldring!" he cried, and to him his voice seemed to split a bell in his ears. It stilled the din. That silence suddenly broke to the scrape and crack of Oldring's chair as he rose, and then, while he paused, a great, gloomy figure—the thronged room stilled in silence yet deeper. "Oldring, a word with you!" continued Venters. "Ho! What have we here?" boomed Oldring in frowning scrutiny. "Come outside, alone. A word for you ... from your Masked Rider!" Oldring kicked a chair out of his way and lunged forward with a stamp of heavy boots that jarred the floor. He waved down his muttering, rising men. Venters backed out of the door and waited, hearing, as no sound had ever before struck into his soul, the rapid heavy steps of the rustler. (Source: *RIDERS OF THE PURPLE SAGE* by Zane Grey)

Change (5)

ACTION: CHANGE: A swift change in the nature of her agitation made him reproach himself for his abruptness. (Source: *RIDERS OF THE PURPLE SAGE* by Zane Grey)

ACTION: CHANGE: She had a trick of changing—and it was not altogether voluntary—from this gay, thoughtless, girlish coquettishness to the silence and the brooding, burning mystery of a woman's mood. The strength and passion and fire of her were in her eyes, and she so used them that Lassiter had to see this depth in her, this flaunting guise of a willful girl. (Source: *RIDERS OF THE PURPLE SAGE* by Zane Grey)

ACTION: CHANGE: Something was changing in her, forming, waiting for decisions to make it a real and fixed thing. (Source: *RIDERS OF THE PURPLE SAGE* by Zane Grey)

ACTION: CHANGE: That night I the moonlit grove she summoned all her courage, and turning suddenly in the path, she faced Lassiter, and leaned close to him, so that she touched him, and her eyes looked up to his. "Lassiter, will you do anything for me? In the moonlight she saw his dark, worn face change, and by that change she seemed to feel him immovable as a wall of stone. (Source: *RIDERS OF THE PURPLE SAGE* by Zane Grey)

ACTION: CHANGE: Thereafter, he came oftener to see Jane and her little protégée. Daily he grew more gentle and kind, and gradually developed a quaintly merry mood. After the meal they [Lassiter, Jane and Fay] walked in the grove of cottonwoods or up by the lake, and little Fay held Lassiter's hand as much as she held Jane's. Thus a strange relationship was established, and Jane liked it. (Source: *RIDERS OF THE PURPLE SAGE* by Zane Grey)

Cherish

ACTION: CHERISH: Although Jane gave with such liberality, she loved her possessions. She loved the rich, green stretches of alfalfa, and the farms, and the grove, and the old stone house, and the beautiful, ever-faithful amber spring, and every one of a myriad of horses and colts and burros and fowls down to the smallest rabbit that nipped her vegetables, but she loved best her noble Arabian steeds. In common with all riders of the upland sage Jane cherished two material thing—the cold, sweet, brown water that made life possible in the wilderness and the horses that were a part of that life. (Source: *RIDERS OF THE PURPLE SAGE* by Zane Grey)

Chill

ACTION: CHILL: Makes cold chills creep up [her] back. (Source: *WEST OF THE PECOS* by Zane Grey)

Climb (7)

ACTION: CLIMB: At the base of this rugged vent, it was dark, cool, and smelled of dry, musty dust. It zigzagged to that he could not see ahead more than a few yards at a time. He noticed tracks of wildcats and rabbits on the dusty floor. As every turn he expected to come upon a huge cavern, full of little square stone houses, each with a small aperture like a staring, dark eye. The passage lightened and widened, and opened at the foot of a narrow, steep, ascending chute. (Source: *RIDERS OF THE PURPLE SAGE* by Zane Grey)

ACTION: CLIMB: He concluded to make the climb and descend into Surprise Valley in one trip. To that end he tied his blanket upon [the dogs] Ring and gave Whitie the extra lasso and the rabbit to carry. Then, with the rifle and saddlebags slung upon his back, he took up the girl. She did not awaken from heavy slumber. (Source: *RIDERS OF THE PURPLE SAGE* by Zane Grey)

ACTION: CLIMB: He tested [the lasso's] strength by throwing all his weight upon it. Then he gathered the girl up, and holding her securely in his left arm, he began to climb, at every few steps jerking his right hand upward along the lasso. It sagged at each forward movement he made, but he balanced himself lightly during the interval when he lacked the support of a taut rope. He climbed as if he had wings, the strength of a giant, and knew not the sense of fear. (Source: *RIDERS OF THE PURPLE SAGE* by Zane Grey)

ACTION: CLIMB: That climb under the rugged, menacing brows of the broken cliffs, in the face of a grim, leaning boulder that seemed to be weary of its age-long wavering, was a tax on strength and nerve that Venters felt equally with something sweet and strangely exulting in its accomplishment. He did not pause until he gained the narrow divide and there he rested. Balancing Rock loomed huge, cold in the gray light of dawn, a thing without life, yet it spoke silently to Venters. (Source: *RIDERS OF THE PURPLE SAGE* by Zane Grey)

ACTION: CLIMB: The next ascent took grip of fingers as well as toes, but he climbed steadily, swiftly, to reach the projecting corner, and slipped around it. Here he faced a notch in the cliff. At the apex he turned abruptly into a rugged vent that split the ponderous wall clear to the top, showing a narrow streak of blue sky. (Source: *RIDERS OF THE PURPLE SAGE* by Zane Grey)

ACTION: CLIMB: The sharp corner of a cliff seemed to be cut out of the darkness. He reached it, and the protruding shelf, and then, entering the black shade of the notch, he moved blindly but surely to the place where he had left the saddlebags. He heard the dogs although he could not see them. Once more he carefully placed the girl at his feet. Then, on hands and knees, he went over the little flat space, feeling for stones. He removed a number, and, scraping the deep dust into a heap, he unfolded the outer blanket from around the girl and laid her upon this bed. Then he went down the slope again for his boots, rifle, and the rabbit, and bringing also his lasso with him, he made short work of that trip. (Source: *RIDERS OF THE PURPLE SAGE* by Zane Grey)

ACTION: CLIMB: With teeth tightly shut he essayed the incline. As he climbed, he bent his eyes downward. This, however, after a little grew impossible; he had to look to obey his eager, curious mind. He raised his glance and saw light between row on row of shafts and pinnacled and crags that stood out from the main wall. Some leaned against the cliff, others against each other; many stood sheer and alone, all were crumbling, cracked rotten. It was a place of yellow, ragged ruin. (Source: *RIDERS OF THE PURPLE SAGE* by Zane Grey)

Close

ACTION: CLOSE: If that secret, intangible power closed its coils around her again, if that great, invisible hand moved here and there and everywhere, slowly paralyzing her with its mystery and its inconceivable sway over her affairs, then she would know beyond doubt that it was not chance, or jealousy, or intimidation, or ministerial wrath at her revolt, ut a cold and calculating policy thought out long before she was born, a dark, immutable will of whose empire she and all that was hers was but an atom. Then might come her ruin. Then might come her fall into black storm. Yet she would rise again, and to the light. God would be merciful to a driven woman who had lost her way. (Source: *RIDERS OF THE PURPLE SAGE* by Zane Grey)

Come

ACTION: COME: Venters had come to meet Tull face to face—if not Tull, then Dyer—if not Dyer, then anyone in the secret of these master conspirators. Such was Venter's passion. (Source: *RIDERS OF THE PURPLE SAGE* by Zane Grey)

Compliment

ACTION: COMPLIMENT: "You are well and strong ... and growing very pretty." Anything in the nature of compliment he had never before said to her, and just now he responded to a sudden curiosity to see its effect. Bess stared as if she had no heard aright, slowly blushed, and completely lost her poise in happy confusion. (Source: *RIDERS OF THE PURPLE SAGE* by Zane Grey)

Conclude (3)

ACTION: CONCLUDE: As far as the state of his mind was concerned, upon the second day after his return the valley with its golden hues and purple shades, the speaking west wind and the cool, silent night, and her watching eyes with their wonderful light so wrought upon Venters that he might never have left them at all. (Source: *RIDERS OF THE PURPLE SAGE* by Zane Grey)

ACTION: CONCLUDE: he concluded the cedars, few as they were, would afford some cover. Therefore he climbed swiftly. (Source: *RIDERS OF THE PURPLE SAGE* by Zane Grey)

ACTION: CONCLUDE: Once for all Venter's quick mind formed a permanent conception of this poor girl. He based it, not upon what the chances of life had made her, but upon the revelation of dark eyes that pierced the infinite, upon a few pitiful, halting words tht betrayed failure and wrong and misery, yet breathed the truth of a tragic rate rather than a natural leaning to evil. (Source: *RIDERS OF THE PURPLE SAGE* by Zane Grey)

Confess

ACTION: CONFESS: a red-hot running iron couldn't burn the name out of her. (Source: *RIDERS OF THE PURPLE SAGE* by Zane Grey)

Construct (2)

ACTION: CONSTRUCT: First, he fitted up the little cave adjoining the girl's room for his own comfort and use. His next work was to build a fireplace of stones and to gather a store of wood.. (Source: *RIDERS OF THE PURPLE SAGE* by Zane Grey)

ACTION: CONSTRUCT: His good fortune in the matter of game [in the valley] brought to mind the necessity of keeping it in the valley. Therefore, he took the axe and cut bundles of aspens and willows, and packed them up under the bridge to the narrow outlet of the gorge. Here he began fashioning a fence, by driving aspens into the ground an lacing them fast with willows. Trip after trip he made down for more building material, and the afternoon had passed when he finished the work to his satisfaction. Wildcats might scale the fence, but no coy9te could come in to search for prey, and no rabbits or other small game could escape from the valley. (Source: *RIDERS OF THE PURPLE SAGE* by Zane Grey)

Cool

ACTION: COOL: The day began with a heightening of the fever. Venters spent the time reducing her temperature, cooling her hot cheeks and temples. He kept close watch over her, and at the least indication of restlessness, that he knew led to tossing and rolling of the body, he held her tightly, so no violent move could reopen her wounds. Hour after hour she babbled and laughed and cried and moaned in delirium. Attended by something somber for Venters, the day passed. At night in the cool winds the fever abated, and she slept. (Source: *RIDERS OF THE PURPLE SAGE* by Zane Grey)

Cover (2)

ACTION: COVER: Jane covered her ears and ran to her own room, and there like a caged lioness she paced to and fro till the coming of little Fay reversed her dark thoughts. (Source: *RIDERS OF THE PURPLE SAGE* by Zane Grey)

ACTION: COVER: Jane shut out the light, and he hands she held over her eyes trembled and quivered against her face. (Source: *RIDERS OF THE PURPLE SAGE* by Zane Grey)

Crawl

ACTION: CRAWL: Like a scouting Indian, Venters crawled through the sage of the oval valley, crossed trail after trail on the north side, and at last entered the canyon out of which the rustlers disappear. (Source: *RIDERS OF THE PURPLE SAGE* by Zane Grey)

Creep

ACTION: CREEP: If he had used caution before, now he strained every nerve to force himself to creeping stealth and to sensitiveness of ear. He crawled along so hidden tht he could not use his eyes except to aid himself in the toilsome progress through the brakes and ruins of cliff wall. Yet, from time to time, as he rested, he sw the massive red walls growing higher and wilder, more looming and broken. He made note of the fact that he was turning and climbing. The sage and thickets of oak and brakes of alder gave place to piñon pine growing out of rocky soil. (Source: *RIDERS OF THE PURPLE SAGE* by Zane Grey)

Cry (4)

ACTION: CRY: "Bern! You're back! You're back!" she cried in a joy that rang of her loneliness. (Source: *RIDERS OF THE PURPLE SAGE* by Zane Grey)

ACTION: CRY: "Spies! My own ...! Oh, miserable!" she cried, with flashing, tearful eyes. (Source: *RIDERS OF THE PURPLE SAGE* by Zane Grey)

ACTION: CRY: Jane felt the hot tears well to her eyes and splash down upon her hands. (Source: *RIDERS OF THE PURPLE SAGE* by Zane Grey)

ACTION: CRY: Jane leaned against him, and with a pressing and breaking in her breast, as if some pent-up force had rent out its way, she fell into a paroxysm of weeping. . (Source: *RIDERS OF THE PURPLE SAGE* by Zane Grey)

ACTION: CRY: Venters felt his eyes grow hot and wet. (Source: *RIDERS OF THE PURPLE SAGE* by Zane Grey)

Cut

ACTION: CUT: He cut spruce boughs and made a bed in the largest cave and laid the [sleeping] girl there. (Source: *RIDERS OF THE PURPLE SAGE* by Zane Grey)

Dance

ACTION: DANCE: He enjoyed this dance with Alice. She was like a fairy on her feet.. (Source: *SUNSET PASS* by Zane Grey)

Daze

ACTION: DAZE: "The longer I live, the stranger life becomes," mused Lassiter with downcast eyes. "I'm reminded of somethin' you once said to Jane Withersteen about hands in her game of life. There's that unseen hand of power, an' Tull's black hand, an' my red one, an' your unfathomable one, an' the girl's little, brown, helpless one. An' Venters, there's another one that's all-wise an' all-wonderful. That's the hand guidin' Jane's game of life! Your story's one to daze a far clearer head than mine. I can't offer no advice, even it you asked for it." (Source: *RIDERS OF THE PURPLE SAGE* by Zane Grey)

Decide

ACTION: DECIDE: These things required tremendous effort, but the last one, concerning Bess, seemed simply and naturally easy of accomplishment. He would marry her. Suddenly, as from roots of poisonous fire, flamed up the forgotten truth concerning her. It seemed to wither and shrivel up all his joy in its hot, tearing way to his heart. (Source: *RIDERS OF THE PURPLE SAGE* by Zane Grey)

Depart (4)

ACTION: DEPART: "Folks, let's shake the dust of Eagle's Nest," suggested Pecos. (Source: *WEST OF THE PECOS* by Zane Grey)

ACTION: DEPART: He packed his saddlebags. The dogs were hungry. They whined about him and nosed his busy hands, but he took no time to feed them or to satisfy his own hunger. He slung the saddlebags over his shoulders and made them secure with his lasso. Then he wrapped the blankets closer about the girl and lifted her in his arms. . (Source: *RIDERS OF THE PURPLE SAGE* by Zane Grey)

ACTION: DEPART: It was about sunset, and she and Fay had finished supper, and were sitting in the court, when Venters's quick steps rang on the stones. As he came up the steps, she felt herself pointing to the pack, and herd herself speaking words that were meaningless to her. He said good bye. He folded her in his arms and kissed her, released her, and turned way. His tall figure blurred in her sight, grew dim through dark, streaked vision, and then he vanished. (Source: *RIDERS OF THE PURPLE SAGE* by Zane Grey)

ACTION: DEPART: The last sunset and twilight and night were the sweetest and saddest they had ever spent in the valley. Morning brought keen exhilaration and excitement. When Venters had saddled the two burros, strapped on the light packs and the two canteens, the sunlight was dispersing the lazy shadows from the valley. Taking a last look at the caves and the silver spruces, they made a reluctant start, leading the burros. (Source: *RIDERS OF THE PURPLE SAGE* by Zane Grey)

Descend (4)

ACTION: DESCEND: Down, down, down Venters strode, more and more feeling the weight of his burden as he descended, and still the valley lay below him. As all other canyons and coves and valleys had deceived him, so had this deep, nestling oval. At length he passed beyond the slope of weathered stone that spread fan-shape from the arch and encountered a grassy terrace running to the right and bout on a level with the tips of the oaks and cottonwoods below. (Source: *RIDERS OF THE PURPLE SAGE* by Zane Grey)

ACTION: DESCEND: He descended the gorge on the other side. The slope was gradual, the space narrow, the course straight for many rods. A gloom hung between the upsweeping walls. In a turn the passage narrowed to scarcely a dozen feet, and here was darkness of night. But light shone ahead, another abrupt turn brought day again, and then wide-open space. (Source: *RIDERS OF THE PURPLE SAGE* by Zane Grey)

ACTION: DESCEND: he put on his belt and boots and prepared to descend. Some consideration was necessary to decide whether or not to leave his rifle there. On the return, carrying the girl and a pack, it would be added encumbrance, and after debating the matter, he left the rifle leaning against the bench. As he went straight down the lope, he halted every few rods to look up at his mark on the rim. It changed, but he fixed each change in memory. When he reached the first cedar tree, he tied his scarf upon a dead branch, and then hurried toward camp, having o more concern about finding his trail upon the return trip. (Source: *RIDERS OF THE PURPLE SAGE* by Zane Grey)

ACTION: DESCEND: Leading the burros down to the spur of rock, he halted at the steep incline. "Bess, here's the bad place I told you about with the cut steps. You start down, leading your burro. Take your time and hold onto him if you slip. I've got a rope on him and a half-hitch on this point of rock, so I can let him down safely." Both burros passed down the difficult stairs cut by the cliff-dwellers, and did it without misstep.. (Source: *RIDERS OF THE PURPLE SAGE* by Zane Grey)

Dim

ACTION: DIM: There was something about [the meeting] that dimmed her sight and softened her toward this foe of her people. (Source: *RIDERS OF THE PURPLE SAGE* by Zane Grey)

Disappear

ACTION: DISAPPEAR: Coincident with the disappearance of [Jane's household helpers] Jane's gardeners and workers in the alfalfa fields and stables quit her, not even asking for their wage.. (Source: *RIDERS OF THE PURPLE SAGE* by Zane Grey)

Discover

ACTION: DISCOVER: At the outset he discovered her to be both a considerable help in some ways, and a very great hindrance in others. Her excitement and joy were spurs, inspirations, but she was utterly impracticable in her ideas, and she flitted from one plan to another with bewildering vacillation. (Source: *RIDERS OF THE PURPLE SAGE* by Zane Grey)

Divulge

ACTION: DIVULGE: Venters did not confide in Bess the alarming fact that he had seen horses and smoke less than a mile up one of the intersecting canyons. He did not talk at all. Long after he had passed this canyon and felt secure once more in the certainty that they had been unobserved, he never relaxed his watchfulness, but he did not walk anymore and kept the burros at a steady trot.. (Source: *RIDERS OF THE PURPLE SAGE* by Zane Grey)

Defy

ACTION: DEFY: The expression in her eyes drove him to pace under the pines, to throw back his head., to fill his lungs with the sage-laden air of the pass, and to cast exultant defiance up at the silent, passionless white stars (Source: *SUNSET PASS* by Zane Grey)

Depart (3)

ACTION: DEPART: "Good day, Mrs. ...," he concluded, rather coldly, and replacing his sombrero he turned away, not, however, without catching a last angry blaze of her eyes. (Source: *SUNSET PASS* by Zane Grey)

ACTION: DEPART: And so they rode away from the gray, dim mansion, out under the huge live oaks with their long streamers of Spanish moss swaying in the breeze, and into the yellow road that stretched away along the green canal. (Source: *WEST OF THE PECOS* by Zane Grey)

ACTION: DEPART: When they reached the outskirts of the hamlet where [her] mother was buried, she looked back until her tear-blurred eyes could no longer distinguish objects. The day before she had taken her leave of her mother's grave—[it was] a rending experience which she could not endure twice. (Source: *WEST OF THE PECOS* by Zane Grey)

Descend

ACTION: DESCEND: He went downstairs to the lobby, where he encountered a heavy-set, ruddy-faced man, whom he well remembered. (Source: *SUNSET PASS* by Zane Grey)

Determined

ACTION: DETERMINED: Trouble, menace, always brought out in him the reckless, dauntless spirit which he shared in common with his type [of cowboy]. Now he waxed stern and calculating, sure of his vision, while outwardly he appeared the old cool cowboy of the range. (Source: *SUNSET PASS* by Zane Grey)

Disapprove

ACTION: DISAPPROVE: At the hotel where they stayed, Terrill regarded herself in the mirror with great disapproval. (Source: *WEST OF THE PECOS* by Zane Grey)

Drink

ACTION: DRINK: There were times when it was bad for him to yield to the bottle. This was one of them. The sudden cold in his very marrow, the blank gray shade stealing over his mind, the [forecast] of a spell of morbid sinking of spirit—these usually preceded his rather are drinking bouts. (Source: *SUNSET PASS* by Zane Grey)

Embarrass

ACTION: EMBARRASS: Jane found it strangely embarrassing to meet the child's gaze. It seemed to her that Little Fay's violet eyes looked through her with piercing wisdom. (Source: *RIDERS OF THE PURPLE SAGE* by Zane Grey)

Enter (3)

ACTION: ENTER: Gage came in late, and his gruff heartiness, his steely glance, embracing Ash and Thiry and Rock, were strangely at variance. Incalculable change had taken place and Rock was about to see a new phase in Gage's complex character. (Source: *SUNSET PASS* by Zane Grey)

ACTION: ENTER: He stepped inside. With the sight of smoke-hazed room and drinking, cursing, gambling, dark-visaged men, reality once more dawned upon Venters. His entrance had been unnoticed, and he bent his gaze upon the drinkers at the bar. Dark-clothed, dark-faced men they all were, burned by the sun, bowlegged as were most riders of the sage, but neither lean nor gaunt. (Source: *RIDERS OF THE PURPLE SAGE* by Zane Grey)

ACTION: ENTER: Jane went in[to the hut]. There was only one room, rather dark and bare, but it was clean and neat. (Source: *RIDERS OF THE PURPLE SAGE* by Zane Grey)

Escape (28)

ACTION: ESCAPE: [Then Bess and Venters took to the sage.] One glance ahead showed him that Bess could pick a course through the sage as well as he. She looked neither back nor at the running riders, and bent forward over Black Star's neck and studied the ground ahead. Venters remembered she had said she could ride, but he had not dreamed she was capable of such superb horsemanship. Then he recalled how the Masked Rider could ride swift as the wind and be gone in the sage! A fleet, dark horse—a slender, dark form—a black mask—a driving run down the slope—a dot on the purple sage—a shadowy, muffled steed disappearing in the night. And this Masked Rider had been Elizabeth Erne! (Source: *RIDERS OF THE PURPLE SAGE* by Zane Grey)

ACTION: ESCAPE: "Venters, ride straight on up the slope," Lassiter was saying, "an', if you don't meet any riders, keep on till you're a few miles from the village, then cut of in the sage an' go 'round to the trace. But you'll most likely meet riders with Tull. Jest keep right on till you're jest out of gunshot an' then make your cut-off into the sage. They'll ride after you, but it won't be no use. You can ride an' Bess can ride. When you're out of reach, turn on 'round to the west an' hit the trail somewhere. Save the hosses all you can, but don't be afraid. Black Star an' Night are good for a hundred miles before sundown, if you have to push them. You can get to Sterlin' by night if you want. But better to make it along about tomorrow mornin'. When you get through The Notch on the Glaze trail, swing to the right. You'll be able to see both Glaze an' Stone Bridge. Keep away from them villages. You won't run no risk of meetin' any of Oldrin's ruslers from Sterlin' on. You'll find water in them deep hollows north of The Notch. There's an old trail there, not much used, an' it leads to Sterlin'. That's your trail. An' one thing more. If Tull pushes you ... or keeps on persistent-like, for a few miles ... jest let the blacks out an' lose him an' his riders." (Source: *RIDERS OF THE PURPLE SAGE* by Zane Grey)

ACTION: ESCAPE: A glistening, wonderful, bare slope with little holes swelled up and up to lose itself in a frowning, yellow cliff. Jane closely watched her steps and climbed behind Lassiter. He moved slowly. Perhaps he was only husbanding his strength. But she was drops of blood on the stones, and then she knew. They climbed and climbed without looking back. Her breast labored; she began to feel as if little points of fiery steel were penetrating her side into her lungs. She heard the panting of Lassiter, and the quicker panting of the dogs. (Source: *RIDERS OF THE PURPLE SAGE* by Zane Grey)

ACTION: ESCAPE: All day he rode slowly and cautiously up the pass, taking time to peer around corners, to pick out hard ground and grassy patches, and to make sure there was no one in pursuit. In the night some time he came to the smooth, scrawled rocks dividing the valley, and here set the burro at liberty. He walked beyond, climbed the slope, and the dim starlit gorge. Then, weary to the point of exhaustion, he crept into a shallow cave and fell asleep. (Source: *RIDERS OF THE PURPLE SAGE* by Zane Grey)

ACTION: ESCAPE: As Jane gazed down that long incline, walled in by crumbling cliffs, awaiting only the slightest jar to make them fall asunder, she saw Tull appear at the bottom and begin to climb. A rider followed him—another—and another. (Source: *RIDERS OF THE PURPLE SAGE* by Zane Grey)

ACTION: ESCAPE: At every open place Lassiter looked back. The shade under the walls [of the canyon] gave place to sunlight, and presently thy came to the dense thicket of slender trees, through which they pressed to rich, green grass and water. Here he rested the burros for a little while, but he was restless, uneasy, silent, always listening, peering under the trees. (Source: *RIDERS OF THE PURPLE SAGE* by Zane Grey)

ACTION: ESCAPE: At his bidding, Jane mounted and rode on, close to the heels of his burro. The canyon narrowed, the walls lifted their rugged rims higher, and the sun shone down hotly rom the center of the blue stream of sky above. (Source: *RIDERS OF THE PURPLE SAGE* by Zane Grey)

ACTION: ESCAPE: At the first hint of gray over the eastern sky he awoke Bess, saddled the burros and began the day's travel. He wanted to get out of the pass before there was any chance of riders coming down. They gained the break as the first red rays of the rising sun colored the rim. (Source: *RIDERS OF THE PURPLE SAGE* by Zane Grey)

ACTION: ESCAPE: Before Jane rose a bulge of stone, nicked with little cut steps, and above that a corner of yellow wall, and over-hanging that a vast, ponderous cliff. The dogs pattered up, disappeared around the corner. Lassiter mounted the steps with Fay, and he swayed like a drunken man, and he, too, disappeared. But instantly he returned alone and half ran, half slipped down to Jane. Then from below pealed up hoarse shouts of angry men. Tull and several of his riders had reached the spot where Lassiter had parted with his guns. (Source: *RIDERS OF THE PURPLE SAGE* by Zane Grey)

ACTION: ESCAPE: Bounding swiftly away, Venters fled around the corner, across the street, and, leaping a hedge, he ran through yard, orchard, and garden to the sage. There, under cover of the tall brush, he turned west and ran on o the place where he had hidden his rifle. Securing that, he again set out in a run and, circling through the sage, came up behind Jane Withersteen's stable and corrals. With laboring, dripping chest and pain as of a knife thrust in his side, he stopped to regain his breath, and, while resting, his eyes roved around in search of a horse. Doors and windows of the stable were open wide and had a deserted look. One dejected, lonely burro stood in the near corral. Strange indeed was the silence brooding over the once happy, noisy home of Jane Withersteen's pets. He went into the corral, exercising care to leave no tracks, and led the burro to the watering trough. Venters, although not thirsty, drank till he could drink no more. Then, leading the burro over hard ground, he struck into the sage and down the slope. He strode swiftly, turning from time to time to scan the slope for riders. His head just topped the level of sagebrush and the burro could not have been seen at all. Slowly the green of cottonwoods sank behind the slope, and at last a wavering, purple like of sage met the blue of the sky. To avoid being seen, to get away, to hide his trail, these were the sole ideas in his mind as he headed for Deception Pass, and he directed all his acuteness of eye and ear, and keenness of a rider's judgment for distance and ground, to stern accomplishment of the task. He kept to the sage far to the left of the trail leading into the pass. He walked ten miles, and looked back a thousand times. Always the graceful, purple wave of sage remained wide and lonely, a clear, un-dotted waste. Coming to a stretch of rocky ground, he took advantage of it to cross the trail, and then continued down on the right. At length he persuaded himself that he would be able to see riders mounted on horses before they could see him on the little burro, and he rode bareback (Source: *RIDERS OF THE PURPLE SAGE* by Zane Grey)

ACTION: ESCAPE: Facing downward with glittering eyes, Lassiter said, "Now, Jane, the last wag. Walk up them little steps. I'll follow an' steady yu. Don't think. Jest go. Little Fay's above. Her eyes are open. She jest said to me ... 'Where's muvver?'" (Source: *RIDERS OF THE PURPLE SAGE* by Zane Grey)

ACTION: ESCAPE: Five riders, surely rustlers, were left. One leaped out of the saddle to secure his fallen comrade's carbine. A shot from Venters, which missed the man but sent the dust flying over him, made him run back to his horse. Then they separated. The crippled rider went one [direction], the one frustrated in his attempt to get the carbine rode another. Venters thought his fleeting glance made out a third rider, carrying a strange bundle, disappearing in the sage. In the rapidity of action and vision he could not discern what it was. Two riders with three horses swung out to the right. Afraid of the long rifle—a burdensome weapon seldom carried by rustlers or riders—they had been put to rout. (Source: *RIDERS OF THE PURPLE SAGE* by Zane Grey)

ACTION: ESCAPE: Hurriedly he strapped on the saddlebags, gave quick glance to girths and cinches and stirrups, then leaped astride. "Get back your nerve, woman! This's life or death now. Stick close to me. Watch where your hoss's goin', and ride!" Jane mounted, somehow found strength to hold the reins, to spur, to cling on, to ride. Lassiter led the swift flight across the wide space, over washes, through sage, into a narrow canyon where the rapid clatter of hoofs rapped sharply from the walls. The wind roared in her ears; the gleaming cliffs swept by; trail and sage and grass moved under her. Lassiter looked back down the pass; he spurred his horse. Jane clung on, spurring likewise. The horses settled from hard, furious gallop into long-striding, driving run. She had never ridden at anything like that pace; desperately she tried to get the swing of the horse. All of life—of good—of use in the world—of life in heaven centered on Lassiter's ride with little Fay to safety. (Source: *RIDERS OF THE PURPLE SAGE* by Zane Grey)

ACTION: ESCAPE: Jane looked back over the long stretch of sage and found the narrow gap in the [canyon] wall, out of which came a file of dark horses with a white horse in the lead. Sight of the riders acted upon Jane as a stimulant. The weight of cold, horrible terror lessened. Gazing forward at the dogs, at Lassiter's limping horse, as the blood on his face, at the rocks growing nearer—lastly at Fay's golden hair, the ice left her veins, and slowly, strangely, she gained hold of strength that she believed would see her to the safety

Lassiter promised. (Source: *RIDERS OF THE PURPLE SAGE* by Zane Grey)

ACTION: ESCAPE: Lassiter dismounted, led his burro, called the dogs in, and proceeded at snail pace through dark masses of rock and dense thickets under the left wall [of the canyon]. Long he watched and listened before venturing to cross the mouths of side canyons. At length he halted, tied his burro, lifted a warning hand to Jane, and then slipped away among the boulders and, followed by the stealthy dogs, disappeared from sight. (Source: *RIDERS OF THE PURPLE SAGE* by Zane Grey)

ACTION: ESCAPE: Lassiter looked back, saying nothing. The bandage had blown from his head, and blood trickled down his face. He was bowing under the strain on injuries, of the ride, of his burden. Yet how cool and gray he looked—how intrepid!. (Source: *RIDERS OF THE PURPLE SAGE* by Zane Grey)

ACTION: ESCAPE: Lassiter picked up the child and turned into a dark cleft. It zigzagged. It widened. It opened. Jane was amazed at a wonderfully smooth and steep incline leading up between ruined, splintered, toppling walls. A red haze from the setting sun filled the passage. Lassiter climbed with slow, measured steps, and blood dripped from him to make splotches on the white stone. The saddlebag began to drag Jane down; she gasped for breath; she thought her heart was bursting. Slower, slower yet, the rider climbed, whistling as he breathed. The incline widened. Huge pinnacles and monuments of stone stood alone, leaning fearfully. Red sunset haze shone through cracks where the wall had split. Jane felt the overshadowing of broken rims above. She felt that it was a fearful, menacing place. She climbed on in heart-rending effort. And she fell beside Lassiter and Fay at the top of the incline on a narrow, smooth divide. (Source: *RIDERS OF THE PURPLE SAGE* by Zane Grey)

ACTION: ESCAPE: Lassiter traveled slower, with more exceeding care as to the ground he chose, and he kept speaking in a low voice to the doge. They were now hunting dogs—keen, alert, suspicious, sniffing the warm breeze. (Source: *RIDERS OF THE PURPLE SAGE* by Zane Grey)

ACTION: ESCAPE: Lassiter was leading the horse up a smooth slope toward cedar trees of twisted and bleached appearance. Among these he halted. "Jane, give me the girl, an' get down," he said. As if it wrenched him, he unbuckled his heavy belt and dropped the empty black guns with a strange air of finality. He then received little Fay in his arms and stood a moment, looking backward. Tull's white horse mounted the ridge of round stone, and several bays or blacks followed. "I wonder what he'll think when he sees them empty guns. Jane, bring your saddlebag and climb after me." (Source: *RIDERS OF THE PURPLE SAGE* by Zane Grey)

ACTION: ESCAPE: Night fell before they reached the last water in the pass, and they made camp by starlight. Venters did not want the burros to stray, so he tied them with long halters in the grass near the spring. (Source: *RIDERS OF THE PURPLE SAGE* by Zane Grey)

ACTION: ESCAPE: Once down in the pass, without leaving a trail, he would hold himself safe for the time being. When, late in the night, he reached the break in the sage, he sent the burro down ahead of him. Then he descended, loosening and dragging boulders behind him, and started an avalanche that all but buried him at the bottom of the trail. Bruised and battered as he was, he had a moment's elation, for he had hidden his tracks. Once more he mounted the burro and rode on. The hour was the blackest of the night when he made the thicket that enclosed his old camp. There he turned the burro loose in the grass near the spring, and then lay down on his old bed of leaves. (Source: *RIDERS OF THE PURPLE SAGE* by Zane Grey)

ACTION: ESCAPE: Pulling at his patient, plodding burro, he climbed the soft, steep trail. Brighter and brighter grew the light. He mounted the last broken edge of rim to have the sun-fired, purple sage slope burst upon him as a glory. (Source: *RIDERS OF THE PURPLE SAGE* by Zane Grey)

ACTION: ESCAPE: The grim rider looked over his shoulder, but said no word. Little Fay's golden hair floated on the breeze. The sun shone, the walls gleamed, the sage glistened, and then it seemed the sun vanished, the walls shaded, the sage paled. Shadows gathered under shelving cliffs. The canyon turned, brightened, opened into long, wide, wall-enclosed valley. Again the sun, now lowering in the west, reddened the sage. Far ahead round, scrawled stones appeared to block the pass. (Source: *RIDERS OF THE PURPLE SAGE* by Zane Grey)

ACTION: ESCAPE: The monotony of the yellow [canyon] walls broke in change of color and smooth surface—and there the pass opened wide at a junction of intersecting canyons.. (Source: *RIDERS OF THE PURPLE SAGE* by Zane Grey)

ACTION: ESCAPE: The sweet sage wind rushed in Venters's face and sang a song in his ears. He heard the dull, rapid beat of Night's hoofs, and he saw Black Star drawing away, farther and farther. He held Night to a trot and rode on, and the sloping upward stretch of sage, and from time to time the receding black riders behind. Soon they disappeared behind a ridge and he turned no more. Hey would go back to Lassiter's trail, and follow it in vain. So Venters rode on with the wind growing sweeter to taste and smell, and the purple sage richer and the sky bluer in his sight, and the song in his ears ringing. (Source: *RIDERS OF THE PURPLE SAGE* by Zane Grey)

ACTION: ESCAPE: They mounted and rode west through the valley and entered the canyon. From time to time Venters walked, leading his burro. When they got by all the canyons and gullies opening into the pass, they went faster with fewer halts. (Source: *RIDERS OF THE PURPLE SAGE* by Zane Grey)

ACTION: ESCAPE: They rested. Then, mounting, they rode side-by-side up the white trail. The sun rose higher behind them.

Far to the left a low line of green marked the site of Cottonwoods. Venters looked once and looked no more. Bess gazed only straight ahead. They put the blacks to the long, swinging rider's canter and at times pulled them to a trot, and occasionally to a walk. The hours passed, the miles slipped behind, and the wall of rock loomed in the foreground. The Notch opened wide. It was a rugged, stony pass, but with level and open trail, and Venters and Bess ran the blacks through it. An old trail led off to the right, taking the line of the wall, and this Venters knew to be the trail mentioned by Lassiter. (Source: *RIDERS OF THE PURPLE SAGE* by Zane Grey)

ACTION: ESCAPE: Tull and his men stopped on a ridge. "They see us, but we're too far yet for them to make out who we are. They'll recognize the blacks first. Bess, we're in good position. We've passed most of the ridges and the thickest sage. Now, when I give the word, let Black Star go and ride!" Venters calculated that a mile or more still intervened between them and the riders. They were approaching at a swift canter. Then Tull and the line of horsemen, perhaps ten or twelve in number, stopped several times and evidently looked hard down the slope. It must have been a puzzling circumstance for Tull. Venters laughed grimly at the thought of what Tull's rage would be, when he finally discovered the trick. Venters meant to sheer out into the sage before Tull could possibly be sure who rode the blacks. The gap closed to a distance of half a mile. Tull halted. His riders came up and formed a dark group around him. Venters thought he saw him wave his arms, an was certain of it when the riders dashed into the sage to right and left of the trail. "Now, Bess!" shouted Venters. "Strike north. Go 'round those riders and turn west." Black Star sailed over the low sage and in few leaps got into his stride and was running. It was hard going in the sage. The horses could not run as well there, but keen eyesight and judgment must constantly be used by the riders in choosing ground. Continuous swerving from aisle to aisle between the brush, and leaping little washes and mounds of the pack rats, and breaking through sage made rough riding. (Source: *RIDERS OF THE PURPLE SAGE* by Zane Grey)

Examine (2)

ACTION: EXAMINE: "I must see your wounds now," he said gently. She made no reply, but watched him steadily as he opened her blouse and untied the bandage. His strong fingers trembled a little as he removed it. If the wounds had reopened! A chill struck him as he saw the angry, red bullet mark and a tiny stream of blood winding from it down her white breast. Very carefully he lifted her to see that the wound in her back had closed perfectly. Then he washed the blood from her breast, bathed the wound, and left it unbandaged, open to the air. Her eyes thanked him. (Source: *RIDERS OF THE PURPLE SAGE* by Zane Grey)

ACTION: EXAMINE: He wondered if the internal bleeding has ceased. There was no more film of blood upon her lips. But no corpse could have been whiter. Opening her blouse, he untied the scarf, and carefully picked away the sage leaves from the wound in her shoulder. It had closed. Lifting her lightly, he ascertained that the same was true of the hole where the bullet had come out. He reflected on the fact that clean wounds closed quickly in the healing upland air. He had no way to tell if internal hemorrhage still went on, but he believed that it had stopped. He marked the entrance of the bullet and concluded that it had just touched the upper lobe of her lung. Perhaps the wound in the lung had also closed. (Source: *RIDERS OF THE PURPLE SAGE* by Zane Grey)

Excite

ACTION: EXCITE: Excitement and trilling expectancy and a painful awakening of numbed and stifled feeling flooded out all Jane's calm. (Source: *RIDERS OF THE PURPLE SAGE* by Zane Grey)

Explore (16)

ACTION: EXPLORE: As he strode down the sloping terrace, rabbits scampered before him, and the beautiful valley quail, as purple in color as the sage on the uplands, ran fleetly along the ground into the forest. It was pleasant under the trees, in the gold-flecked shade, with the whistle of quail and twittering of birds everywhere. Soon he passed the limit of his former excursions and entered new territory. Here, the woods began to show open glades and brooks running [down] from the slope, and presently he emerged from shade into the sunshine of a meadow. (Source: *RIDERS OF THE PURPLE SAGE* by Zane Grey)

ACTION: EXPLORE: Bess never rested for long. Soon she was exploring, and he followed. She dragged forth from corners and shelves a multitude of crudely fashioned and pained pieces of pottery, and he carried them. They peeped down into the dark holes of the kivas, and Bess gleefully dropped a stone, and waited for the long-coming hollow sound to rise. They peeped into the little globular homes, like mud-wasp's nests, and wondered if these had been storage places for grain or baby cribs, or what, and they crawled into the larger houses, and laughed when they bumped their heads on the low roofs, and they dug in the dust of the floors and they brought from dust and darkness armloads of treasure that they carried to the light. Flints and stones and strange, curved sticks and pottery they found, and twisted grass rope that crumbled in their hands, and bits of whitish stone that crushed to powder at a touch and seemed to vanish in the air. "That white stuff was bone" said Venters slowly. (Source: *RIDERS OF THE PURPLE SAGE* by Zane Grey)

ACTION: EXPLORE: During all these waiting days he had scarcely gone out of sight of camp and never out of hearing. His desire to explore Surprise Valley was keen, and on the morning after his long talk with the girl he took his rifle and, calling Ring [the dog], made a move to start. (Source: *RIDERS OF THE PURPLE SAGE* by Zane Grey)

ACTION: EXPLORE: He climbed he terrace, and then faced a long, gradual ascent of weathered rock and dust that made climbing too difficult for attention to anything else. At length he entered a zone of shade, and looked up. He stood just within the hollow of a cavern so immense that he had no conception of its real dimensions. The curved roof, stained by ages of leakage, with buff an black and rust-colored streaks, swept up and loomed higher and seemed to soar to the rim of the cliff. Here again was a magnificent arch, such as formed the grand gateway to the valley, only in this instance it formed the dome of a cave instead of the span of a bridge. (Source: *RIDERS OF THE PURPLE SAGE* by Zane Grey)

ACTION: EXPLORE: He leaped [over] the stream, and headed toward the southern wall. Once out of the oaks he found again the low terrace of aspens, and above that the wide, open terrace fringed by silver spruces. This side of the valley contained wind- or water-worn caves. As he pressed on, keeping to the upper terrace, cave after cave opened out of the cliff, now a large one, now a small one. Then yawning, quite suddenly and wonderfully above him, was, the great cavern of the cliff-dwellers. (Source: *RIDERS OF THE PURPLE SAGE* by Zane Grey)

ACTION: EXPLORE: On and on they wandered to the wild jumble of massed and broken fragments of cliff at the west end of the valley. Into this maze of rocks they threaded a tortuous way, climbing, descending, halting to gather wild plums and great lavender lilies, and going on at the will of fancy. Idle and keep perceptions guided them equally. (Source: *RIDERS OF THE PURPLE SAGE* by Zane Grey)

ACTION: EXPLORE: Part of the time Ring and Whitie led the way, then Venters, then Bess, and the direction was not an objective. They left the sun-streaked shade of the oaks, brushed the long grass of the meadow, entered the green and fragrant swaying willows, to stop, at length, under the huge old cottonwoods, where the beaver were busy. (Source: *RIDERS OF THE PURPLE SAGE* by Zane Grey)

ACTION: EXPLORE: Pointing upward to a small space of terrace left green and shady between hugs abutments of broken cliff, they climbed to the nook and rested and looked out across the valley to the curling column of blue smoke from their campfire. But the cool shade and the rich grass and the fine view were not what they had climbed for. They could not have told, although whatever had drawn them was all satisfying. Light, surefooted as a mountain-goat, Bess pattered down at Venter's heels, and they went on, calling the dogs, eyes dreamy and wide, listening to the wind and the bees and the crickets and the birds. (Source: *RIDERS OF THE PURPLE SAGE* by Zane Grey)

ACTION: EXPLORE: So he set out. It still wanted several hours before dark. This trip he turned to the left and wended his skulking way southward a mile or more in the opening of the valley, where lay the strange, scrawled rocks. He did not, however, venture boldly out into the open sage, but clung to the right-hand wall and went along that till its perpendicular line broke into the long incline of bare stone. (Source: *RIDERS OF THE PURPLE SAGE* by Zane Grey)

ACTION: EXPLORE: Then Venters and Bess wandered farther, and perhaps not all unconsciously this time, wended their slow steps to the cave of the cliff-dwellers, where she liked best to go. The tangled thicket and the long slant of dust and little chips of weathered rock, and he steep bench of stone, and the worn steps—all were arduous work for Bess in the climbing. But she gained the shelf, gasping, hot of cheek, glad of eye, with her hand in Venter's. Here they rested. The beautiful valley glittered below with its millions of wind-turned leaves bright-faced in the sun, and the mighty bridge towered heavenward, crowned with blue sky.. (Source: *RIDERS OF THE PURPLE SAGE* by Zane Grey)

ACTION: EXPLORE: There were tangled thickets of wild plum trees [in the oak forest] and other thorny growths that made passage extremely laborsome. He found innumerable tracks of wildcats and foxes. Rustlings in the thick undergrowth told him of stealthy movement of these animals. (Source: *RIDERS OF THE PURPLE SAGE* by Zane Grey)

ACTION: EXPLORE: They left camp to wander along the terraces, into the aspen ravines, under the gleaming walls. The dogs wandered in the foreground, often turning, often trotting back, open-mouthed and solemn-eyed and happy. Venters lifted his gaze to the grand archway over the entrance to the valley, and both [he and Bess] were silent. Sometimes the bridge held their attention for a long time. Today a soaring eagle attracted them. (Source: *RIDERS OF THE PURPLE SAGE* by Zane Grey)

ACTION: EXPLORE: They wandered on, down the terrace, into the shady, sun-flecked forest. (Source: *RIDERS OF THE PURPLE SAGE* by Zane Grey)

ACTION: EXPLORE: Venters approached the willow and cottonwood belt that he had observed from the height of the slope. He penetrated it to find considerable stream of water and great, half-submerged mounds of brush and sticks, and all about him were old and new gnawed circles at the base of the cottonwoods. "Beaver!" he exclaimed. (Source: *RIDERS OF THE PURPLE SAGE* by Zane Grey)

ACTION: EXPLORE: Venters felt the sublimity of that marvelous, vaulted arch, and it seemed to gleam with a glory of something that was gone. How many years had passed since the cliff-dwellers gazed out across the beautiful valley, as he was gazing now? How long had it been since women ground grain in those polished holes? What time had rolled by since men of an unknown race lived, loved, fought, and died here? Had disease destroyed them, or only that greatest destroyer—time? Venters saw a long line of blood-red hands painted low down upon the yellow roof of stone.

Here was a strange portent, if not an answer to his queries. The place oppressed him. It was light, but full of a transparent gloom. It smelled of dust and musty stone, or age and disuse. It was sad. It was solemn. It had the look of a place where silence had become master and was not irrevocable and terrible and could not be broken. (Source: *RIDERS OF THE PURPLE SAGE* by Zane Grey)

ACTION: EXPLORE: Venters passed onward and upward [as he explored the cavern]. The stones he dislodged rolled down with strange, hollow crack and roar. He had climbed 100 rods inward, and yet he had not reached the base of the shelf where the cliff-dwellings rested, a long half circle of connected stone houses with little dark holes that he had fancied were eyes. At length he gained the base of the shelf, and here fund steps cut in the rock. These facilitated climbing, and, as he went up, he thought how easily this vanished race of men might once have held that stronghold against an army. There was only one possible place to ascend, and this was narrow and steep. Venters had visited cliff-dwellings before, and they had been in ruins and of no great character or size, but this place was of proportions that stunned him, and it had not been desecrated by the hand of man, nor had it been crumbled by the hand of time. It was a stupendous tomb. It had been a city. It was just as it had been left by its builders. The little houses were there, the smoke-blackened stains of fires, the pieces of pottery scattered about cold hearths, the stone hatchets, stone pestles and mealing stones lay beside round holes polished by years of grinding maize—lay there as if they had been dropped yesterday. But the cliff-dwellers were gone! They were dust on the floor or at the foot of the shelf, but their habitations and utensils endured. (Source: *RIDERS OF THE PURPLE SAGE* by Zane Grey)

Faith

ACTION: FAITH: The glimmer of the first star was like the peace and beauty of the night. Her faith welled up in her heart and said that all would soon be right in her little world. (Source: *RIDERS OF THE PURPLE SAGE* by Zane Grey)

Fall (2)

ACTION: FALL: Jane ... fell to her knees. This was the long-pending hour of fruition. The habit of years—the religious passion of her life—leaped from lethargy—and the long months of gradual drifting to doubt were as ity had never been. (Source: *RIDERS OF THE PURPLE SAGE* by Zane Grey)

ACTION: FALL: Terrill fell back spent and blind in her overwhelming reaction to the stampede that just passed. (Source: *WEST OF THE PECOS* by Zane Grey)

Fear (2)

ACTION: FEAR: ... stepped out as if impelled, yet she was evidently clamped with fear. (Source: *SUNSET PASS* by Zane Grey)

ACTION: FEAR: Venters felt how foolish it was for him to fear these broken walls, to fear that, after they had endured for thousands of years, the moment of his passing should be the one for them to slip. Yet he feared it. (Source: *RIDERS OF THE PURPLE SAGE* by Zane Grey)

ACTION: FEEL: (See FEEL)

Fidget (2)

ACTION: FIDGET: Lassiter acted queerly, all at once beginning to turn his sombrero around with hands that actually shook. (Source: *RIDERS OF THE PURPLE SAGE* by Zane Grey)

ACTION: FIDGET: The low voice ceased, and Lassiter closely turned his sombrero around and around, and appeared to be counting the silver ornaments on the band. (Source: *RIDERS OF THE PURPLE SAGE* by Zane Grey)

Fight (3)

ACTION: FIGHT: The half-breed's lean, small face, black almost as his stiff sombrero, underwent a hideous change that ended in a fixed yellow distortion. Fangs protruded from under his stretched lips. His slim frame vibrated under the thin black garments. And that vibration culminated in a spasmodic jerk for his gun. As it left the sheath Pecos fired to break his arm, but the heavy bullet struck the gun, spinning it away to the feet of the cowhands. Then a swifter and a different hange transfixed the half-breed. He appeared to shrink, all except his beadlike eye. Pecos aligned his gun a little higher, where it rose on a level, spurted red, and thundered. The bullet tore Felipe's stiff sombrero from his head an never touched a hairs. (Source: *WEST OF THE PECOS* by Zane Grey)

ACTION: FIGHT: There might have been, to the strained sight of a madman, an indefinable break in Pecos. Then Sawtell bawled and lunged. There was a red flash, a burst, a boom and a cloud of smoke. Sawtell's gun went flipping high. He staggered back to fall upon the porch, a great spurt of blood squirting from his heart. (Source: *WEST OF THE PECOS* by Zane Grey)

ACTION: FIGHT: There was a swift interchange of blows, then one from Rock staggered Preston. Another swift and hard, hitting solid like an ax on beef, sent Preston in a long fall. (Source: *SUNSET PASS* by Zane Grey)

Fill

ACTION: FILL: Little Fay so completely filled a long aching void in her heart. In fettering the hands of this Lasiter, she was accomplishing the greatest good of her life, and to do good even in a small way rendered happiness to Jane. (Source: *RIDERS OF THE PURPLE SAGE* by Zane Grey)

Find

ACTION: FIND: The afternoon hd well advanced when Venters [found] struck the trail of the red herd and found where it had grazed the night before. (Source: *RIDERS OF THE PURPLE SAGE* by Zane Grey)

ACTION: FIND: Whatever Fay seemed to be searching for in his sun-reddened face and quiet eyes, she evidently found. (Source: *RIDERS OF THE PURPLE SAGE* by Zane Grey)

Flee

ACTION: FLEE: Her father had inherited that temper, and at times, like antelope fleeing before fire on the slope, his people fled from his red rages. (Source: *RIDERS OF THE PURPLE SAGE* by Zane Grey)

Flick

ACTION: FLICK: He paused a moment and flicked a sagebrush with his quirt. (Source: *RIDERS OF THE PURPLE SAGE* by Zane Grey)

Flirt

ACTION: FLIRT: he had grown past flirting with any woman. Life had suddenly become sweet, strange, full of fears and hopes, something real and poignant, such as he had never experienced before. (Source: *SUNSET PASS* by Zane Grey)

Float

ACTION: FLOAT: When Jane did get out to the court, Fay was here alone and at the moment embarking on a dubious voyage down the stone-lined amber stream upon a craft of two brooms and a pillow. Fay was as delightfully wet as she could possible wish to get. Clatter of hoofs distracted Fay and interrupted the scolding she was gleefully receiving from Jane. (Source: *RIDERS OF THE PURPLE SAGE* by Zane Grey)

Flush

ACTION: FLUSH: In this plain of sage he flushed birds and rabbits, and, when he had proceeded about a mile, he caught sight of the bobbing white tails of a herd of running antelope. (Source: *RIDERS OF THE PURPLE SAGE* by Zane Grey)

Free

ACTION: FREE: They let the eight calves out of the corral, and kept only two of the burros. These they intended to ride. Bess freed all her pets, the quail and rabbits and foxes. (Source: *RIDERS OF THE PURPLE SAGE* by Zane Grey)

Gasp (2)

ACTION: GASP: a low, gasping intake of breath and a sudden twitching of body told Venters the rider still lived. (Source: *RIDERS OF THE PURPLE SAGE* by Zane Grey)

ACTION: GASP: Jane found herself gasping, passionately. She had not been conscious of it till Lassiter ended his story, and she experienced exquisite pain and relief in shedding tears. Long had her eyes been dry, her grief deep, long had her emotions been dumb. Lassiter's story put her on the rack. The appalling nature of Venters' act and speech had o parallel as an outrage; I was worse than bloodshed. Men like Tull had been shot, but had one ever been so terribly denounced in public? Over-mounting her horror, an uncontrollable, quivering passion shook her very soul. It was sheer human glory in the deed of a earless man. It was hot, primitive instinct to live—to fight. It was a kind of mad joy in Venters' chivalry. It was close to the wrath that had first shaken her in the beginning of this war waged upon her . (Source: *RIDERS OF THE PURPLE SAGE* by Zane Grey)

Gaze (5)

ACTION: GAZE: "I promise not to take you back to him or to Cottonwoods or to Glaze." The mournful earnestness of her gaze suddenly shone with unutterable gratitude and wonder. (Source: *RIDERS OF THE PURPLE SAGE* by Zane Grey)

ACTION: GAZE: He gazed ahead to make out a dust-clouded dark group of horsemen riding down the slope. . (Source: *RIDERS OF THE PURPLE SAGE* by Zane Grey)

ACTION: GAZE: Jane gazed down the wide purple slope with dreamy and troubled eyes. (Source: *RIDERS OF THE PURPLE SAGE* by Zane Grey)

ACTION: GAZE: She lay there under the cedars, gazing up through the delicate, lacy-like foliage at the blue sky. (Source: *RIDERS OF THE PURPLE SAGE* by Zane Grey)

ACTION: GAZE: Venters found the clear gaze embarrassing to him, yet, like wine, it had an exhilarating effect. (Source: *RIDERS OF THE PURPLE SAGE* by Zane Grey)

Gesture

ACTION: GESTURE: Lassiter paused, and for the thousandth time in her presence moved his black sombrero around and around, as if counting the silver pieces on the band. (Source: *RIDERS OF THE PURPLE SAGE* by Zane Grey)

Give

ACTION: GIVE: Venters said, "On, if we were only across that wide open waste of sage." "Bern, the trip's as good as made. It'll be safe ... easy. It'll be a glorious ride," she said softly. "You're a rider. She's a rider. This will be the ride of your lives," added Jane in that same soft undertone, almost as if she were musing to herself. "I give you Black Star and Night!" "Black Star and Night?" he echoed in stupid reiteration. "Lassiter, put our saddlebags on the burros." "No ... no? he said. "I won't take her racers." "Son ... cool down," returned Lassiter in a voice he might have used to a child. But with the grip with which he tore away Venter's grasping hands was that of a giant. "The burros'll do for us. We'll sneak along an' hide. I'll take your dogs an' your rifle. The blacks are yours, an', sure as I can throw a gun, you're goin' to ride safe out of the sage." (Source: *RIDERS OF THE PURPLE SAGE* by Zane Grey)

Glance (2)

ACTION: GLANCE: "Where's Fay?" asked Jane, hurriedly glancing around the shady knoll. The bright-haired child, who had appeared to be close all the time, was not in sight. "Fay!" called Jane. No answering shout of glee! No patter of flying feet! Jane saw Lassiter stiffen. "Fay ... oh, Fay! Jane almost screamed. (Source: *RIDERS OF THE PURPLE SAGE* by Zane Grey)

ACTION: GLANCE: Venter's swift glance took in the brightening valley, and Bess, and her pets, and [the dogs] Ring and Whitie. (Source: *RIDERS OF THE PURPLE SAGE* by Zane Grey)

Glare

ACTION: GLARE: He plainly was handicapped by the presence of others. He fumed, and chewed his lont mustache, and glared at his ally as if he suspected hitherto unconsidered possibilities. (Source: *WEST OF THE PECOS* by Zane Grey)

Go (2)

ACTION: GO: Jane went to the room that had once been her father's, and from a secret chamber in the thick stone wall she took a bag of gold. (Source: *RIDERS OF THE PURPLE SAGE* by Zane Grey)

ACTION: GO: She appeared to be wandering mind. Venters felt her face and hands and found them burning with fever. He went for water, and was glad to find it almost as cold as if flowing from ice. That water was the only medicine he had, and he put faith in it. She did not want to drink, but he made her swallow, and then he bathed her face and head and cooled her wrists. (Source: *RIDERS OF THE PURPLE SAGE* by Zane Grey)

Greet (2)

ACTION: GREET: "Howdy, Rock! Glad to see you," he greeted, cordially, if not heartily, extending a hand. "I seen your name on the book. Couldn't be sure till I'd had a peep at you." "Howdy, Bill!" returned Rock, as they gripped hands. (Source: *SUNSET PASS* by Zane Grey)

ACTION: GREET: It had been long since he had experienced friendly greeting from a man. Lassiter's warmed in him something that had drown cold from neglect. When he had returned it, with a strong grip of the iron hand that held his and met the gray eyes, he knew that Lassiter and he were to be friends. (Source: *RIDERS OF THE PURPLE SAGE* by Zane Grey)

Handshake

ACTION: HANDSHAKE: The grasp of his hand was rough, hard, but lacked warmth or response. (Source: *SUNSET PASS* by Zane Grey)

Hang

ACTION: HANG: This led [his] startled gaze to something dark and moving. It jerked. A man hung by his neck. Williams! He was kicking in a horribly grotesque manner. His distorted face, eyes distended, mouth wide, tongue out, was in plain sight. (Source: *WEST OF THE PECOS* by Zane Grey)

Happy

ACTION: HAPPY: To ride through the long days and at night to creep into her snug bed in the wagon brought her an ever-growing joy. (Source: *WEST OF THE PECOS* by Zane Grey)

Hate

ACTION: HATE: there was hate in the set glare of his deep gray eyes. (Source: *SUNSET PASS* by Zane Grey)

Hear

ACTION: HEAR: She had heard of Bishop Dyer's forgetting the minister in the fury of a common man, and now she was to feel it. The glance by which she measured him in turn momentarily veiled the diving in the ordinary. He looked a rancher, he was booted, spurred, and covered with dust, he carried a gun at his hip, and she remembered that he had been known to use it. But, during the long moment while he watched her, there was nothing commonplace in the slow-gathering might of his wrath. (Source: *RIDERS OF THE PURPLE SAGE* by Zane Grey)

Help

ACTION: HELP: He helped her to a seat beside him on the bench, and he respected her silence that he divined was full of a woman's deep emotion beyond his understanding. (Source: *RIDERS OF THE PURPLE SAGE* by Zane Grey)

Hesitate

ACTION: HESITATE: Venters hesitated. It would be a foolhardy man who risked his life under the leaning, waiting avalanches of rock in that gigantic split.. (Source: *RIDERS OF THE PURPLE SAGE* by Zane Grey)

Hide (4)

ACTION: HIDE: "That's the worst of our trail past. We've only men to fear now. If we can get up in the sage, we can hide and slip long like coyotes." (Source: *RIDERS OF THE PURPLE SAGE* by Zane Grey)

ACTION: HIDE: He hid his rifle in the sage, marking its exact location with extreme care. Then he faced down the lane and strode toward the center of the village. (Source: *RIDERS OF THE PURPLE SAGE* by Zane Grey)

ACTION: HIDE: He hurried to the spot where the first rustler had been dragged by his horse. The man lay in deep grass, dead, jaw fallen, eyes protruding. The first man at whom Venters had ever aimed a weapon he had shot through the heart. With the clammy sweat oozing from every pore, Venters dragged the [dead] rustler in among some boulders and covered him with slabs of rock. Then he smoothed out the crushed trail in grass and sage. The rustler's horse had stopped a quarter of a mile off and was grazing. (Source: *RIDERS OF THE PURPLE SAGE* by Zane Grey)

ACTION: HIDE: He was not disposed to run. His cool mood tightened under grip of excitement, as he reflected that whoever the approaching riders were they could not be friends. He slipped out of the saddle and led [the horse] behind the tallest sage bush. It might serve to conceal them till the riders were close enough for him to see who they were; after that, he would be indifferent to how soon they discovered him. (Source: *RIDERS OF THE PURPLE SAGE* by Zane Grey)

Hope

ACTION: HOPE: "Pecos, you've got my hopes so high now I'm riding the clouds instead of my saddle," replied Terrill. (Source: *WEST OF THE PECOS* by Zane Grey)

Hug (2)

ACTION: HUG: ... smile was like a warm hug. (Source: *Author*)

ACTION: HUG: She sprang up in despairing, breaking spirit, and encircled his neck with her arms, and held him in an embrace that he strove vainly to loosen. (Source: *RIDERS OF THE PURPLE SAGE* by Zane Grey)

Humor

ACTION: HUMOR: "What you shakin' aboot boy?" queried Smith, in a cool, drawling voice, suggestive of humor. (Source: *WEST OF THE PECOS* by Zane Grey)

Hungry

ACTION: HUNGRY: "I reckon, I'll only stay a little while," Lassiter was saying. "An' if you don't mind troublin', I'm hungry. I fetched some biscuits along, but they're gone. Venters, this place is sure wonderfulest I ever seen. Them cut step on the slope! That outlet into the gorge! An' it's like climbin' up through hell into heaven to climb through that gorge into this valley! There's a queer-lookin' rock at the top of the passage. I didn't have time to stop. I'm wonderin' how you ever found this place. It's sure interestin'." (Source: *RIDERS OF THE PURPLE SAGE* by Zane Grey)

Hurry

ACTION: HURRY: He hurried out, bareheaded and in his shirt sleeves. (Source: *SUNSET PASS* by Zane Grey)

Imagine (2)

ACTION: IMAGINE: Rick pictured in his mind the wild range south of [tongue] and particularly the broken Sunset Pass country with its sage flats and cedar ridges and pinioned gorges and the purple timber uplands. There had never been a more beautiful wilderness known to Rock or one harder on riders, horses, and cattle. (Source: *SUNSET PASS* by Zane Grey)

ACTION: IMAGINE: She pictured Venters about his lonely campfire sitting between his faithful dogs. (Source: *RIDERS OF THE PURPLE SAGE* by Zane Grey)

Interrupt (2)

ACTION: INTERRUPT: "I promise you this," he interrupted in stern passion that thrilled while it terrorized her. "If you say one more word for that damned plotter, I'll kill him s I would a mad coyote!" (Source: *RIDERS OF THE PURPLE SAGE* by Zane Grey)

ACTION: INTERRUPT: Trampling of hoofs interrupted the rider. More restless movements on the part of Tull's men broke up the little circle, exposing the reasoner Venters. (Source: *RIDERS OF THE PURPLE SAGE* by Zane Grey)

Itch

ACTION: ITCH: "Smith, if you've got thet queer hand-itch fer a gun, won't you grease it with axle grease or somethin'?" (Source: *WEST OF THE PECOS* by Zane Grey)

Kill (2)

ACTION: KILL: One more trip he undertook to the rustler's valley, and this time he roped a yearling steer from the rustled herd and killed it and cut out a small quarter of beef. The howling of coyotes told him he need have no apprehension that the work of his knife would be discovered. He packed the beef back to camp and hung it upon a spruce tree. (Source: *RIDERS OF THE PURPLE SAGE* by Zane Grey)

ACTION: KILL: The border was a bloody place. But life had always been bloody. Men were blood spillers. Phases of the history of the world flashed through her mind—Greek and roman wars—dark medieval times—the crimes in the name of religions. On sea, on land, everywhere—shooting, stabbing, cursing, clashing, fighting men!
Greed—power—oppression—fanaticism—love—hate—revenge—justice-these men killed one another. (Source: *RIDERS OF THE PURPLE SAGE* by Zane Grey)

Kiss (3)

ACTION: KISS: Quick as a bird she pecked his cheek, to lift a flushing radiant face. "There! The first sisterly one I ever gave you.". (Source: *SUNSET PASS* by Zane Grey)

ACTION: KISS: Instantly, as if by some divine insight, he knew himself in the remaking—tried—found wanting—but stronger, better, surer—and he wheeled to her eager, joyous, passionate, wild exalted. He bent to her; he left tears and kisses on her hands. (Source: *RIDERS OF THE PURPLE SAGE* by Zane Grey)

ACTION: KISS: The kiss he gave her seemed singular in that it held an element of finality. He never kissed her again. (Source: *WEST OF THE PECOS* by Zane Grey)

Know

ACTION: KNOW: He knew that behind the corner of stone would be a cave or a crack that could never be suspected from below. Chance that had sported with him of late, now directed him to a probable hiding place. (Source: *RIDERS OF THE PURPLE SAGE* by Zane Grey)

Laugh (5)

ACTION: LAUGH: "Do oo love my new muvver?" she asked with bewildering demureness. Jane laughed, and not for the first time in many a day she felt a stir of her pulse and warmth in her cheek. (Source: *RIDERS OF THE PURPLE SAGE* by Zane Grey)

ACTION: LAUGH: ... there at the sight of her face he laughed outright. (Source: *RIDERS OF THE PURPLE SAGE* by Zane Grey)

ACTION: LAUGH: As many times as he had ridden out from ... and other towns, and from the innumerable range camps all over the West, not one of them had ever been like this venture. He laughed at himself. His boyhood had returned. There was nothing but good and joy in the world. (Source: *SUNSET PASS* by Zane Grey)

ACTION: LAUGH: There was a dark blue merry flashing of eyes, and a parting of lips—then she laughed. In that moment she was naïve and wholesome. (Source: *RIDERS OF THE PURPLE SAGE* by Zane Grey)

ACTION: LAUGH: Venters uttered a short laugh. (Source: *RIDERS OF THE PURPLE SAGE* by Zane Grey)

Lay (2)

ACTION: LAY: Outstretched upon the stable floor lay Blake, ghastly white—dead—one hand clutching a gun and the other twisted in his bloody blouse. (Source: *RIDERS OF THE PURPLE SAGE* by Zane Grey)

ACTION: LAY: Venters lay under the silver spruces, recuperating from his almost prostrating exertion in dragging packs and burros up the slope and through the entrance to Surprise Valley. (Source: *RIDERS OF THE PURPLE SAGE* by Zane Grey)

Lead (4)

ACTION: LEAD: He unstrapped the saddlebags from the burros, slipped the saddles, and let them lie [on the ground], turned the burros loose, and, calling the dogs, led the way through stones and cedars to an open where two horses stood. (Source: *RIDERS OF THE PURPLE SAGE* by Zane Grey)

ACTION: LEAD: Then Venters flipped Black Star's bridle and, sharply trotting, led the other horses to the center of the village. Here at the intersecting streets and in front of the stores he halted once more. The usual, lounging atmosphere of that prominent corner was not now in evidence. Riders and ranchers and villagers broke up what must have been absorbing conversation. There was a rush of many feet, and then the walk was lined with faces. (Source: *RIDERS OF THE PURPLE SAGE* by Zane Grey)

ACTION: LEAD: Up on the stone-flag drive, nicked with the marks made by the iron-shod hoofs of her racers, Lassiter led her. (Source: *RIDERS OF THE PURPLE SAGE* by Zane Grey)

ACTION: LEAD: Venters saddled and led [the horse] out of the oak thicket and, leaping astride, rode up the canyon, with [the dogs] Ring and White trotting behind. (Source: *RIDERS OF THE PURPLE SAGE* by Zane Grey)

Lean

ACTION: LEAN: " [He] has men watch the herds ... they would kill you. You must never go again!" When she had spoken, the strength and the blaze of her died, and she swayed toward Venters. "I'll not go again!" he said, catching her. She leaned against him, an her body was limp and vibrated to a long, wavering tremble. But as her fear was instinctive, so was her clinging to this one and only friend. (Source: *RIDERS OF THE PURPLE SAGE* by Zane Grey)

Leap

ACTION: LEAP: [Wrangle's] rider leaped off, throwing the bridle, and held hard on a lasso looped around Wrangle's head and neck. (Source: *RIDERS OF THE PURPLE SAGE* by Zane Grey)

Learn

ACTION: LEARN: In the end, when her awakening came, she learned that she had built better than she knew. Lassiter, although kinder and gentler than ever, had parted with his quaint humor, and his coldness, and his tranquility, to become a restless and unhappy man. Whatever the power of his deadly intent toward Mormons, that passion now had a rival and one equally burning and consuming. Jane had one moment of exultation before the dawn of a strange uneasiness/ What if she had made of herself a lure, at tremendous cost to him and to her, and all in vain?. (Source: *RIDERS OF THE PURPLE SAGE* by Zane Grey)

Lift

ACTION: LIFT: She lift her head with the singular, wild grace always part of her actions, with that old unconscious intimation of innocence that always tortured him, but now with something more—a spirit rising from the depts.—tat linked itself to his brave words. "I've been thinking ... too," she said with quivering smile and swelling breast. (Source: *RIDERS OF THE PURPLE SAGE* by Zane Grey)

Listen (4)

ACTION: LISTEN: At intervals he put his hand on the dog, and stopped to listen. There was a drowsy hum of insects, but no other sound disturbed the warm midday stillness. (Source: *RIDERS OF THE PURPLE SAGE* by Zane Grey)

ACTION: LISTEN: Every little while certainty of her death came to him with a shock, and then he would bend over and lay his ear on her breast. Her heart still beat. (Source: *RIDERS OF THE PURPLE SAGE* by Zane Grey)

ACTION: LISTEN: From time to time he stopped to listen and herd only the usual familiar bark of coyote and sweep of wind and rustle of sage.. (Source: *RIDERS OF THE PURPLE SAGE* by Zane Grey)

ACTION: LISTEN: Jane leaned toward him, petrified in a position of waiting, listening intensity. She could have shrieked, but power of tongue and lips was denied her. She saw only this sad, gray, passion-worn man, and she heard only the faint rustling of the leaves. (Source: *RIDERS OF THE PURPLE SAGE* by Zane Grey)

Look (19)

ACTION: LOOK: [As they descended out of the gorge] Venters had an irresistible desire to look upward at Balancing Rock. It had always haunted him and now he wondered if he were really to get through the outlet before the huge stone thundered down. Every few steps he answered to the strange, nervous fear and turned to make sure the rock still stood—like a giant statue. As in a dream, he saw this long-standing thunderbolt of the little Stone Age men plunge down to close forever the outlet to Deception Pass. While he was giving way to unaccountable imaginings of dread, the descent was accomplished without mishap. "I'm glad that's over," he said, breathing more freely. "I hope I'm past that hanging rock for good and all. Since almost the moment I first saw it, I've had an idea that it was waiting for me. Now, when it does fall, if I'm thousands of miles away, I'll hear it [fall]." (Source: *RIDERS OF THE PURPLE SAGE* by Zane Grey)

ACTION: LOOK: [She] looked up into a face that she trusted instinctively and which riveted her attention. . (Source: *RIDERS OF THE PURPLE SAGE* by Zane Grey)

ACTION: LOOK: ... her clear gray eyes on him. (Source: *SUNSET PASS* by Zane Grey)

ACTION: LOOK: As if compelled against her will—answering to an irresistible voice—Bess raised her bowed head, looked at him with sad, dark eyes, and tried to whisper with tremulous lips. (Source: *RIDERS OF THE PURPLE SAGE* by Zane Grey)

ACTION: LOOK: Ash Preston measured Rock again, a long penetrating look that was neither insolent nor curious, but which added something to his first impression. (Source: *WEST OF THE PECOS* by Zane Grey)

ACTION: LOOK: From the cover of a cedar, he peered out and down the slope. It sheered steep and rough, down to an open draw. This draw appeared green, with a dry winding wash in the center. It led up to a wide pocket, where yellow water gleamed.. (Source: *SUNSET PASS* by Zane Grey)

ACTION: LOOK: He carefully cleaned and reloaded his guns. When he rose to go, be bent a long glance down upon the unconscious girl. Then ordering [the dogs] Whitie and Ring to keep guard, he left the camp. (Source: *RIDERS OF THE PURPLE SAGE* by Zane Grey)

ACTION: LOOK: In the dimming, pale light Venters looked down upo the girl. She had sunk into his arms, upon his breast, burying her face. She clung to him. He felt the softness of her, and the warmth, and the quick heave of her breast. He saw the dark, slender, graceful outline of her form. A woman lay in his arms! And he held her closer. He who had been alone in the sad, silent watches of the night was not now and never must be again alone. He who had yearned for the touch of a hand felt the long tremble and the heartbeat of a woman. (Source: *RIDERS OF THE PURPLE SAGE* by Zane Grey)

ACTION: LOOK: Lassiter looked at the grave and then out into space. At that moment he seemed a figure of bronze. (Source: *RIDERS OF THE PURPLE SAGE* by Zane Grey)

ACTION: LOOK: Lassiter suddenly moved forward, and with that beautiful light in his face now strangely luminous he looked at Jane and Venters, and then let his soft bright gaze rest on Bess. "Well, I reckon you're all had your say, an' now it's Lassiter's turn." (Source: *RIDERS OF THE PURPLE SAGE* by Zane Grey)

ACTION: LOOK: Looking at him—he was so terrible of aspect—she could not comprehend his words. Who was this man with the face gray as death, with eyes that would have made her shriek had she the strength, with the strange, ruthlessly bitter lips?

Where had vanished the gentle Lassiter? What was this presence in the hall, about him, about her—this cold, invisible presence? "Yes, it's ended, Jane," he was saying, so awfully quiet and cool and implacable, "an' I'm going' to make a little call." (Source: *RIDERS OF THE PURPLE SAGE* by Zane Grey)

ACTION: LOOK: She looked long [in the mirror] at the stately form with its gracious contours, at the fair face with its strong chin and full, firm lips, at the dark blue, proud, and passionate eyes. (Source: *RIDERS OF THE PURPLE SAGE* by Zane Grey)

ACTION: LOOK: She looked strongly into his eyes, and for the life of her could not quite subdue an imperiousness that rose within her spirit. (Source: *RIDERS OF THE PURPLE SAGE* by Zane Grey)

ACTION: LOOK: She shot him a gray glance not wholly doubtful or unforgiving. And meeting his eyes caused her to look down again with a tinge of color staining her cheeks. (Source: *SUNSET PASS* by Zane Grey)

ACTION: LOOK: The intense blue of his eyes, steady on Rock, changed only with a flare. (Source: *SUNSET PASS* by Zane Grey)

ACTION: LOOK: The trail driver gave a sly look at Mary, which made her blush flamingly. (Source: *WEST OF THE PECOS* by Zane Grey)

ACTION: LOOK: The younger rider had been bending his intent, clear gaze upon Rock and had formed conclusions. (Source: *SUNSET PASS* by Zane Grey)

ACTION: LOOK: Then he gave her one long look as she stood now in the moonlight. Then he strode away, and when he turned, at quite some distance, she was still standing like a white statue. (Source: *SUNSET PASS* by Zane Grey)

ACTION: LOOK: Venters rose cautiously and looked over the sage. A band of struggling horsemen were riding across the oval ground. He sank down, startled and trembling. Hurriedly he glanced about for a place to hide. He dared not risk crossing the open patches to reach the rocks. Again he peeped over the sage. The rustlers were approaching, but not directly in line with him. That was relief for a cold deadness that seemed to be creeping inward along his veins. He crouched down with bated breath and held the bristling dog. (Source: *RIDERS OF THE PURPLE SAGE* by Zane Grey)

Love (5)

ACTION: LOVE: Aloud he spoke—unburdened his heart—confessed his secret. For an instant the golden valley swam before his eyes, and the walls waved, and all about him whirled with the tumult within. "I love her!" (Source: *RIDERS OF THE PURPLE SAGE* by Zane Grey)

ACTION: LOVE: Hope had not died. Doubt and fear, subservient to her will, no longer gave her sleepless nights and tortured days. Love remained. All that she had loved she now loved the more. She seemed to feel that she was defiantly flinging the wealth of her love in the face of misfortune and of hate. (Source: *RIDERS OF THE PURPLE SAGE* by Zane Grey)

ACTION: LOVE: No more did he listen to the rush and roar of thunderstorm. For with the touch of clinging hands and throbbing bosom he grew conscious of an inward storm—the tingling of new chords of thought. Strange music of unheard joyous bells—sad dreams dawning to wakeful delight—dissolving doubt, resurging hope, force, fire, and freedom—unutterable wetness of desire. [There was] a storm in his heart—a storm of real love. (Source: *RIDERS OF THE PURPLE SAGE* by Zane Grey)

ACTION: LOVE: She loved it all—the grove of cottonwoods, the old stone house, the amber-tinted water, and the droves of shaggy, dusty horses and mustangs, the sleek, clean-limbed, blooded racers, and the browsing herds of cattle, and the lean sun-bronzed riders of the sage. (Source: *RIDERS OF THE PURPLE SAGE* by Zane Grey)

ACTION: LOVE: That ever was the burden on [the] tidings [of the wind],—youth in the shady woods—waders through the wet meadows—boy and girl at the hedgerow stile—bathers in the booming surf—sweet, idle hours on grassy, windy hills—long strolls down moonlit lanes—everywhere in far-off lands, fingers locked and bursting hearts and longing lips—from all the world tidings of unquenchable love. (Source: *RIDERS OF THE PURPLE SAGE* by Zane Grey)

Miss

ACTION: MISS: Jane missed the rattle and trot, canter and gallop of the incoming riders on the hard trails. (Source: *RIDERS OF THE PURPLE SAGE* by Zane Grey)

Moan

ACTION: MOAN: The girl's eyes were open; a feverish spot burned in her cheeks; she moaned something unintelligible to Venters, but he took the movement of her lips to mean that she wanted water. Lifting her head, he tipped the canteen to her lips. After that she again lapsed into unconsciousness or a weakness that was its counterpart. Venters noted, however, that the burning flush had faded into the former pallor. (Source: *RIDERS OF THE PURPLE SAGE* by Zane Grey)

Move (14)

ACTION: MOVE: "Dad, I'm sorrowful at leavin' home." "I am, too!" he replied with tears in his eyes. (Source: *WEST OF THE PECOS* by Zane Grey)

ACTION: MOVE: He backed out the door, his blue eyes like fire under ice, and then he stalked off the porch toward his cabin. (Source: *SUNSET PASS* by Zane Grey)

ACTION: MOVE: He climbed over rough, broken rock, picking his way carefully, and then went down where it was darker and sheltered from the wind. A white object guided him. It was another dog, and this one was asleep, curled up between a saddle and a pack. He placed the saddle for a pillow, rolled in his blankets, with his face upward to the stars. The white dog snuggled close to him. The other whined and pattered a few yards to the rise of ground, and there crouched on guard. (Source: *RIDERS OF THE PURPLE SAGE* by Zane Grey)

ACTION: MOVE: He passed the black cottonwoods and, entering the sage, climbed the gradual slope. He kept his direction in line with a western star. (Source: *RIDERS OF THE PURPLE SAGE* by Zane Grey)

ACTION: MOVE: he threw up his head so that the ruddy firelight played upon his tanned face. (Source: *WEST OF THE PECOS* by Zane Grey)

ACTION: MOVE: He waited until the faint slam of a door assured him she had reached the house, and then, taking up his rifle, he noiselessly slipped through the bushes, down the knoll, and on under the dark trees to the edge of the grove. (Source: *RIDERS OF THE PURPLE SAGE* by Zane Grey)

ACTION: MOVE: He wheeled in his chair to regard Lassiter in amazement. (Source: *RIDERS OF THE PURPLE SAGE* by Zane Grey)

ACTION: MOVE: Keeping close to the edge of the cottonwoods, he went swiftly and silently westward. (Source: *RIDERS OF THE PURPLE SAGE* by Zane Grey)

ACTION: MOVE: She made a fierce, passionate movement, clutched the [spy}glass tightly, shook as with the passing of a spasm, and then dropped her head. (Source: *RIDERS OF THE PURPLE SAGE* by Zane Grey)

ACTION: MOVE: That brought her erect, trembling and ashy pale, with dark, proud eyes and mute lips refuting his insinuation. (Source: *RIDERS OF THE PURPLE SAGE* by Zane Grey)

ACTION: MOVE: The outgoing riders moved swiftly and came sharply into sight as they topped a bridge to show wild and black above the horizon, and then passed down dimming into the purple of the sage. (Source: *RIDERS OF THE PURPLE SAGE* by Zane Grey)

ACTION: MOVE: Then she left him and moved away, a white, gliding shape that soon vanished in the shadows. (Source: *RIDERS OF THE PURPLE SAGE* by Zane Grey)

ACTION: MOVE: They were stirring long before the red burst of sun glorified the eastern wall. (Source: *WEST OF THE PECOS* by Zane Grey)

ACTION: MOVE: When she returned from this, her last walk along the beloved old canal with its water-lily pads floating on the still surface, she found the horses in the yard, and Sambo carrying out her little brass-bound French trunk. (Source: *WEST OF THE PECOS* by Zane Grey)

Nod

ACTION: NOD: The rider responded with a curt nod. The wide brim of a black sombrero cast a dark shade over his face. For a moment he closely regarded Tull and his comrades, and then, halting in his slow walk, he seemed to relax. "'Evenin' ma'am," he said to Jane, and removed his sombrero with quaint grace. (Source: *RIDERS OF THE PURPLE SAGE* by Zane Grey)

Open

ACTION: OPEN: "Open [the locket]," he said with a singularly rich voice. Bess complied, but listlessly. "Take a look at the pictures. Don't you know the woman?" Jane, after one glance, drew back. "Milly erne! She cried wonderingly. "Yes, that's Milly," said Lassiter softly. "Bess, did you ever see her face ... look hard ... with all your heart an' soul?" "The eyes seem to haunt me," whispered Bess. Lassiter's strong arm went around her, and he bent his head. "Lass, I thought you'd remember her eyes. They're the same beautiful eyes you'd see if you looked in a mirror or a clear spring. They're your mother's eyes. You are Milly Erne's child. Your name is Elizabeth Erne. You're the daughter of Frank Erne, a man once my best friend." "And I'm Milly's brother, an' your uncle! Uncle Jim!" (Source: *RIDERS OF THE PURPLE SAGE* by Zane Grey)

Outline

ACTION: OUTLINE: Briefly, in few words, Jane outlined the circumstances of her undoing in the weeks of his absence. Under his beard and bronze she saw his face whiten in terrible wrath. (Source: *RIDERS OF THE PURPLE SAGE* by Zane Grey)

Pace (2)

ACTION: PACE: Pecos lowered his gun, but he kept up his pacing to and fro, his strange eyes pivoting like the oscillations of a compass needle. He had the lunge, the standing hair, the savageness of a wild animal. (Source: *WEST OF THE PECOS* by Zane Grey)

ACTION: PACE: Pecos took to pacing the porch, his hands behind his back, his brow knitted in thought. He was no longer the smiling, cool, and kindly Pecos. The picture faintly resembled a somber Pecos. (Source: *WEST OF THE PECOS* by Zane Grey)

Pass

ACTION: PASS: He passed shady pockets [in the rock] half full of water, and as he marked the location for possible future need, he reflected that there had been no rain since the winter snows. (Source: *RIDERS OF THE PURPLE SAGE* by Zane Grey)

Pause

ACTION: PAUSE: Here Lassiter paused while he turned his sombrero around and around in his familiar habit and his eyes had the look of a man seeing over again some thrilling spectacle, and under his red bronze there was strange animations and play of feature. (Source: *RIDERS OF THE PURPLE SAGE* by Zane Grey)

Penetrate

ACTION: PENETRATE: Venters penetrated into one of these offshoot [pockets], and, as he had hoped, he found abundant grass. He had to bend the oak saplings to het his horse through. Deciding to make this a hiding place, if he could find water, he worked back to the limit of the shelving walls. In a little cluster of silver spruces he found a spring. This enclosed nook seemed n ideal place to leave his horse and to camp at night, and from which to make stealthy trips on foot. The thick grass hid his trail; the dense growth of oaks in the opening would serve as a barrier to keep his horse in, if indeed the luxuriant browse would not suffice for that. So Venters, leaving Whittie with the horse, called Ring to his side and, rifle in hand, worked his way out to the open. A careful photographing in mind of the formation of the bold outlines of rim rock assured him he would be able to return to his retreat even in the dark. (Source: *RIDERS OF THE PURPLE SAGE* by Zane Grey)

Perceive

ACTION: PERCEIVE: Perceptions flashed upon him,—faint, cold touch of breeze, a cold, silvery trickle of flowing water, a cold sun shining out of a cold sky, song of birds and laughter of children coldly distant. (Source: *RIDERS OF THE PURPLE SAGE* by Zane Grey)

Plan (2)

ACTION: PLAN: After a day of rest he recovered his strength, and shared her pleasure in rummaging over the endless packs, and began to plan for the future. (Source: *RIDERS OF THE PURPLE SAGE* by Zane Grey)

ACTION: PLAN: He had so grown into the habit of passing from one dreamy pleasure to another, like a bee going from flower to flower in the valley, that he found this wandering habit likely to extend to his labors. Nevertheless, he made a start. (Source: *RIDERS OF THE PURPLE SAGE* by Zane Grey)

Point

ACTION: POINT: He pointed to several moving specks of black and puffs of dust in the purple sage [from those who stampeded the herd]. (Source: *RIDERS OF THE PURPLE SAGE* by Zane Grey)

Proceed

ACTION: PROCEED: Early in the morning he proceeded on his way and about the middle of the forenoon reached the constricted gap that marked the southerly end of the pass and through which led the trail up to the sage level. (Source: *RIDERS OF THE PURPLE SAGE* by Zane Grey)

Proud

ACTION: PROUD: "Miss Withersteen, I make proud to say I've not lost a steer." (Source: *RIDERS OF THE PURPLE SAGE* by Zane Grey)

Push

ACTION: PUSH: Instinctively he put his hands on it and pushed; then his shoulder and heaved. The [giant] stone seemed to groan, to stir, to grate, and then to move. It tipped a little downward and hung balancing for a long instant, slowly returned, rocked slightly, groaned, and settled back to its former position. (Source: *RIDERS OF THE PURPLE SAGE* by Zane Grey)

Perspire

ACTION: PERSPIRE: The day was hot, and what with brisk exercise and the emotion under which he labored, he was wet with perspiration. (Source: *SUNSET PASS* by Zane Grey)

Please

ACTION: PLEASE: A subtle change had begun to affect his pleasure in returning to the town. He left the station, giving a wide berth to the street corner that had clouded his happy reflections. (Source: *SUNSET PASS* by Zane Grey)

Pursue (31)

ACTION: PURSUE: "Now Wrangle!" cried Venters. "Run! You big devil! Run!" Venters laid the reins on Wrangle's neck and dropped the loop over the pommel. The sorrel needed no guiding on that smooth trail. He was surer-footed in a run than at any other fast gait, and his running gave the impression of something devilish. He might now have been activated by Venters's spirit; undoubtedly his savage running fitted the mood of his rider. Venters bent forward, swinging with the horse, and gripped his rifle. His eye measured the distance between him and Jerry Card. (Source: *RIDERS OF THE PURPLE SAGE* by Zane Grey)

ACTION: PURSUE: "Wrangle, the race is on," said Venters grimly. "We'll canter with them and gallop with them and run with them. We'll let them set the pace." (Source: *RIDERS OF THE PURPLE SAGE* by Zane Grey)

ACTION: PURSUE: Again Venters began slipping fresh cartridges into the magazine of his rifle, and his hand was so sure and steady that he did not drop a single cartridge. With the eye of a rider and the judgment of a marksman he once more measured the distance between him and Jerry Card. Wrangle had gained, bringing him into rifle range. Venters was hard put to it now to resist shooting but thought it better to withhold his fire. Jerry, who in anticipation of a running fusillade had huddled himself into a little, twisted ball on Black Star's neck, now surmising that his pursuer would make sure of not wounding one of the blacks rose to his natural seat in the saddle. (Source: *RIDERS OF THE PURPLE SAGE* by Zane Grey)

ACTION: PURSUE: As the afternoon wore away, Venters concern diminished, yet he kept close watch on the blacks [black horses], and the trail, and the sage. There was no telling what Jerry Card might be capable of. Venters sullenly acquiesced to the idea that the rider had been too quick and too shrewd for him. Strangely, and doggedly, however, Venters clung to his foreboding of Card's downfall. (Source: *RIDERS OF THE PURPLE SAGE* by Zane Grey)

ACTION: PURSUE: Cruelly he struck his spurs into Wrangle's flanks. A light touch of spur was sufficient to make Wrangle plunge. Now with a ringing, wild snort, he seemed to double up in muscular convulsion and to shift forward with an impetus that almost unseated Venters. The sage blurred by, the trail flashed by—and the wind robbed him of breath and hearing. (Source: *RIDERS OF THE PURPLE SAGE* by Zane Grey)

ACTION: PURSUE: For the hundredth time Venters measured the width of space separating him from Jerry Card. Wrangle had ceased to gain. The blacks were proving their fleetness. Venters watched Jerry Card, admiring the little rider's horsemanship. He had the incomparable seat of the upland rider, born in the saddle. It struck Venters that Card had changed his position, or the position of the horses. Presently Venters remembered positively that Jerry had been leading Night on the right hand side of the trail. The racer was now on the side to the left. No, it was Black Star. But, Venters argued in amazement, Jerry had been mounted on Black Star. Another clearer, keener gaze assured Venters that Black Star was really riderless. Night now carried Jerry Card. (Source: *RIDERS OF THE PURPLE SAGE* by Zane Grey)

ACTION: PURSUE: From time to time he glanced backward, as a wise general in retreat calculating his chances and the power and speed of pursuers, and the moment for the last, desperate burst. No doubt Card, with his life at stake, gloried in that race, perhaps more wildly than Venters. He had been born to the sage and the saddle and the wild. He was more than half horse. Not until the last call—the sudden, up-flashing instinct of self-preservation—would he lose his skill and judgment and nerve—and the spirit of that race. Venters seemed to read Jerry's mind. (Source: *RIDERS OF THE PURPLE SAGE* by Zane Grey)

ACTION: PURSUE: He considered the [pursuit] with cunning mind. The rider on Bells would probably drop behind and take to the sage. What he did was of little moment to Venters. To stop Jerry Card, his evil, hidden career as well as his present flight, and then to catch the blacks—that was all that concerned him. (Source: *RIDERS OF THE PURPLE SAGE* by Zane Grey)

ACTION: PURSUE: In a few miles of that swinging canter Wrangle [the horse] had crept appreciably closer to the three horses [of the escaping rustlers]. Jerry Card turned again. When he saw the sorrel had gained, he put Black Star to a gallop. The horses running on either side of Black Star swept into the same stride. (Source: *RIDERS OF THE PURPLE SAGE* by Zane Grey)

ACTION: PURSUE: In his mind perhaps, as certainly as in Venters's, this moment was the beginning of the real race. Venters leaned forward to put his hand on Wrangle's neck, then backward to put it on his flank. Under the shaggy, dusty hair trembled and vibrated a wonderful muscular activity. But Wrangle's flesh was still cold. What a cold-blooded brute, thought Venters, and felt in him a love for the horse he had never given to any other. It would not have been humanly possible for any rider, even though clutched by hate or revenge, or a passion to save a loved one or ear of his own life, to be astride the sorrel, to swing with his swing, to see his magnificent stride and hear the rapid thunder of his hoofs, to ride him in that race and not glory in the ride. (Source: *RIDERS OF THE PURPLE SAGE* by Zane Grey)

ACTION: PURSUE: In less than two miles of running Bells began to drop behind the blacks and Wrangle began to overhaul him. Venters anticipated that the rustler would soon take to the sage. Yet he did not. Not improbably he reasoned that the powerful sorrel could more easily overtake Bells in the heavier going outside of the trail. Soon only a few hundred yards lay between Bells and Wrangle. (Source: *RIDERS OF THE PURPLE SAGE* by Zane Grey)

ACTION: PURSUE: In searching around in the little hollows, Venters, much to his relief, found water. He composed himself to rest and eat some bread and meat, while he waited for a sufficient time to elapse so that he could safely give the horses a drink. He judged the hour to be somewhere around noon. Wrangle lay down to rest, and Night followed suit. So long as they were down, Venters intended to make no move. The longer they rested, the better, and the safer it would be to give them water. (Source: *RIDERS OF THE PURPLE SAGE* by Zane Grey)

ACTION: PURSUE: Jerry Card bent forward with his teeth fast in the front of Wrangle's nose! Venters saw it. Moreover, there flashed over him a memory of this trick of a few desperate riders. He even though of one rider who had worn off his teeth in this terrible hold to beak or control wildly fierce horses. Wrangle had, indeed, gone mad. The marvel was what guided him. Was it the half-brute—the more than half-horse instinct of Jerry Card? Whatever the mystery, it was true. In a few more rods Jerry would have the sorrel turning into the trail, leading down into the canyon. (Source: *RIDERS OF THE PURPLE SAGE* by Zane Grey)

ACTION: PURSUE: Jerry Card turned once more. The way he shifted to Black Star showed he had to make his last, desperate running. Venters aimed to the side of the trail and sent a bullet puffing the dust beyond Jerry. Venters hoped to frighten the rider and get him to take to the sage. But Jerry returned the shot, and his ball struck dangerously close in the dust at Wrangle's flying feet. Venters held his fire then, while Card emptied his revolver. For a mile, with Black Star leaving Night behind and doing his utmost, Wrangle did not gain—for another mile he gained little if at all. In the third he caught up with the now galloping Night and began to gain rapidly on the other black. (Source: *RIDERS OF THE PURPLE SAGE* by Zane Grey)

ACTION: PURSUE: Jerry Card wheeled once more [to look back at the pursuer]. Venters distinctly saw the flash of his red face in the sun. This time he looked long. Venters laughed. He knew what passed in Card's mind. The rider was trying to make out what horse it happened to be that gained on Jane's peerless racers. Wrangle had been away from the village that not improbably Jerry Card had forgotten. Besides, whatever Jerry's qualifications for his fame as the greatest rider of the sage, certain it was that his best point was not farsightedness. He had not recognized Wrangle. After what must have been a searching gaze, he got his comrade to face about. The action gave Venters amusement. It spoke so surely of the fact that neither Card nor the rustler actually knew their danger. Yet if they kept to the trail—and the last thing such men would do would be to leave it—they were both doomed. (Source: *RIDERS OF THE PURPLE SAGE* by Zane Grey)

ACTION: PURSUE: So with his passion to kill still keen and unabated, Venters lived out that ride, and drank a rider's sage-sweet cup of wilderness to the dregs. When Wrangle's long mane, lashing in the wind, stung Venters in the cheek, the sting add a beat to his flying pulse. He bent a downward glance to try to see Wrangle's actual stride, and saw only twinkling, darting streaks, and the white rush of the rail. He watched the sorrel's savage head, pointed level, his mouth still closed and dry, but his nostrils distended as if her were snorting unseen fire. Wrangle was he horse for a race with death. Upon each side Venters saw the sage merged into a sailing, colorless wall. In the front sloped the lay of ground with its purple breadth split by the white [herd] [cattle] trail. The wind, blowing heavy, steady blast into his face, sickened him with enduring, sweet odor, and filled his ears with a hollow, rushing roar. (Source: *RIDERS OF THE PURPLE SAGE* by Zane Grey)

ACTION: PURSUE: The long-kindling, stormy fire in his heart burst into flame. He spurred his horse, and, as the horse got going, he slipped cartridges into the magazine of his rifle till it was once again full. Card and his companion were now half a mile or more in advance, riding easily down the slope. (Source: *RIDERS OF THE PURPLE SAGE* by Zane Grey)

ACTION: PURSUE: Thenceforth, while Wrangle sped on, Venters glued his eyes to the little rider. Jerry Card rode as only he could ride. Of all the daring horsemen of the uplands Jerry was the one rider best fitted to bring out the greatness of the blacks in that long race. He had them on a dead run, but not yet at the last strained and killing pace. (Source: *RIDERS OF THE PURPLE SAGE* by Zane Grey)

ACTION: PURSUE: This comrade of Card's whirled far around in his saddle, and he even shaded is eyes from the sun. He, too, looked long. Then, all at once, he faced ahead again and, bending low in the saddle, began to fling his right arm up and down. That flinging Venters knew to be the lashing of Bells. Jerry also became active. The three racers [horses] lengthened out into a run. (Source: *RIDERS OF THE PURPLE SAGE* by Zane Grey)

ACTION: PURSUE: Turning, he drew Black Star close and closer toward Night till they ran side-by-side as one horse. Then Card raised himself in the saddle, slipped out of the stirrups, and, somehow twisting himself, leaped upon Black Str. He did not even lose the swing of the horse. Like a leech he was there on the other saddle, and as the horses separated, his right foot that had been doubled under him, shot down to catch the stirrup. The grace and dexterity and daring of that rider's act won something more than admiration from Venters. For the distance of a mile, Jerry rode Black Star, and then changed back to Night. But all Jerry's skill and the running of the blacks could avail little more against the sorrel. (Source: *RIDERS OF THE PURPLE SAGE* by Zane Grey)

ACTION: PURSUE: Unable to stay there to see Jane's favorite racer die, Venters hurried up the trail to meet the other black [horse]. On the way he kept a sharp look-out for Jerry Card. Venters imagined the rider would keep well out of range of the rifle, but, as he would be lost on the sage without a horse, not improbably he would linger in the vicinity on the chance of getting back one of the blacks. Night soon came trotting up hot and wet and run out. Venters led him down near the others and, unsaddling him, let him loose to rest. Night wearily lay down in the dust and rolled, which action proved he was not in bad condition. (Source: *RIDERS OF THE PURPLE SAGE* by Zane Grey)

ACTION: PURSUE: Venters gasped in amazement. Had the wild sorrel gone mad? His head was high and twisted, in most singular position for a running horse. Suddenly Venters decried a froglike shape clinging to [the horse's neck. Jerry Card! Somehow he had straddled Wrangle and now stuck like a huge burr. But it was his strange position and the sorrel's strange, horrid neigh that strung Venter's nerves. Wrangle was pounding toward the turn where the trail went down. Like a blind horse he plunged. More than one of his jumps took him near the verge of the precipice. (Source: *RIDERS OF THE PURPLE SAGE* by Zane Grey)

ACTION: PURSUE: Venters knew he bestrode the strongest, swiftest, most tireless horse ever ridden by any rider across the Utah uplands. Recalling Jane's assurance that Night could run neck and neck with Wrangle and Black Star could show his heels to him, Venters wished that Jane were there to see the race to recover her blacks and in the unqualified superiority of the giant sorrel. (Source: *RIDERS OF THE PURPLE SAGE* by Zane Grey)

ACTION: PURSUE: Venters looked back, Black Star stood riderless in the trail. Jerry Card had taken to the sage. Far up the white trail Night came trotting faithfully down. Venters leaped off [Wrangle], still half blind, reeling dizzily. In a moment he had recovered sufficiently to have a care for Wrangle. Rapidly he took off the saddle and bridle. The sorrel was reeking, heaving, whistling, [and] shaking. But he had still the strength to sand, and for him Venters had no fears. (Source: *RIDERS OF THE PURPLE SAGE* by Zane Grey)

ACTION: PURSUE: Venters loosened the rein on Wrangle and let him break into a gallop. The sorrel saw the horses ahead and wanted to run, but Venters restrained him, and in the gallop he gained more than in the canter. The horse Bells was fast in that gait, but Black Star and Night had been trained to run. Slowly Wrangle closed the gap down to a quarter of a mile, and crept closer and closer. (Source: *RIDERS OF THE PURPLE SAGE* by Zane Grey)

ACTION: PURSUE: Venters peered far ahead, studying the lay of land. Straight away for five miles the trail stretched, and then it disappeared in hummocky ground. T the right some few rods Venters saw a break in the sage and this was the rim of Deception Pass. Across the dark cleft gleamed the red of the opposite [canyon] wall. Venters imagined that the trail went down the pass somewhere north of those ridges, and He realized that he must, and would overtake Jerry Card in this straight course of five miles. (Source: *RIDERS OF THE PURPLE SAGE* by Zane Grey)

ACTION: PURSUE: Venters saw Jerry Card look back over his shoulder; the other rider did likewise. Then the three racers lengthened their stride to the point where the swinging canter was ready to break into a gallop. (Source: *RIDERS OF THE PURPLE SAGE* by Zane Grey)

ACTION: PURSUE: Venters saw with a rider's keen vision then, fifteen, twenty miles of clear purple sage. There were no oncoming riders or rustlers to aid Jerry Card. His only chance to escape lay in abandoning the stolen horses and creeping away in the sage to hide. (Source: *RIDERS OF THE PURPLE SAGE* by Zane Grey)

ACTION: PURSUE: Venters seemed to read Jerry's mind. That little, crime-stained rider was actually thinking of his horses, husbanding their speed, handling them with knowledge of years, glorying in their beautiful swift racing stride, and wanting them to win the race—when his own life hung suspended in quivering balance. Again Jerry whirled in his saddle and the sun flashed redly on his face. (Source: *RIDERS OF THE PURPLE SAGE* by Zane Grey)

ACTION: PURSUE: Venters seemed to see the expanse before him as a vast, sheeted, purple plain sliding under him. Black Star moved in it as a blue. The rider [being pursued], Jerry Card, appeared a mere dot, bobbing dimly. In that red haze before him, he suddenly seemed to see Black Star riderless and with broken gait. (Source: *RIDERS OF THE PURPLE SAGE* by Zane Grey)

ACTION: PURSUE: Whatever the risk, Venters was compelled to stay right where he was, or comparatively near, for the night. The horses must rest and drink. Venters would have to find water. He was now seventy miles from Cottonwoods and he believed close to the canyon where the cattle trail must surely turn off and go down into the pass. After a while he rose to survey the valley. His position was very near to the ragged edge of a deep canyon into which the trail turned. The ground lay in uneven ridges divided by washes and these sloped into the canyon. Following the canyon line, he saw where its rim was broken by other intersection canyons, and farther down red walls and yellow cliffs leading toward a deep blue cleft that he made sure was Deception Pass. Walking out a few rods to a promontory, he found where the trail went down. The descent was gradual, along a stone-walled trail, and Venters felt sure that this was the place where cattle were driven into the pass. (Source: *RIDERS OF THE PURPLE SAGE* by Zane Grey)

Question (3)

ACTION: QUESTION: "Did you jest drop in to say hello to old friends, or do you aim to stay?" inquired Clark, his speculative eye lighting. (Source: *SUNSET PASS* by Zane Grey)

ACTION: QUESTION: "Where is ... Dyer?" "Wal, when I seen him last ... he was on his knees. He was some busy, but he wasn't prayin'!" "He was pressin' his big hands over his bowels tryin' to hold 'em in, but his hands wasn't in no shape jest then to hold. (Source: *RIDERS OF THE PURPLE SAGE* by Zane Grey)

ACTION: QUESTION: In the music of the singing birds—in the murmur of the running water—he heard a presaging warning sound. Where on earth did gaiety of children mean what it meant here? Quiet beauty—sweet music—innocent laughter! By what monstrous abortion of fate did these abide in the shadow of [him] Dyer? (Source: *RIDERS OF THE PURPLE SAGE* by Zane Grey)

Raise (2)

ACTION: RAISE: Pecos raised himself to peep down, the voices guiding him. His eyes nearly popped out at [the] sight of four men holding Adams on a horse. He was cursing, bellowing, entreating. They had a lasso round his neck, with an end thrown up over the branch of a tree. (Source: *WEST OF THE PECOS* by Zane Grey)

ACTION: RAISE: Venters held up both hands as if to ward of a blow. (Source: *RIDERS OF THE PURPLE SAGE* by Zane Grey)

Reach (2)

ACTION: REACH: He reached as if to take her hand, drew back, and wheeled away. (Source: *WEST OF THE PECOS* by Zane Grey)

ACTION: REACH: Toward sundown he reached the south slope of the valley and entered the zone of the cedars. . (Source: *WEST OF THE PECOS* by Zane Grey)

Realize (2)

ACTION: REALIZE: She was [his] nameless daughter. Oldring had loved her [as a father]. He had so guarded her, so kept her from women and men, and knowledge of life, that her mind was that of a child's. That was part of the secret—part of the mystery. That was the wonderful truth—not only was she not bad but good—pure—innocent, above all innocence in the world—the innocence of lonely girlhood.. (Source: *RIDERS OF THE PURPLE SAGE* by Zane Grey)

ACTION: REALIZE: What had been incredible from the lips of men became, in the tone, look, and gesture of a woman, a wonderful truth for Bess. With little tremblings of her slender body, she rocked to and fro on her knees. The yearning wistfulness of her eyes changed to solemn splender of joy. She was realizing happiness. (Source: *RIDERS OF THE PURPLE SAGE* by Zane Grey)

Recline (3)

ACTION: RECLINE: Her rigidity loosened in one long quiver, and she lay back limply, still, white as snow, with closed eyes. He thought then that she died. But the faint pulsation of her breast assured him that life yet lingered. Death seemed only a matter of moments, for the bullet had gone clear through her. Nevertheless, he tore sage leaves from a bush, and, pressing them tightly over her wounds, he bound the black scarf around her shoulder, tying it securely under her arm. Then he closed the blouse, hiding from his sight that blood-stained accusing breast. (Source: *RIDERS OF THE PURPLE SAGE* by Zane Grey)

ACTION: RECLINE: The grove seemed dreamy and silent. She found a grassy seat, and reclining there in the sun-flecked shade, with sweet fragrance all around and pale-blue flowers peeping up at her from the green, she felt the slow receding of excitement and fear and nausea. (Source: *WEST OF THE PECOS* by Zane Grey)

ACTION: RECLINE: When he got to the cedars and mounted a slope to a lonely spot he was grateful for the cool shade. He threw aside coat and sombrero, and lay down on the fragrant mat of cedar needles. He became aware of his labored breathing, of moist, restless hands, of hot face. (Source: *SUNSET PASS* by Zane Grey)

Recognize (3)

ACTION: RECOGNIZE: [His] Venters's glance swept down the line of silent, stone-faced men. He recognized many riders and villagers, but none of those he had hoped to meet. There was not enough expression in the whole crowd to give a single man an animated face. All of them knew him, most were inimical to him, but surely there were few who were not burning up with curiosity and wonder in regard to the return of Jane Withersteen's racers. Yet all were as silent and expressionless as dummies. Here was the thing—that masked feeling—that strange secretiveness—that expressionless expression of mystery and hidden power. (Source: *RIDERS OF THE PURPLE SAGE* by Zane Grey)

ACTION: RECOGNIZE: Jane tried to recognize the rider. Something familiar stuck her in the lofty stature, in the sweep of powerful shoulders, but this bearded, long-haired, unkempt man, who wore ragged clothes patched with pieces of skin, and boots that showed bare legs and feet, this dusty, dark, and wild rider could not possibly be Venters. (Source: *RIDERS OF THE PURPLE SAGE* by Zane Grey)

ACTION: RECOGNIZE: Suddenly Venters discovered that one of the two men who swung out to the right was riding Jane Withersteen's horse, Bells—the beautiful bay racer that she had given to Lassiter. Venters uttered a savage outcry. Then the small, wiry-frog-like shape of the second rider and the ease and grace of his seat in the saddle—things so strikingly incongruous—grew more and more familiar in Venters sight. "Jerry Card!" cried Venters. It was Tull's right-hand man. Such a white-hot wrath inflamed Venters that he fought himself to see with clearer gaze. "It's Jerry Card! And he's riding Black Star and leading Night!" (Source: *RIDERS OF THE PURPLE SAGE* by Zane Grey

Recover (8)

ACTION: RECOVER: ... from [the meat of the rabbits and quail] he made broths and soups as best he could, and fed her with a spoon. It came to him that the human body, like the human soul, was a strange thing and capable of recovering from terrible shocks. For almost immediately she showed faint signs of gathering strength. She would live, and the somber gloom lifted out of the valley, and he felt relief that was pain. (Source: *RIDERS OF THE PURPLE SAGE* by Zane Grey)

ACTION: RECOVER: ... the girl rested easier when she could see him near at hand. On the first day her languor appeared to leave her in a renewed grip of life. She awoke stronger from each short slumber; she ate greedily, and she moved about in her bed or boughs, and always, it seemed to Venters, her eyes followed him. He knew now that her recovery would be rapid.. (Source: *RIDERS OF THE PURPLE SAGE* by Zane Grey)

ACTION: RECOVER: Day by day he watched he white of he face slowly change to brown, and he wasted cheeks fill out by imperceptible degrees. There came a time when he could just trace the line of demarcation between the part of her face hidden by a mask and that left exposed to wind and sun. When that line disappeared in clar bronze tan, it was if she had been washed clean of the stigma of the Masked Rider. The suggestion of the mask always made him remember; now that it was gone, he seldom thought of her past. (Source: *RIDERS OF THE PURPLE SAGE* by Zane Grey)

ACTION: RECOVER: In those ensuing days, however, it became clear as clearest light that Bess was rapidly regaining strength, that she seemed to have forgotten [her long association with the rustlers] that, like an Indian who lives slowly from moment to moment, she was utterly absorbed in the present. (Source: *RIDERS OF THE PURPLE SAGE* by Zane Grey)

ACTION: RECOVER: On the third [day] he seemed to see her wither and waste away before his eyes. That day he scarcely went from her side for a moment, except to run for fresh, cool water, and he did not eat. The fever broke on the fourth day and left her spent and shrunken, a slip of a girl with life only in her eyes. They hung upon Venters with a mute observance, and he found hope in that. To rekindle the spark that had nearly flickered out, to nourish the little life and vitality that remained in her, were Venter's problems. (Source: *RIDERS OF THE PURPLE SAGE* by Zane Grey)

ACTION: RECOVER: The darkness lightened, turned to slow-drifting haze, and lifted. Through a thin film of blue smoke she saw the rough-hewn timbers of the court roof. A cool, damp touch moved across her brow. She smelled powder, and it was that which galvanized her suspended thought. She moved to see that she lay prone upon the stone flags with her head on Lassiter's knee, and he was bathing her brow with water from the stream. The same swift glance, shifting low, brought into range of her sight a smoking gun and splashes of blood. (Source: *RIDERS OF THE PURPLE SAGE* by Zane Grey)

ACTION: RECOVER: Upon his return [from hunting rabbits], he was amazed and somewhat anxiously concerned to see his invalid sitting with her bare feet swinging out. Hurriedly he approached, intending to advise her to lie down gain. The sun shone upon her, glinting on the little head with its tangle of bright hair and the small, oval face with its pallor, and dark blue eyes underlined by dark blue circles. She looked t him. "Help me down," she said "I'm weak ... dizzy. But I want to get down.". (Source: *RIDERS OF THE PURPLE SAGE* by Zane Grey)

ACTION: RECOVER: Upon the second morning she sat up, when he awakened her, and would not permit to bathe her face and feed her, which actions she performed for herself.. (Source: *RIDERS OF THE PURPLE SAGE* by Zane Grey)

Register

ACTION: REGISTER: He registered [at the hotel], gave the clerk his baggage checks, and went to the room assigned him, where he further resisted the mood encroaching upon him by shaving and making himself look presentable to his exacting eyes. (Source: *SUNSET PASS* by Zane Grey)

Relieve

ACTION: RELIEVE: "Bess, this is a friend of mine." The embarrassment of the moment did not extend to Lassiter. Almost at once his manner, as he shook hands with Bess, relieved Venters and put the girl at east. After Venter's words and the quick look at Lassiter, her agitation stilled, and although she was shy, if she were conscious of anything out of the ordinary in the situation, certainly she did not show it. (Source: *RIDERS OF THE PURPLE SAGE* by Zane Grey)

Remain

ACTION: REMAIN: "For some reason or other he wants us holed up out here like a lot of gophers." (Source: *SUNSET PASS* by Zane Grey)

Remember (8)

ACTION: REMEMBER: [In his mind] he saw Oldring's magnificent eyes—inquisitive—searching—softening. He saw them flare in amazement, in gladness, with love, then suddenly strain in terrible effort of will. He heard Oldring whisper and saw him sway like a log, and fall. Then a million billowing, thundering voices—gunshots of conscience—thunderbolts of remorse—dinned horribly in his ears. He had killed Bess's father. He dropped to his knees and hid his face against her and grasped her with hands of a drowning man. (Source: *RIDERS OF THE PURPLE SAGE* by Zane Grey)

ACTION: REMEMBER: ... the clinging clasp of her arms, the sweetness of her lips, and the sense of a new and exquisite birth of character in her remained hauntingly and thrillingly in his mind. (Source: *RIDERS OF THE PURPLE SAGE* by Zane Grey)

ACTION: REMEMBER: A chord of the past vibrated in her frozen and inhibited emotions. (Source: *WEST OF THE PECOS* by Zane Grey)

ACTION: REMEMBER: He recalled instances of riders who had been cut and shot, apparently to fatal issues, yet the blood had clotted, the wounds closed, and they had recovered. (Source: *RIDERS OF THE PURPLE SAGE* by Zane Grey)

ACTION: REMEMBER: Herein lay the secret that had clamored to him through all the tumult and stress of his emotions. What a look in the eyes of a man shot through the heart! It had been neither hate nor ferocity, or ear of man, or fear of death. It had been no p0assionate, glinting spirit of a fearless foe, willing shot for shot, life for life, but lacking physical power. Distinctly recalled now, never to be forgotten, Venters saw in Oldring's magnificent eyes the rolling of great, glad surprise—softness—love! Then came a shadow, and the terrible superhuman striving of a spirit to speak. Oldring, shot through the heart, had fought and forced back death, not for a moment in which to shoot or curse, but to whisper strange words. What words for a dying man to whisper! Why had not Venters waited! For what? That was no plea for life. It was regret that there was not a moment of life left in which to speak. Bess was ...? Herein lay renewed torture for Venters. What had Bess been to Oldring? The old question, like a specter, stalked from its grave to haunt him. He had overlooked, he had forgiven, he had loved, and he had forgotten, and now, out of the mystery of a dying man's whisper, rose again that perverse, unsatisfied jealous uncertainty. Bess had loved that splendid, black-crowned giant—by her own confession she had loved him—and in Venters's soul again flamed up the jealous hell. Then into the clamoring hell burst the shot that had killed Oldring, and it rang in a wild, fiendish gladness, a hateful, vengeful joy. That passed to the memory of the love and light in Oldring's eyes and the mystery in his whisper. So the changing, swaying emotions fluctuated in Venters's heart. (Source: *RIDERS OF THE PURPLE SAGE* by Zane Grey)

ACTION: REMEMBER: Memory stirred to the sight of the familiar [street] corner. He had been in several bad gun fights in this town, and the scene of one of them lay before him. The warmth and intimacy of old pleasant associations suffered a chill. (Source: *SUNSET PASS* by Zane Grey)

ACTION: REMEMBER: Reviving memory of Jane and thought of the complications of the present amazed him with proof of how far he had drifted from his old life. He discovered that he hated to take up the broken threads, to delve into dark problems and difficulties. (Source: *RIDERS OF THE PURPLE SAGE* by Zane Grey)

ACTION: REMEMBER: She remembered the all Sawtell, even to his shirt sleeves, his black vest and sombrero, his long mustache and deep-set black eyes. (Source: *WEST OF THE PECOS* by Zane Grey)

Reply

ACTION: REPLY: "Sooner or later I shall rise out of this stupor. I'm awaiting the hour." "It'll soon come, Jane, "replied Lassiter soberly. (Source: *RIDERS OF THE PURPLE SAGE* by Zane Grey)

Resend

ACTION: RESEND: He appeared what he had become—sullen, conceited, resentful, remote and secret in the pain and perplexity of his pubescence, a dreadful, harrowing time when he must bite everyone near, even himself, like a dog in a trap—a miserable discontent. (The Winter of Our Discontent)

Respect

ACTION: RESPECT: The more she saw of Lassiter, the more she respected him, and the greater her respect, the harder it became to lend herself to mere coquetry. (Source: *RIDERS OF THE PURPLE SAGE* by Zane Grey)

Restock

ACTION: RESTOCK: Bess was in transports over the stored of supplies and the outfit he had packed from Cottonwoods. Certain it was that he had fetched a hundred times more than he had gone for, enough, surely, for years, perhaps to make permanent home in the valley.. (Source: *RIDERS OF THE PURPLE SAGE* by Zane Grey)

Retrace

ACTION: RETRACE: Venters waited no longer, and turned swiftly to retrace his steps. He named the canyon Surprise Valley and the huge boulder that guarded the outlet Balancing Rock. Going down, he did not find himself attended by such fears as had beset him in the climb, still, he was not easy in mind and could not occupy himself with plans of moving the girl and his outfit until he had descended to the notch. (Source: *RIDERS OF THE PURPLE SAGE* by Zane Grey)

Return (4)

ACTION: RETURN: "Soon after that I left home ... an I went to the bad, as to prosperin', I saw some pretty hard life in the Panhandle, an' then I went north. In them days Kansas an' Nebraska was as bad, come to think of it, as these days right here on the border of Utah. I got to be pretty handy with guns. An' there wasn't many riders as could beat me ridin', an' I can say all modest-like that I never seen the white man who could track a hoss or a steer or a man with me. Afore I knew it, two years slipped by, an' all at once I got homesick an' pulled a bridle south." (Source: *RIDERS OF THE PURPLE SAGE* by Zane Grey)

ACTION: RETURN: Venters returned to camp. He remembered that but for the bobbing of the white tail [rabbit] catching his eye he would not have espied the rabbit, and he would never have discovered Surprise Valley. Little incidents of chance like this had turned him here and there in Deception Pass, and now they had assumed to him the significance and direction of destiny. (Source: *RIDERS OF THE PURPLE SAGE* by Zane Grey)

ACTION: RETURN: Venters, sighing, gathered up an armful of pottery, such pieces as he thought strong enough and suitable for his own use, and bent his steps toward camp. He mounted the terrace at an opposite point than by which he had left. His footsteps made no sound in the deep grass, and he approached closely without her being aware of his presence.. (Source: *RIDERS OF THE PURPLE SAGE* by Zane Grey)

ACTION: RETURN: When Venters got back to the valley with another calf, it was close upon daybreak. He crawled into his cave and slept late. Bess had no inkling that he had been absent from camp nearly all night and only remarked solicitously that he appeared to be more tired than usual, and more in need of sleep. (Source: *RIDERS OF THE PURPLE SAGE* by Zane Grey)

Ride (11)

ACTION: RIDE: "Judkins, you're a good fellow," interrupted Venters. "Now take the horses to Jane." Judkins stared, and then, muttering to himself, he mounted Bells, and stared again at Venters, and then, leading the other horses, he rode into the grove and disappeared. (Source: *RIDERS OF THE PURPLE SAGE* by Zane Grey)

ACTION: RIDE: He rode through a dark constriction of the pass no wider than the lane in the grove, and he came out into a great amphitheater into which jutted huge towering corners of a confluence of intersections canyons. Venters sat his horse and, with a rider's eye, studied this wild cross-cut of hug stone gullies. Then he went on, guided by the course of water. If it had not been for the main stream of water flowing north, he would never have been able to tell which of these many openings was a continuation of the pass. In crossing this amphitheater he went by the mouths of five canyons, fording little streams that flowed into the larger one. Gaining the outlet that he took to be the pass, he rode on again under overhanging walls. One side was dark in shade, the other light in sun. This narrow passageway turned and twisted and opened into a valley that amazed Venters. Here was a sweep of purple sage, richer than upon the higher levels. (Source: *RIDERS OF THE PURPLE SAGE* by Zane Grey)

ACTION: RIDE: He rode through sage and clumps of piñon trees and grassy plots where long-petaled, purple lilies bloomed. (Source: *RIDERS OF THE PURPLE SAGE* by Zane Grey)

ACTION: RIDE: Lassiter lengthened the stirrup straps on one of the burros and bade Jane mount and ride close to him. She was to keep the burro from cracking his little, hard hoofs on stone. Then she was riding on between dark, gleaming walls. There were quiet and rest and coolness in this canyon. (Source: *RIDERS OF THE PURPLE SAGE* by Zane Grey)

ACTION: RIDE: She knew Lassiter rode beside her. "Don't ... look ... back!" he said, and his voice, too, was not clear. Facing straight ahead, seeing only the waving, shadowy sage, Jane held out her gauntleted hand, to feel it enclosed in strong clasp. So she rode on without a backward glance at the beautiful grove of cottonwoods. She did not seem to think of the past, of what she left forever, but of the color and mystery and wildness of the sage slope leading down to Deception Pass, and of the future. (Source: *RIDERS OF THE PURPLE SAGE* by Zane Grey)

ACTION: RIDE: She rode out of the court, through the grove, across the wide lane into the sage. She realized that she was leaving forever, and she did not look back. A strange, dreamy, calm peace pervaded her soul. Her doom had fallen upon her, but, instead of finding life no longer worth living, she found it doubly significant, full of sweetness as the western breeze, beautiful and unknown as the sage slope stretching its purple sunset shadows before her. (Source: *RIDERS OF THE PURPLE SAGE* by Zane Grey)

ACTION: RIDE: Slowly he rode in, holding in his white horse that scented water and grass. (Source: *WEST OF THE PECOS* by Zane Grey)

ACTION: RIDE: So they rode on down the old trail, and the sun sloped to the west and a golden sheen lay on the sage. The hours sped now; the afternoon waned. Often they rested the horses. The glisten of a pool of water in a hollow caught Venters's eye, and here he unsaddled he blacks and let them roll and drink and browse. When he and Bess rode up out of the hollow, the sun was low, a crimson ball, and the valley seemed veiled in purple fire and smoke. It was that short time when the sun appeared to rest before setting, and silence, like a cloak of invisible life, lay heavily on all that shimmering world of sage. They watched the sun begin to bury its red curve under the dark horizon. (Source: *RIDERS OF THE PURPLE SAGE* by Zane Grey)

ACTION: RIDE: Some forty hours or more later, Venters created a commotion in Cottonwoods [the town] by riding down the main street on Black Star and leading Bells and Night. He had come upon Bells, grazing near the body of a dead rustler, and no other incident had marked his quick ride into the village. Nothing was further from Venter's mind than bravado. (Source: *RIDERS OF THE PURPLE SAGE* by Zane Grey)

ACTION: RIDE: They mounted and, with Jane in the lead, rode down the lane, nd, turning off into a cattle trail, proceeded westward. Venter's dogs trotted behind them. (Source: *RIDERS OF THE PURPLE SAGE* by Zane Grey)

ACTION: RIDE: Without more ado Pecos headed the horse into the river, taking a diagonal course downstream toward the opposite shore. (Source: *WEST OF THE PECOS* by Zane Grey)

Rise

ACTION: RISE: Then he rose. The rustlers were riding into a canyon. Their horses were tired, and they had several pack animals; evidently they had traveled far. Venters watched these horsemen disappear under a bold canyon wall. (Source: *RIDERS OF THE PURPLE SAGE* by Zane Grey)

Roll

ACTION: ROLL: "Lassiter! Roll the stone!" she cried. Ghastly, with protruding jaw, he arose, tottering, and again he placed the bloody hand on the balancing rock. Jane gazed from him down the passageway. Tull was climbing. Almost, she thought, she saw his dark, relentless face. Behind him more riders climbed. Under all Lassiter's deathly pallor, and the blood, and the iron of seared cheek and lined brow, worked a great change. Lassiter placed both hands on the rock, and then leaned his shoulder there and braced his powerful body. The stone stirred, groaned, and moved with slow grind, as of wrathful relief, it began to lean. It had waited ages to fall and now was slow in starting. Wondrously it heaved, with sullen low roar as it loosed its hold, to sway, to fall with loud crunch. Then, as if suddenly instinct with life, it leaped hurtling down to alight on the steep incline, to bound swifter into the air, to gather momentum, to plunge into the lofty, leaning crag below. The crag thundered into atoms. A wave of air—a splitting shock! Dust shrouded the sunset red of shaking rims; dust shrouded Tull as he fell on his knees with flinging, uplifted arms. Shafts and monuments and sections of wall fell majestically. [There was a] deep, weird, detonating, deafening boom of doom! The outlet to Deception Pass closed forever. (Source: *RIDERS OF THE PURPLE SAGE* by Zane Grey)

Rope

ACTION: ROPE: The first peep of day found him stirring, and as soon as it was light enough to distinguish objects, he took his lasso off his saddle and went out to rope the sorrel. (Source: *RIDERS OF THE PURPLE SAGE* by Zane Grey)

Rouse

ACTION: ROUSE: "Jane, Lassiter called you blind," said Venters. "It must be true. But I won't upbraid you. Only for God's sake don't rouse the devil in me by praying for Tull! I'll try to keep cool when I meet him. That's all." (Source: *RIDERS OF THE PURPLE SAGE* by Zane Grey)

ACTION: ROUSE: Jane's question had roused Bess out of stupefaction. Her eyes suddenly darkened and dilated. (Source: *RIDERS OF THE PURPLE SAGE* by Zane Grey)

Rub

ACTION: RUB: The wind sweetly fanned Venters's hot face. [Then Bess called] "Bern ... look!" She pointed up the long slope. A small, dark, moving dot split the line where purple sage met blue sky. That dot was a band of riders. The black dot grew to be a dark patch, moving under low dust clouds. It grew all the time, although very slowly. (Source: *RIDERS OF THE PURPLE SAGE* by Zane Grey)

Run (2)

ACTION: RUN: Action brightened her. Beside him, holding her hand, she slipped down the shelf, ran down the long steep slant of sliding stones, out of the cloud of dust, and likewise out of the pale gloom. (Source: *RIDERS OF THE PURPLE SAGE* by Zane Grey)

ACTION: RUN: The lad gave Pecos a wondering, grateful look, and bounded away, proving in his flight that whatever the issue might have been before, it was not something to lend wings to his feet. (Source: *WEST OF THE PECOS* by Zane Grey)

Sag

ACTION: SAG: Pecos sheathed his gun, and with that motion appeared to sag. He ceased his cat-like stride. Freckles no one had ever seen stood out on his clammy face. His hair was wet. He stooped to pick up his sombrero which had fallen when he leaped to confront Sawtell's men. (Source: *WEST OF THE PECOS* by Zane Grey)

Scan

ACTION: SCAN: The slope before him seemed to swell into obscurity, to lose its definite outline in a misty, opaque cloud that shaded into the over-shadowing wall. He scanned the rim where the serrated points speared the sky, and he found the zigzag crack. It was thin, only a shade lighter than the dark ramparts, but he distinguished it, and that served. (Source: *RIDERS OF THE PURPLE SAGE* by Zane Grey)

Seal

ACTION: SEAL: Venters closed up the opening of the cave with a thatch of willows and aspens so that not even a bird or a rat could get in to the sacks of grain. (Source: *RIDERS OF THE PURPLE SAGE* by Zane Grey)

Search (7)

ACTION: SEARCH: "Eighteen years in all I've been on the trail. An' it led me to the last, lonely villages on the Utah border. Eighteen years! I feel pretty old now. I was only twenty when I hit that trail. Well, back here a ways a Gentile said Jane Withersteen could tell me about Milly Erne an' show me her grave!" (Source: *RIDERS OF THE PURPLE SAGE* by Zane Grey)

ACTION: SEARCH: "Then come a change in my luck. Along in central Utah I rounded up Hurd, an' I whispered somethin' in his ear, an' watched his face, an' then threw a gun against his bowels. An' he died with his teeth so tight shut I couldn't have pried them open with a knife. Slack and Metzger that same year both heard me whisper the same question, an' neither would they speak a word when they lay dyin'. Long before, I learned no man of this breed or class ... or g=God knows what ... would give up any secrets. I had to see in a man's fear of death the connection with Milly Erne's fate. An', as the years passed, at long intervals I would find such a man. So I drifted on the long trail down into southern Utah, my name preceded me, an' I had to meet a people prepared for me, an' ready with guns. They made me a gunman. An' that suited me." (Source: *RIDERS OF THE PURPLE SAGE* by Zane Grey)

ACTION: SEARCH: First I went to the town outside where she'd been kept and where she'd had heer baby after her conversion in that cave. I got that skunk who owned the place, an' took him out in the woods, an' made him tell all he knew. That wasn't much as to length, but it was pure hell's fire in substance. This time I left him some incapacitated for any more skunk work short of hell. Then I hit the trail for Utah. That was fourteen years ago. I saw the incomin' of most of the Mormons. It was a wild country an' a wild time. I rode from town to own, village to village, ranch to ranch, camp to camp. I never stayed long in one place. I never had but one idea. I never rested. Four years went by, an' I knew every trail in northern Utah. I kept on, an', as time went by an' I'd begun to grow old in my search.

I had firmer, blinder faith in whatever was guidin' me. I never really lost the trail, though for years it was the dimmest trail ever followed by any man." (Source: *RIDERS OF THE PURPLE SAGE* by Zane Grey)

ACTION: SEARCH: He knew that rustlers, being riders, would not make much of a day's or night's absence from camp for one or two of their number, but when the missing ones failed to show up in reasonable time, there would be a search . (Source: *RIDERS OF THE PURPLE SAGE* by Zane Grey)

ACTION: SEARCH: In all this time, signs of the proselyter an' the giant with the blue-ice eyes an' the gold beard seemed to fade dimmer out of the trail. Only twice in ten years did I find a trace of that mysterious man who had visited the proselyter at my home village. What he had to do with Milly's fate was beyond all hope for me to learn, unless my guidin' spirit led me to him. As for the other man, I knew, as sure as I breathed an' the stars shone an' the wind blew, that I'd meet him someday. (Source: *RIDERS OF THE PURPLE SAGE* by Zane Grey)

ACTION: SEARCH: She was searching the very depths of him, her eyes keen with jealous intuition. (Source: *SUNSET PASS* by Zane Grey)

ACTION: SEARCH: They confined their search efforts to riding the river canyon, the intersecting brakes, and up these as far as the heads, where dense thickets never failed to yield calves and yearlings that had never smelled burned [branding] hair. (Source: *WEST OF THE PECOS* by Zane Grey)

Seclude

ACTION: SECLUDE: It would not do to dream—at least until he had settled things with himself. [He] always went to the loneliness and silence of desert or forest when in any kind of trouble. (Source: *SUNSET PASS* by Zane Grey)

See (44)

ACTION: SEE: "Don't be losin' no more time," put in Lassiter. "I ain't certain but I think I seen a speck up the sage slope. Mebbe I was mistaken. But, anyway, we must all be movin'. (Source: *RIDERS OF THE PURPLE SAGE* by Zane Grey)

ACTION: SEE: "I'm learning much, my friend. Some of those blinding scales have fallen from my eyes." (Source: *RIDERS OF THE PURPLE SAGE* by Zane Grey)

ACTION: SEE: "Judge Dyeer was layin' down the law. An' if ever any man turned to stone he was thet man. I looked back to see what hed acted so powerful strange on the judge. An' there halfway up the room, in the middle of the wide aisle, stood Lassiter! All white an' black he looked, an' I can't think of anythin' he resembled, onless it's death. I went cold to my very marrow. I don't know why but Lassiter has a way about him thet's awful. He spoke a word ... a name. I couldn't understand it, though he spoke clear as a bell. Judge Dyer must hev' understood it, an' a lot more thet was mystery to me, fer he pitched forward out of his chair right onto the platform.. (Source: *RIDERS OF THE PURPLE SAGE* by Zane Grey)

ACTION: SEE: "Look! a rider!" [She] wheeled and saw a horseman, silhouetted against the western sky, coming out of the sage. He had ridden down from the let, in the golden glare of the un, and had been unobserved till close at hand. (Source: *RIDERS OF THE PURPLE SAGE* by Zane Grey)

ACTION: SEE: About mid-afternoon Pecos espied the first bunch of cattle, wilder than deer—an old mossy-horn, a cow, two yearlings and a calf, for all he could tell unbranded. This encounter was in a shallow rock-bottomed gorge where clear water ran. From that point on cattle tracks increased markedly, and mixed stock showed on the ridges. (Source: *WEST OF THE PECOS* by Zane Grey)

ACTION: SEE: Across the mounds of rock and sage Jane caught sight on a band of [approaching] riders filing out of the narrow neck of the pass, and in the lead was a white horse, which even at distance of a mile or more she knew. "Tull!" she almost screamed. (Source: *RIDERS OF THE PURPLE SAGE* by Zane Grey)

ACTION: SEE: As twilight was fast falling, a group of horsemen crossed the dark line of low ground to become more distinct as they climbed the slope. (Source: *RIDERS OF THE PURPLE SAGE* by Zane Grey)

ACTION: SEE: Desperately she tried to meet his gray eyes—in vain—desperately she tried again, fought herself as feeling and thought resurged in torment—and she succeeded—and then she knew. "No ... no ... no!" she wailed. "You promised not to kill Bishop Dyer." "You'll ... kill him?" "If God lets me live another hour. If not God ... then the devil who drives me." "You'll ... kill him ... for your vengeful hate?" "No!" "For Milly Erne's sake?" "No!" "... for whose?" "For yours!" (Source: *RIDERS OF THE PURPLE SAGE* by Zane Grey)

ACTION: SEE: For days on end dim blue hills led Terrill's gaze on to dimmer and bluer mountains, like ghosts above the hazy horizon. Those mountains lay across the Pecos and must be the Guadaloupes. The blue hills, however, were the brakes of the Pecos. (Source: *WEST OF THE PECOS* by Zane Grey)

ACTION: SEE: He cursed himself and the unerring aim of which he had been so proud. He had seen that look in the eyes of a crippled antelope that he was about to finish with his knife. But in her it held infinitely more—a revelation of mortal spirit. The instinctive clinging to life was there, and the divining helplessness and the terrible accusation of the stricken.. (Source: *RIDERS OF THE PURPLE SAGE* by Zane Grey)

ACTION: SEE: He felt his eyes stretch and fix at the sight of Lassiter, leading Black Star and Night out of the sage, with Jane, in rider's costume, close beside them. For an instant he felt himself whirl dizzily in the center of vast circles of sage. He recovered partially, enough to see Lassiter standing with a glad smile and Jane riveted in astonishment. (Source: *RIDERS OF THE PURPLE SAGE* by Zane Grey)

ACTION: SEE: He had come quite high up the slope, and he could see the town below, and beyond it, to the south. [The town] had grown considerably, and from this vantage-point it looked promising. Some day it would grow into an important center. (Source: *SUNSET PASS* by Zane Grey)

ACTION: SEE: He opened his eyes to another surprise of this valley of beautiful surprises. Outside his cave he saw the exquisitely fine foliage of the silver spruces crossing a round space of blue morning sky, and in this lacy leafage fluttered a number of gray birds. (Source: *RIDERS OF THE PURPLE SAGE* by Zane Grey)

ACTION: SEE: He saw Bess under the spruces. Upon her complete recovery of strength she always rose with the dawn. At the moment she was feeding the quail she had tamed, and she had begun to tame the mockingbirds. They fluttered among the branches overhead, and some left off their songs to flit down, and shyly hop near the twittering quail. Little gray-and-white rabbits crouched in the grass, now nibbling, now laying long ears flat and watching the dogs. (Source: *RIDERS OF THE PURPLE SAGE* by Zane Grey)

ACTION: SEE: He saw the front line of savages spread to left and right. At least six of these, in their thirst for blood charged out of the thicket. Pecos saw arrows flying like glints of light through the air, some to stick in the carcass of the horse, others in the tree. (Source: *WEST OF THE PECOS* by Zane Grey)

ACTION: SEE: He saw the girl's color fade and her face turned white. A swift shadow darkened the great gray eyes. (Source: *SUNSET PASS* by Zane Grey)

ACTION: SEE: He sighted a bunch of Indians, a glimpse of lean wild forms and ragged mustangs crossing a brake back from the high bank. (Source: *WEST OF THE PECOS* by Zane Grey)

ACTION: SEE: He was startled to see something, dark and moving. It jerked. A man hung by his neck. He was kicking in a horribly grotesque manner. His distorted face, distended eyes, mouth wide, tongue out, was in plain sight. (Source: *WEST OF THE PECOS* by Zane Grey)

ACTION: SEE: In her unutterable bitterness he saw a darkness of mood that could not have been caused by her present weak and feverish state. She hated the life she had led, that she probably had been compelled to lead. She had suffered some unforgivable wrong at the hands of Oldring. With that conviction Venters felt a flame throughout his body, and it marked the rekindling of fierce anger and ruthlessness. In the past long year he had nursed resentment. He had hate the wilderness—the loneliness of the uplands. He had waited for something to come to pass. It had come. (Source: *RIDERS OF THE PURPLE SAGE* by Zane Grey)

ACTION: SEE: In the sand before the door, he saw little boot tracks that surely had been made by her. (Source: *SUNSET PASS* by Zane Grey)

ACTION: SEE: It was Jane's gaze riveted upon the rider that wheeled Bishop Dyer. There clear sight filled her. Dizzily, in a blue, she saw the bishop's hand jerk to his hip. She saw gleam of blue and spout of red. In her ears burst a thundering report. The court floated in darkening circles around her and she fell [fainted] into utter blackness. (Source: *RIDERS OF THE PURPLE SAGE* by Zane Grey)

ACTION: SEE: Jane climbed a few more paces with him, and then peeped over the ridge. Just beyond began a shallow swale that deepened and widened into a valley and then swung to the left. Following the undulating sweep of sage, Jane saw the straggling lines and then the great body of the white herd [of cattle]. (Source: *RIDERS OF THE PURPLE SAGE* by Zane Grey)

ACTION: SEE: Jane did not look back. A misty veil obscured the clear, searching gaze she had kept steadfastly upon the purple slope and the dim lines of canyons ... and she saw the valley deepening into the shades of twilight. (Source: *RIDERS OF THE PURPLE SAGE* by Zane Grey)

ACTION: SEE: Presently he descried two mounted men riding toward him. He hugged the shadow of a tree. Again the starlight, brighter now, aided him, and he made out Tull's stalwart figure, and beside him the short, frog-like shape of the rider, Jerry. They were silent, and they rode on to disappear. (Source: *RIDERS OF THE PURPLE SAGE* by Zane Grey)

ACTION: SEE: She returned to the main street and bent her thoughtful steps toward the center of the village. A string of wagons drawn by oxen was lumbering along. These sage freighters, as they were called, hauled grain and flour and merchandise from Sterling. (Source: *RIDERS OF THE PURPLE SAGE* by Zane Grey)

ACTION: SEE: She saw a creeping lizard, cactus flowers, the drooping burros, the resting dogs, an eagle high over a yellow crag. (Source: *RIDERS OF THE PURPLE SAGE* by Zane Grey)

ACTION: SEE: She saw him rapidly saddle Black Star and Night. Then he was drawing her into the light of the huge window, standing over her, gripping her arm with fingers of steely ice. "... you're not goin' to Dyer. I'm goin' instead." (Source: *RIDERS OF THE PURPLE SAGE* by Zane Grey)

ACTION: SEE: She saw him shake his tall form erect, look at her strangely and steadfastly, and then, noiselessly, stealthily slip away amid the rocks and trees. (Source: *RIDERS OF THE PURPLE SAGE* by Zane Grey)

ACTION: SEE: She saw the line of cattle lengthening. Then, like a stream of white bees pouring from a huge swarm, the steers stretched out from the main body. In a few moments, with astonishing rapidity, the whole herd got into motion. A faint roar of trampling hoofs came to Jane's ears, and gradually swelled, low, rolling clouds of dust began to rise above the sage. "It's a stampede, an' a hummer," said Lassiter. (Source: *RIDERS OF THE PURPLE SAGE* by Zane Grey)

ACTION: SEE: Shrinkingly Venters removed the rider's wide sombrero and the black cloth mask. The action disclosed bright chestnut hair, inclined to curl, and a white, youthful face. Along the lower line of cheek and jaw was a clear demarcation where the brown of tanned skin met the white that had been hidden from the sun. (Source: *RIDERS OF THE PURPLE SAGE* by Zane Grey)

ACTION: SEE: Terrill sustained a peculiar feeling at her first close sight of a Texas long-horn steer. The enormously wide-spreading, bow shaped horns had inspired the name of this Mexican breed, and they quite dwarfed the other characteristics of the animal.. (Source: *WEST OF THE PECOS* by Zane Grey)

ACTION: SEE: The stragglers were restless; the more compactly massed steers were browsing. Jane brought the glass back to the big sentinels of the herd, and saw them trot with quick steps, stop short, and toss wide horns, look everywhere, and then trot in another direction. (Source: *RIDERS OF THE PURPLE SAGE* by Zane Grey)

ACTION: SEE: Then dots of white and black told Venters there were cattle of other colors in tis enclosed valley. (Source: *RIDERS OF THE PURPLE SAGE* by Zane Grey)

ACTION: SEE: Then from out of the sage on the ridge flew up a broad, white object, flashed in the sunlight, and vanished. Like magic it was, and bewildered Jane.. "I reckon there's someone behind that ridge throwin' up a sheet or a white blanket to reflect the sunshine. To stampede the herd" (Source: *RIDERS OF THE PURPLE SAGE* by Zane Grey)

ACTION: SEE: Then in the white rapt face, in the unfathomable eyes, Venters saw Jane in the supreme moment of her sacrifice. This moment was one wherein she reached up to the height for which her noble soul had ever yearned.. (Source: *RIDERS OF THE PURPLE SAGE* by Zane Grey)

ACTION: SEE: They mounted and rode out to the cattle trail and began to climb. From the height of the ridge, where they had started down, Venters did not see Lassiter, but his glance, drawn irresistibly father out on the gradual slope, caught sight of a moving cloud. [A rider was moving fast.] The horse disappeared in the sage, and then puffs of dust marked his course—making straight for the corrals . (Source: *RIDERS OF THE PURPLE SAGE* by Zane Grey)

ACTION: SEE: Under the clump of silver spruce hung a denser mantle of darkness, yet not so thick that Venter's night-practiced eyes could not catch the white oval of a still face {of the girl]. He bent over it with a slight suspension of breath that was both caution lest he frighten her and chill uncertainty of feeling lest he find her dead. But she slept, and he arose to renewed activity. (Source: *RIDERS OF THE PURPLE SAGE* by Zane Grey)

ACTION: SEE: Venters and Lassiter were turning toward the house when Jane appeared in the lane, leading a horse. She was bright, smiling, and her greeting was warmly cordial. (Source: *RIDERS OF THE PURPLE SAGE* by Zane Grey)

ACTION: SEE: Venters saw ahead a turn, more abrupt than any yet. Warily he rounded this corner, once again to halt, bewildered. The canyon opened fan-shaped into a great oval of green and gray growths. It was the hub of an oblong wheel, and from it, at regular distances, like spokes, ran the outgoing canyons. Here a dull red color predominated over the fading yellow. The corners of wall bluntly rose, scarred and scrawled, to taper into towers and serrated peaks and pinnacled domes. (Source: *RIDERS OF THE PURPLE SAGE* by Zane Grey)

ACTION: SEE: When Venters rapidly strode toward the [other rustler] Masked Rider, not even the cold nausea that gripped him could wholly banish curiosity.. His curious eagerness and expectations had not prepared him for the shock he received when he stood over a slight, dark figure. The rustler wore the black mask that had given him his name, but he had no weapon. Venters glanced at the drooping horse; there were no gun sheaths on the saddle. {He] shot an unarmed man. (Source: *RIDERS OF THE PURPLE SAGE* by Zane Grey)

ACTION: SEE: While yet far off he discerned Bess, moving under the silver spruces, and soon the barking of the dogs told him they had seen him. [The dogs] Ring and Whitie came bounding toward him, and behind them ran Bess, her hands outstretched. (Source: *RIDERS OF THE PURPLE SAGE* by Zane Grey)

ACTION: SEE: With a cold prickling of her skin, with a queer thrumming in her ears, with fixed and staring eyes, Jane saw a gun lying at her feet with the chambers swung and empty, and discharged shells scattered near. (Source: *RIDERS OF THE PURPLE SAGE* by Zane Grey)

ACTION: SEE: With a pulse beginning to beat and hammer away his calmness, he eyed that indistinct line of steps, up to where the buttress of wall hid farther sight of them. (Source: *RIDERS OF THE PURPLE SAGE* by Zane Grey)

ACTION: SEE: With the first glimpse of the smooth slope leading down to the grotesque cedars and out to the pass, his cool nerve returned. One long survey to the left, then one to the right, satisfied his caution.. (Source: *RIDERS OF THE PURPLE SAGE* by Zane Grey)

Sense

ACTION: SENSE: Jane sensed then a slight alteration in Venters and what it was, in her own confusion, she could not tell. It had always been her intention to acquaint him with the deceit she had fallen to in her zeal. She did not mean to spare herself. Yet now, at the moment, before these riders who in a measure she had betrayed, it was an impossibility to explain. (Source: *RIDERS OF THE PURPLE SAGE* by Zane Grey)

Shake (4)

ACTION: SHAKE: But a flush of fire flamed in her cheeks, and her trembling hands shook Black Star's bridle, and her eyes fell before Lassiter's. (Source: *RIDERS OF THE PURPLE SAGE* by Zane Grey)

ACTION: SHAKE: His big shaking hand, with its tobacco-stained fingers, tore out sheafs of greenbacks that had been neatly and compactly folded. (Source: *WEST OF THE PECOS* by Zane Grey)

ACTION: SHAKE: Like a tree once cut deeply in its roots, she began to quiver and shake. (Source: *RIDERS OF THE PURPLE SAGE* by Zane Grey)

ACTION: SHAKE: Rock seized Preston b the neck, coked and shook him like a terrier with a rat. (Source: *SUNSET PASS* by Zane Grey)

Shine

ACTION: SHINE: The pale sheet lightning shined live silver fire on her bare head. (Source: *SUNSET PASS* by Zane Grey)

Shame

ACTION: SHAME: "What's your name?" he inquired. "Bess," she answered. "Bess what?" "That's enough...just Bess." The red that deepened in her cheeks was not all the flash of fever. Venters marveled anew, and, this time at the hint of shame in her face, at the momentary drooping of long lashes. (Source: *RIDERS OF THE PURPLE SAGE* by Zane Grey)

Shoot (11)

ACTION: SHOOT: "Lassiter! The gun here ... the blood?" "So that's troublin' you. I reckon it needn't. You see it now this way. I come 'round the house an' seen that fat party an' heard him talkin' loud. Then he seen me, an' very impolite goes straight for his gun. He mightn't have tried to throw a gun on me...whatever the reason was.

For that's meetin' me on my own round. I've seen runnin' molasses that was quicker'n him. Now I didn't know who he was, a visitor or friend or relation of yours, though I seen he was Mormon all over, an' I couldn't get serious about shootin'. So I winged him ... put a bullet through his arm as he was pullin' at his gun. An' he dropped the gun, an' a little blood. I told him he'd introduced himself sufficient an' to please move out of my vicinity. An' he went." (Source: *RIDERS OF THE PURPLE SAGE* by Zane Grey)

ACTION: SHOOT: "No, Jerry," whispered Venters, stepping forward and throwing up his rifle. He tried to catch the little, humped, frog-like shape [of Jerry Card] over the sights. [The horse] was moving too fast—it was too small. Yet Venters shot—once—twice—the third time—four times—five! All wasted shots and precious seconds!. (Source: *RIDERS OF THE PURPLE SAGE* by Zane Grey)

ACTION: SHOOT: "Oldring! Bess is alive! But she's dead to you ... dead to the life you made her lead ... dead as you will be in one second!" Swift as lightning Venter's glance dropped from Oldring's rolling eyes to his hands. One of them, the right, swept out, then down toward his gun—and Venters shot him through the heart. Slowly Oldring sank to his knees, and the hand, dragging at the gun, fell away. Venter's exquisitely acute faculties grasped the meaning of that linp arm, of the swaying hulk, o the gasp and heave of the quivering beard. "Man! Why ... didn't ... you ... wait! Bess ... was ..." Oldring's whisper died under his beard, and with a heavy lurch, he fell forward. (Source: *RIDERS OF THE PURPLE SAGE* by Zane Grey)

ACTION: SHOOT: "Swift as lightning Venter's glance dropped from Oldring's rolling eyes to his hands. One of them, the right, swept out, then down toward his gun—and Venters shot him through the heart. Slowly Oldring sank to his knees, and the hand, dragging at the gun, fell away. Venter's exquisitely acute faculties grasped the meaning of that linp arm, of the swaying hulk, o the gasp and heave of the quivering beard. Oldring's whisper died under his beard, and with a heavy lurch, he fell forward. (Source: *RIDERS OF THE PURPLE SAGE* by Zane Grey)

ACTION: SHOOT: he shot once—twice. The foremost rustler dropped his weapon and toppled from his saddle, to fall with his foot catching in a stirrup. The horse snorted wildly and plunged away, dragging the rustler through the sage. The [other] rider huddled over his pommel, slowly swaying to one side, and then, with a faint, strange cry slipped out of the saddle. (Source: *RIDERS OF THE PURPLE SAGE* by Zane Grey)

ACTION: SHOOT: I had a good look at Lassiter. He stood sort of stiff, bendin' a little, an' both his arms was crooked, an' his hands looked like a hawk's claws. But there ai't no tellin' how his eyes looked. I know this, though, an' thet in his eyes could read the mind of any man about to throw a gun. An' in watchin' him, of course, I couldn't see the three men go for thir guns. An' though I was lookin' hard ... I couldn't see how he drew. He was qucker'n eyesight ... thet's all. But I seen the red spurtin' of his guns, an' heard the shots of the riders. An' when I turned, Wright an' Carter was down, an' Jengessen who's tough like a steer was pullin' the trigger of a wobblin' gun. But it was plain he was shot through, plumb center. An' sudden he fell with a crash, an' is gun clattered on the floor." "Then there was a hell of a silence. Nobody breathed. I didn't, anyway. I saw Lassiter slip a smokin' gun back in a belt. But he hadn't drawn either of the big black guns, an' I though thet strange. Then there come a scrapin' on the floor, an' Dyer got up, his face like lead. I wanted to watch Lassiter, but Dyer's face, oncet I seen it like thet, glued my eyes. I seen him go fer his gun. An' then there was a thunderin' shot from Lassiter, an it hit Dyer's right arm, an' his gun went off as it dropped. Like some cornered sage wolf he looked at Lassiter, an' sort of howled, an' reached down fer his gun. He'd jest picked it off the floor an' was raisin' it when another thunderin' shot almost tore that arm off. So it seemed to me. He gun dropped again, an' he went down on his knees, kind of flounderin' after it. It was some strange an' terrible to see his awful earnestness. Anyway, he got the gun with his left hand, an' was raisin' it, pullin' trigger in his weakness when the third thunderin' shot his his left arm, an' he dropped the gun again. But thet left arm wasn't useless yet, fer he grabbed up the gun, an' with a shakin' aim thet would hev' been pitiful to see ... he began to shoot. One wild bullet struck a man twenty feet from Lassiter. An' it killed thet man. Then come a bunch of thunderin' shots ... nine I calculated after, fer they come so quick. I couldn't count them ... an' I knew Lassiter had turned the black guns loose on Dyer. I remember distinctly it was the smell of gun-powder. The court had about adjourned fer thet judge. He was on his knees an' he wasn't prayin'. He was gaspin', and' trying' to press his big, floppin' cripple hands over his bowels. Lassiter had sent all those last, thunderin' shots through Dyer's bowels. An' he looked up at Lassiter. An' then he stared horrible at somethin' thet wasn't Lassiter, nor anyone there, nor the room, nor the branches of purple sage peepin' into the winder. Whatever he seen, it was with the look of a man who discovers somethin' too late. Thet's a terrible look. An' with a horrible understandin' cry he slid forrard on his face." (Source: *RIDERS OF THE PURPLE SAGE* by Zane Grey)

ACTION: SHOOT: No great distance was covered, however, before Bells swerved to the left, out of line with Black Star and Night. Then Venters, aiming high and waiting for the pause between Wrangle's great strides, began to take snap shots at the rustler. The fleeing rider presented a broad target for a rifle, but he was moving swiftly forward and bobbing up and down. Moreover, shooting from Wrangle's back was shooting from a speeding thunderbolt. Added to that was the danger of a low-placed bullet [hitting] Bells. Yet despite these considerations, making the shot exceedingly difficult, Venters's confidence, like his implacability, saw a speedy and final termination of that rustler's race. On the sixth shot the rustler threw up his arms and took a flying tumble off his horse. He rolled over and over, hunched himself to a half-erect position, fell, and then dragged himself into the sage. As Venters went thundering by, he peered keenly into the sage, but caught no sign of the man. Bells ran a few hundred yards, slowed up, and had stopped when Wrangle passed him. (Source: *RIDERS OF THE PURPLE SAGE* by Zane Grey)

ACTION: SHOOT: The rustler bent forward [in the saddle], as if keenly peering ahead. Then, with a swift sweep, he jerked a gun from its sheath and fired. The bullet zipped through the sagebrush. Flying bits of wood struck Venters, and the hot, stinging pain seemed to lift him in one leap. Like a flash the blue barrel of his rifle gleamed level and he shot once—twice. (Source: *RIDERS OF THE PURPLE SAGE* by Zane Grey)

ACTION: SHOOT: Turning in his saddle, he rustler began to shoot, and the bullets beat up little whiffs of dust. Venters raised his rifle, ready to take snap shots, and waited for favorable opportunity when Bells was out of line with the forward horses. Venters had it in him to kill these men as if they were skunk-bitten coyotes, but, also, he had restraint enough to keep from shooting one of Jane's beloved Arabians. (Source: *RIDERS OF THE PURPLE SAGE* by Zane Grey)

ACTION: SHOOT: When the riders were within 300 yards, he deliberately led [his horse] out into the trail. Then her heard shouts, and the hard scrape of sliding hoofs, and saw horses rear and plunge back with upflung heads and flying manes. Several little white puffs of smoke appeared sharply against the black background of riders and horses, and shots rang out. Bullets struck far in front of him, whipped up the dust, and then hummed into the sage. The range was great for revolvers, but whether the shots were meant to kill him or merely check advance, they were enough to fire that waiting ferocity in him. Slipping his arm through the bridle so that [his horse] could not get away, he lifted his rifle and pulled the trigger twice. (Source: *RIDERS OF THE PURPLE SAGE* by Zane Grey)

ACTION: SHOOT: With a deep-muttered, broken curse Venters caught [the horse] through his sights and pulled the trigger. Plainly he heard the bullet thud. Wrangle uttered a horrible, strangling sound. In swift nimbleness of death action he whirled, and, in a last, magnificent stride, he cleared the canyon rim. Down—down—down with the little, frog-like shape [of Jerry Card] humped on his neck! Unending pause—shock—silence—paralyzed Venters. Then up rolled a heavy crash—long roar of sliding rock—rumble dying away in distant echo—into dead silence. Wrangle's race was run. (Source: *RIDERS OF THE PURPLE SAGE* by Zane Grey)

Shootout

ACTION: SHOOTOUT: "Well, I was hid pretty good, enough to keep them from shootin' me deep, but they was slingin' lead close all the time. I used up all the rifle shells, an' then I went after them. Mebbe you heard. It was then I got hit. I had to use up every shell in my own guns, an' they did, too, as I seen. An' now I'm packin' five bullet holes in my carcass, an' guns without shells. (Source: *RIDERS OF THE PURPLE SAGE* by Zane Grey)

Show (5)

ACTION: SHOW: "Here," he added, and showed Jane where little Fay lay on the grass. Jane dropped on her knees. By that long, beautiful golden hair she recognized the beloved Fay. But Fay's loveliness was gone. Her face was drawn and looked old with grief. Yet her heart beat—she was not dead—and Jane gathered strength and lived again. (Source: *RIDERS OF THE PURPLE SAGE* by Zane Grey)

ACTION: SHOW: "Well, I came to Cottonwoods," went on Lassiter, "an' you showed me Milly's grave. An' though your teeth have been shut tighter'n them of all the dead men lyin' back along that trail ... jest the same you told me the secret I've lived these eighteen years to hear. Jane, I said you'd tell me without ever me askin'. I didn't need to ask any question here." "I seen in your face that Dyer, now a bishop, was the proselyter who had brought Milly Erne to her ruin!" (Source: *RIDERS OF THE PURPLE SAGE* by Zane Grey)

ACTION: SHOW: No thought came to him of the defiance, and boldness of riding Jane's racers straight into the arch-plotter's stronghold [of rustlers]. He wanted men to see the famous Arabians; he wanted men to see them dirty, and dusty, bearing all the signs of having been driven to their limits; he wanted men to see and to know that the thieves who had ridden them out into the sage had not ridden them back. Venters had come for that. (Source: *RIDERS OF THE PURPLE SAGE* by Zane Grey)

ACTION: SHOW: She ran through the spruces to the cave, and returned carrying something that was manifestly heavy. Upon neared view he saw that whatever she held with such evident importance had been bound up in a black scarf. She carefully deposited the black bundle. With deft fingers she spread open the black scarf and the bright sun shone upon a dull, glittering heap of gold. (Source: *RIDERS OF THE PURPLE SAGE* by Zane Grey)

ACTION: SHOW: Venters led his comrade to a shady bower and showed him Amber Spring. It was a magnificent outburst of clear, amber water pouring from a dark, stone-lined hole. This spring was the most beautiful and remarkable known to the upland riders of southern Utah. It was the spring that made old Withersteen, a feudal lord and now enabled his daughter to return the roll that her father had exacted from the toilers of the sage. (Source: *RIDERS OF THE PURPLE SAGE* by Zane Grey)

Sigh

ACTION: SIGH: Jane sighed. Another shadow had lengthened down the sage slope to cast further darkness upon her. A melancholy sweetness pervaded her resignation. The boy who had left her had returned a man, nobler, stronger, one in whom she divined something unbending as steel. (Source: *RIDERS OF THE PURPLE SAGE* by Zane Grey)

Sit (3)

ACTION: SIT: He seated himself on the counter and put aside his sombrero, to find his brow clammy and cold. (Source: *SUNSET PASS* by Zane Grey)

ACTION: SIT: "Son, tell me all about this," Lassiter said, as he seated himself on a stone and wiped his moist brow. (Source: *RIDERS OF THE PURPLE SAGE* by Zane Grey)

ACTION: SIT: They all sat around on the porch and grass enjoying the cool breeze coming up the Pass. (Source: *SUNSET PASS* by Zane Grey)

Skulk

ACTION: SKULK: Up in that dark grove dwelt a woman who had been his friend, and he had skulked about her home, gripping a gun stealthily as an Indian, a man without place or people or purpose. (Source: *RIDERS OF THE PURPLE SAGE* by Zane Grey)

Sleep (5)

ACTION: SLEEP: Bess, tired out and silent, laid her head in a saddle, and went to sleep between the two dogs. (Source: *RIDERS OF THE PURPLE SAGE* by Zane Grey)

ACTION: SLEEP: He sought his own bed of fragrant boughs, and, as he lay back, somehow grateful for the comfort and safety, the night seemed to steal away from him, and he sank softly into intangible space and rest and slumber. (Source: *RIDERS OF THE PURPLE SAGE* by Zane Grey)

ACTION: SLEEP: In that wild covert he shut his eyes under the great white stars and intensely vaulted blue, bitterly comparting their [the dogs] loneliness to his own, and fell asleep. (Source: *RIDERS OF THE PURPLE SAGE* by Zane Grey)

ACTION: SLEEP: Little Fay slept dreamlessly upon the bed, her golden curls streaming over the pillow. (Source: *RIDERS OF THE PURPLE SAGE* by Zane Grey)

ACTION: SLEEP: When the storm abated, Venters sought his own cave, and late in the night, as his blood cooled and the stir and throb and thrill subsided, he fell asleep. (Source: *RIDERS OF THE PURPLE SAGE* by Zane Grey)

Slip

ACTION: SLIP: He slipped from cedar to cedar, keeping them between him and the open valley. As he progressed, the belt of trees widened, and he kept to its upper margin. (Source: *RIDERS OF THE PURPLE SAGE* by Zane Grey)

Smile (8)

ACTION: SMILE: "Be merciful ... spare him!" His answer was a ruthless smile. (Source: *RIDERS OF THE PURPLE SAGE* by Zane Grey)

ACTION: SMILE: "Uncle Jim," she said tremulously with a smile different from any Venters had ever seen on her face. (Source: *RIDERS OF THE PURPLE SAGE* by Zane Grey)

ACTION: SMILE: A smile softened the set of his lean hard face, but did not change those light piercing eyes. (Source: *WEST OF THE PECOS* by Zane Grey)

ACTION: SMILE: A smile, like a shadow, flickered across his face. (Source: *RIDERS OF THE PURPLE SAGE* by Zane Grey)

ACTION: SMILE: He smiled a flinty smile that was more than inhuman, yet seemed to give out of its dark aloofness a gleam of righteousness. (Source: *RIDERS OF THE PURPLE SAGE* by Zane Grey)

ACTION: SMILE: He smiled as if he meant that bad news came swiftly enough without being presaged by speech. (Source: *RIDERS OF THE PURPLE SAGE* by Zane Grey)

ACTION: SMILE: She smiled in understanding of his speechless gratitude.. (Source: *RIDERS OF THE PURPLE SAGE* by Zane Grey)

ACTION: SMILE: The gentle smile that she liked, which made of him another person, slowly overspread his face. (Source: *RIDERS OF THE PURPLE SAGE* by Zane Grey)

Sneak (3)

ACTION: SNEAK: Like an Indian stealing hoses he had skulked into he recesses of the canyons. He had found Oldring's retreat, he had killed a rustler, he had shot an unfortunate girl, then had saved her from this unwitting act, and he meant to save her from the consequent wasting of blood, from fever and weakness. Where he had been sick at the letting of blood, now he remembered it in grim, cold calm. As he lost that softness of nature, so he lost his fear of men. He would watch for Oldring, biding his time, and he would kill this great, black-bearded rustler who once held a girl in bondage, who had used her to his infamous ends. Venters surmised this much of the change in him—idleness had passed; keen, fierce vigor flooded his mind and body, all that had happened to him at Cottonwoods seemed remote and hard to recall, the difficulties and perils of the present absorbed him, held him in a kind of spell. (Source: *RIDERS OF THE PURPLE SAGE* by Zane Grey)

ACTION: SNEAK: That very night he stole out of camp, climbed up under the stone bridge, and entered the outlet to the pass. The gorge was full of luminous gloom. Balancing Rock loomed dark and leaned over the pale descent. Transformed in the shadowy light, it took shape and dimensions of a spectral god, waiting—waiting for the moment to hurl himself down upon the tottering walls and close forever the outlet to Deception Pass. At night more than by day Venters felt something fearful and fateful in that rock, and that it had leaned and waited through a thousand years to have somehow to deal with his destiny. (Source: *RIDERS OF THE PURPLE SAGE* by Zane Grey)

ACTION: SNEAK: The safest cover lay closely under the wall of the canyon, and here through the dense thickets Venters made his slow, listening advance toward the oval [open space]. Upon gaining the wide opening, he decided to cross it and follow the left wall till he came to the cattle trail. He scanned the oval as keenly as if hunting for antelope. Then, stooping, he stole from one cover to another, taking advantage of rocks and bunches of sage, until he had reached the thickets under the opposite wall. Once there, he exercised extreme caution in his surveys of the ground ahead, but increased his speed when moving. Dodging from bush to bush, he passed the mouths of two canyons, and in the entrance of a third canyon he crossed a wash of swift, clear water to come abruptly upon the cattle trail. (Source: *RIDERS OF THE PURPLE SAGE* by Zane Grey)

Snub

ACTION: SNUB: "... son, if you snub your old girl for this new one—wal, son, you'll have a rough row to hoe.". (Source: *SUNSET PASS* by Zane Grey)

Spasm

ACTION: SPASM: Consciousness of death was there, a blended terror and pin, but no consciousness of sight. She did not see Venters. She stared into the unknown. Then came a spasm of vitality. She writhed in a torture of reviving strength., and in her convulsions she almost tore from Venter's grasp. Slowly she released and sank partly back. The ungloved hand sought the wound, and pressed so hard that her wrist half buried itself in her bosom. Blood trickled between her spread fingers. Now she looked at Venters with eyes that saw him.. (Source: *RIDERS OF THE PURPLE SAGE* by Zane Grey)

Speak (48)

ACTION: SPEAK: [He] spoke with the arrogance of a Mormon whose power could not be brooked and with the passion of a man in whom jealousy had kindled a consuming fire. (Source: *RIDERS OF THE PURPLE SAGE* by Zane Grey)

ACTION: SPEAK: "Are ... you ... there?" The girl's low voice came from the blackness.. (Source: *RIDERS OF THE PURPLE SAGE* by Zane Grey)

ACTION: SPEAK: "Black Star an' Night are ready," he said simply. His quiet mention of the black racers spurred Jane to action. Hurrying to her room, she changed to her rider's suit, packed her jewelry, and the gold that was left, and all the women's apparel for which there was space in the saddlebags, and then returned to the hall. Black Star stamped his iron-shod hoofs, and tossed his beautiful head and eyed her with knowing eyes. (Source: *RIDERS OF THE PURPLE SAGE* by Zane Grey)

ACTION: SPEAK: "Child, be still," said Lassiter with a dark dignity that had in it something of pity. "You are a woman, fine an' big an' strong, an' your heart matches you size. But no mind. You're a child. Among many thousands of women, you're one who has bucked against your churchmen. They tried you out, an' failed of persuasion, an' finally threats. You meet now the cold steel of a will as far from Christ-like as the universe is wide. You're to be broken But your soul? What the hell do they care for your soul?" (Source: *RIDERS OF THE PURPLE SAGE* by Zane Grey)

ACTION: SPEAK: "Dear ... you look strange to me," faltered Bess. "Never mind that. I'm all right. There's nothing for you to be scared about. ... Only now, right now ... I must know the truth about you." "Truth about me?" echoed Bess shrinkingly. She seemed to be casting back into her mind for a forgotten key. Venters himself, as he saw her, received a pang. "Yes ... the truth. Bess, don't misunderstand. I haven't changed ... that way. I love you still. I'll love you more afterward' Life will be just as sweet... sweeter to us. We'll be married as soon as ever we can. We'll be happy. But there's a devil in me. A perverse, jealous devil! Then I've queer fancies, I forgot for a long time. Now all those fiendish little whispers of doubt and faith and fear and hope come torturing me again. I've got to kill them with the truth." "Bess ... did Oldring love you?" "Certainly he did." "Did ... did you love him?" "Of course. I told you so." "How can you tell it so lightly?" cried Venters passionately. "Haven't you any sense of ... of ...?" He choked back speech. He felt the rush of pain and passion. He seized her in rude, strong hands and drew her close. He looked straight into her dark eyes. They were shadowing with the old, wistful light, but they were as clear as the limpid water of the spring. They were earnest, solemn in unutterable love and faith and abnegation. Venters shivered. He knew he was looking into her soul. He knew she could not lie in that moment, but that she might tell the truth, looking at him with those eyes, almost killed his belief in purity. "What are ... what were you to ... to Oldring?" he panted fiercely. "I am his daughter." She replied instantly. Venters slowly let go of her. There was a violent break in the force of his feeling—then creeping blankness. "What ... was it ... you said?" he asked in a kind of dull wonder. "I am his daughter." (Source: *RIDERS OF THE PURPLE SAGE* by Zane Grey)

ACTION: SPEAK: "Did you send for me?" "Yes, several times." "But I had no word ... no messages ever got to me." "I sent the boys, and they left word with your women that I was ill and would you please come." A sudden, deadly sickness seized Jane. She fought the weakness, as she fought to be above suspicious thoughts, and it passed, leaving her conscious of her utter impotence. That, too, passed as her spirit rebounded. But she had again caught a glimpse of dark, underhand domination, running its secret lines this time into her own household. Like a spider in the blackness of night an unseen hand had begun to run these dark lines, to turn and twist them about her life, to plait and weave a web. Jane knew it now, and in the realization further coolness and sureness came to her, and the fighting courage of her ancestors. (Source: *RIDERS OF THE PURPLE SAGE* by Zane Grey)

ACTION: SPEAK: "He spoke the ringin', lightin' truth. Then he accused Tull of the underhand, miserable robbery of a helpless woman. He told Tull where the red herd was ... of a deal made with Oldrin' ... that Jerry Card had made the deal. I thought Tull was going' to drop, an' that little frog-legged cuss, he looked some limp an' white. But Venters's voice would have kept anybody's legs from bucklin'. I was stiff myself. He went on, an' called Tull ... called him every bad name ever known to a rider, and then some. He cursed Tull. I never heard a man get such a cursin'. He laughed in white, terrible scorn at the idea of Tull bein' a minister. He said Tull an' a few more dogs of hell built their campfire out of the hearts of such innocent an' God-fearin' women as Jane Withersteen. He called Tull a binder of women ... a callous beast who hid behind a mock mantle of righteousness ... an' the last an' lowest coward on the face of the earth. To prey on weak women through their religion ... that was the last, unspeakable crime! Then he finished, an' by this time he'd almost lost his voice. But the whisper was enough. 'Tull,' he said, 'she begged me not to draw on you today. She would pray for you if you burned her at the stake. But listen, ... I swear if you and I ever come face to face again ... I'll kill you!' We backed out the door then, an' up the road. But nobody followed us." (Source: *RIDERS OF THE PURPLE SAGE* by Zane Grey)

ACTION: SPEAK: "He's changed from one to the other!" ejaculated Venters, realizing the astounding fest with unstinted admiration. "Changed at full speed! Jerry Card, that's what you've done, unless I'm drunk on the smell of sage. But I've got to see the trick before I believe it." (Source: *RIDERS OF THE PURPLE SAGE* by Zane Grey)

ACTION: SPEAK: "I heard it from a rider who said you'd know where to tell me to find .. Milly Erne's grave," and the words came with a wrench. (Source: *RIDERS OF THE PURPLE SAGE* by Zane Grey)

ACTION: SPEAK: "I knew it was a lie," replied the mother, and she sank back upon her pillow with something of peach in her white worn face. (Source: *RIDERS OF THE PURPLE SAGE* by Zane Grey)

ACTION: SPEAK: "I knew it! I knew all along that Wrangle was the best hoss!" exclaimed Judkins with his lean face working and his eyes lighting. (Source: *RIDERS OF THE PURPLE SAGE* by Zane Grey)

ACTION: SPEAK: "I want ... to live! I'm afraid ... to die. But I'd rather ... die ... than go back ... to ... to ..." "To Oldring?" asked Venters interrupting her in turn. Her lips moved in an affirmative. (Source: *RIDERS OF THE PURPLE SAGE* by Zane Grey)

ACTION: SPEAK: "I'll steal up here, and push and push with all my might to roll the rock and close forever the outlet to the pass!" She said it lightly, but in the undercurrent of her voice was a heavier note, a ring deeper than any ever given mere play of words. (Source: *RIDERS OF THE PURPLE SAGE* by Zane Grey)

ACTION: SPEAK: "I'll tell you now what I couldn't tell you when you was ... was still engaged to Jane. She turned his head. He's mad in love over her ... follers her like a dog. He ain't no more Lassiter! He's lost his nerve. He doesn't look like the same feller. It's village talk. Everybody knows it. He hasn't thrown a gun, an' he won't ...." (Source: *RIDERS OF THE PURPLE SAGE* by Zane Grey)

ACTION: SPEAK: "I'll tell you one thing," he said bluntly as the gray lightning formed in his eyes. (Source: *RIDERS OF THE PURPLE SAGE* by Zane Grey)

ACTION: SPEAK: "I'll try ... to live," she said. The broken whisper just reached his ears. "Do what ... you want ... with me." "Rest, then ... don't worry ... sleep," he replied. (Source: *RIDERS OF THE PURPLE SAGE* by Zane Grey)

ACTION: SPEAK: "Is Oldring here now?" whispered Venters. He could not speak above a whisper. "He's at Snell's yet. I hev'n't told you yet then the rustlers hev' been raisin' hell. They shot up Stone Bridge an' Glaze, an' fer three days they've been here, drinkin' an' gamblin' and' throwin' gold. These rustlers hev' reason to think, but it's new coin gold, as if it hed jest come from the United Sates Treasury/ An' the coin's genuine. Tet's all been proved. The truth is Oldring's on a rampage. A while back he lost his Masked Rider, an' they say he's wild about thet. I'm wonderin' if Lassiter could hev' told the rustler anythin' about thet little, masked, hard-ridin' devil. Ride! He was 'most as good as Jerry Card. An', Bern, I've been wonderin' if you know ...." (Source: *RIDERS OF THE PURPLE SAGE* by Zane Grey)

ACTION: SPEAK: "It'll take a good deal to kill me. A man couldn't have a faster horse or keener dog. And, I've guns, nd I'll use them, if I'm pushed. But don't worry." "I've faith in you. I'll not worry until after four days. Only ... because you mightn't come ... I must tell you ..." She lost her voice. Her pale face, her great glowing, earnest eyes, seemed to stand alone out of the gloom of the gorge. The dog whined, breaking the silence. "I must tell you ... because you mightn't come back," she whispered. "You must know what ... what I think of your goodness ... of you. Always I've been tongue-tied. I seemed not to be grateful. It ... was deep in my heart. Even now ... if I were ... other than I am ...I couldn't tell you. But I'm nothing. You've saved me ... and I'm ... I'm yours to do with as you like. With all my heart and soul ... I love you!". (Source: *RIDERS OF THE PURPLE SAGE* by Zane Grey)

ACTION: SPEAK: "Jane Withersteen, either you're a fool or noble beyond my understandin'. Mebbe you're both. I know you're blind. What you meant is one thing ... what you did ws to make me love you." "I reckon I'm a human bein', though I never loved anyone but my sister Milly Erne." (Source: *RIDERS OF THE PURPLE SAGE* by Zane Grey)

ACTION: SPEAK: "Jane, are you strong?" "I think I can bear anything." "I didn't tell you why I jest had to go after them fellers. I couldn't tell you. I believe you'd have died. But I can tell you now ... I've got little Fay! Alive ... bad hurt ... but she'll live!" (Source: *RIDERS OF THE PURPLE SAGE* by Zane Grey)

ACTION: SPEAK: "Jud, I'll bet he does," replied Venters earnestly. "Remember what I say. This Lassiter is something more than a gunman. Jud, he's big ... he's great! I feel that in him. God help Tull and Dyer when Lassiter does go after them. Horses and riders and stone walls won't save them." (Source: *RIDERS OF THE PURPLE SAGE* by Zane Grey)

ACTION: SPEAK: "Leave me ... here." "Alone ... to die?" "Yes." "I will not." Venters spoke shortly with a kind of ring in his voice. "What ... do you want ... to do ... with me?" Her whispering grew difficult, so low and faint that Vernters had to stoop to hear her. (Source: *RIDERS OF THE PURPLE SAGE* by Zane Grey)

ACTION: SPEAK: "Listen," he said earnestly, "I've had some wounds, and I've seen many. I know a little about them. The hole in our back has closed. If you lie still three days, the one in your breast will close and you'll be safe. The danger from hemorrhage will be over." He had spoken with earnest sincerity, almost eagerness. (Source: *RIDERS OF THE PURPLE SAGE* by Zane Grey)

ACTION: SPEAK: "Look at that one [beaver] ... he puddles in the mud," said Bess. "And there! See him dive. Hear them gnawing. I'd think they'd break their teeth. How's it they can stay out of the water and under the water?" And she laughed. (Source: *RIDERS OF THE PURPLE SAGE* by Zane Grey)

ACTION: SPEAK: "Look here, Carson," went on Jane hurriedly, and now her cheeks were burning. "You and Black and Willet pick your goods and move your families up to my cabins in the grove. They're far more comfortable than these. Then go to work for me. And if aught happens to you there, I'll give you money ... gold enough to leave Utah!". (Source: *RIDERS OF THE PURPLE SAGE* by Zane Grey)

ACTION: SPEAK: "No, it won't do," he said, when he had somewhat recovered himself."... there are things that you don't know, and there's not a soul among us who can tell you". (Source: *RIDERS OF THE PURPLE SAGE* by Zane Grey)

ACTION: SPEAK: "Oh, listen! He waterfall! I hear it! You've brought me back!" Venters heard a murmuring moan that one moment swelled to a pitch almost softly shrill and the next lulled to a low, almost inaudible sigh. "That's ... wind blowing ... in the ... cliffs," he panted. "You're far ... from Oldring's ... canyon." (Source: *RIDERS OF THE PURPLE SAGE* by Zane Grey)

ACTION: SPEAK: "Sure it was Oldring. What the hell's wrong with you, anyway? Venters, I tell you something's wrong. You're whiter'n a sheet. You can't be scared of the rustler. I don't believe you're got a scare in you. Wal, now, jest let me talk. You know I like to talk, an', if I' slow, I allus git there sometime. As I said, Lassiter was talkin' chummy wih Oldring. There isn't no hard feelin's. and the gang wasn't payin' no particular attention. But like a cat watchin' a mouse I had my eyes on them two fellers. It was strange to me, that confab. I'm gittin' to think a lot fer a feller who doesn't know much. There'd been some queer deals lately an' this seemed to me the queerest. These men stood to the bar alone, an' so close their big gun hilts butted together. I seen Oldring was some surprised at first, an' Lassiter was cool as ice. They talked, an' presently at somethin' Lasssiter said the rustler bawled out a curse, an' then he jest fell off against the bar, an' sagged there. The gang in the saloon looked around, an' laughed, an' thet's about all. Finally Oldring turned, an' it was easy to see somethin' hed shook him. Yes, sir, thet big rustler ... you know he's as broad as he is long an' the powerfulest build of a man. Yes sir, the nerve had been taken out of him. Then, after a little he begun to talk, an' said a lot to Lassiter, an' by and by it didn't take much of an eye to see that Lassiter was gittin' hit hard. I never saw him anyway but cooler'n ice ... til then. He jest kind of sunk in, an' looked an' looked, an' he didn't see a living' soul in that saloon. Then he sort of comes to, an', shakin' hands, mind you ... shakin' hands ... with Oldring, he went out. I couldn't help thinkin' how easy even a boy could hev' dropped the great gunman then! Wal, the rustler stood at the bar for a long time, an' he was seein' things far off, too, then he came to an' roared for whisky, and' gulped a drink thet was big enough to drown me." (Source: *RIDERS OF THE PURPLE SAGE* by Zane Grey)

ACTION: SPEAK: "That's powerful kind of you, now," he said. Sarcasm and scorn made his voice that of a stranger. (Source: *RIDERS OF THE PURPLE SAGE* by Zane Grey)

ACTION: SPEAK: "Then, listen. Saving you, I saved myself. Living here in this valley with you, I've found myself. I've learned to think while I was dreaming. I never troubled myself about God. But God ... or some wonderful ... has whispered to me here. I can't explain it. There are things too deep to tell. . (Source: *RIDERS OF THE PURPLE SAGE* by Zane Grey)

ACTION: SPEAK: "These bones that fly into dust ... they make me sick, and a little afraid. Did the people who lived here have he same feelings as we have? What was the good of their living at all? They're gone! What's the meaning of it all ... of us?" "You ask more than I can tell. It's beyond me. Only there was laughter here once ... and now there's death. Men cut these little steps [in the rock], made these arrowheads and mealing stones, plaited the ropes we found, and left their bones to crumble in our fingers. As far as time is concerned, it might all have been yesterday. We're here today. Maybe we're higher in the scale of human beings ... in intelligence. But who knows? We can't be any higher in the things for which life is lived at all." (Source: *RIDERS OF THE PURPLE SAGE* by Zane Grey)

ACTION: SPEAK: "Venters yelled ... 'Don't anybody pull guns! We ain't come for that!' Then he tramped in, an' I was some put to keep alongside of him. There was a hard, scrapin' sound of feet, a loud cry, an' the some whisperin', an' after that stillness you could cut with a knife." (Source: *RIDERS OF THE PURPLE SAGE* by Zane Grey)

ACTION: SPEAK: "Wal, hev' it your way. I hope you're right. Nat'rully I've been some sore on Lassiter fer gitten soft. But I ain't denyin' his nerve, or whatever's great in him thet sort of paralyzes people. Not later'n this mornin' I seen him come saunterin' down the lane, quiet and slow. An like his guns he comes black ... black, thet's Lassiter. Wal, the cowd on the corner never batted an eye, an' I'll gamble my hoss thet there wasn't one who had a heartbeat till Lassier got by. He went in Snell's saloon, an', there, darn my pictures, if Lassiter wasn't standin' at the bar, drinkin' an' talkin' with Oldring." (Source: *RIDERS OF THE PURPLE SAGE* by Zane Grey)

ACTION: SPEAK: "Where are we?" "I'm taking you to a safe place where o one will ever find you. I must climb a little here and call the dogs. Don't be afraid. I'll soon come for you." She said no more. Her eyes watched him steadily for a moment and then closed. Venters pulled off his boots and felt for the little steps in the rock. The shade of the cliff above obscured the point he wanted to gain, but he could see dimly a few feet before him. What he had attempted with care he now went at with surpassing lightness. Buoyant, rapid, sure, he attained the corner of wall and slipped round it. Here he could not see a hand before his face, so he groped along, found a little flat space, and there removed the saddlebags. The lasso he took back with him to the corner and looped the noose over the spur of rock. (Source: *RIDERS OF THE PURPLE SAGE* by Zane Grey)

ACTION: SPEAK: "Why ... do yu ... want me ... to get well?" she asked wonderingly. The simple question seemed unanswerable except on grounds of humanity. But the circumstances under which he had shot his strange girl, the shock and realization, the waiting for death, the hope, had resulted in a condition of mind wherein Venters wanted her to live more than he had ever wanted anything. Yet he could not tell why. He believed the killing of the rustler and the subsequent excitement had disturbed him. For how else could he explain the throbbing of his brain, the heat of his blood, the undefined sense of full hours, charged, vibrant with pulsating mystery where once they had dragged in loneliness? "I shot you," he said slowly, "and I want you to get well so I shall not have killed a woman. But ... for your own sake, too ..." A terrible bitterness darkened her eyes, and her lips quivered. (Source: *RIDERS OF THE PURPLE SAGE* by Zane Grey)

ACTION: SPEAK: "Will you take me over there [to the cliff-dwellings], and all around in the valley ... pretty soon, when I'm well?" she asked. "Indeed, I shall. It's a wonderful place. Rabbits so thick you can't step without kicking one. And quail, beaver, foxes, wildcats. We're in a regular den." he replied. (Source: *RIDERS OF THE PURPLE SAGE* by Zane Grey)

ACTION: SPEAK: "You see, I jest had to go after Fay," Lassiter was saying, as he knelt to bathe the little [child's], pale face, "But I reckon I don't want no more choices like the one I had to make. There was a crippled feller in that bunch. Mebbe Venters crippled him. Anyway, that's why they were holdin' up here. I seen little Fay first thing, an' was hard put to it to figure out a way to get her. An' I wanted hosses, too. I had to take chances. So I crawled close to their camp. One feller jumped a hoss with little Fay, an', when I shot him, she dropped. She's stunned an' bruised ... she fell right on her head. Jane! She's comin' to! She ain't bad hurt." (Source: *RIDERS OF THE PURPLE SAGE* by Zane Grey)

ACTION: SPEAK: "You shot me ... you've killed me," she whispered in panting gasps. Upon her lips appeared a fluttering, bloody froth. By that he knew the air in her lungs was mixing with blood. (Source: *RIDERS OF THE PURPLE SAGE* by Zane Grey)

ACTION: SPEAK: "Yes," she said with a throb in her voice. (Source: *RIDERS OF THE PURPLE SAGE* by Zane Grey)

ACTION: SPEAK: During the preparation and eating of dinner, Lassiter listened mostly, as was his wont, and occasionally he spoke in his quaint and dry way. (Source: *RIDERS OF THE PURPLE SAGE* by Zane Grey)

ACTION: SPEAK: he replied with the red color in his face. (Source: *RIDERS OF THE PURPLE SAGE* by Zane Grey)

ACTION: SPEAK: Lassiter spoke with slow, cool, soothing voice in which there was a hint of levity, and his touch, as he continued to bath her brow, was gentle and steady. His impassive face, an the kind gray eyes, further stilled her agitation. (Source: *RIDERS OF THE PURPLE SAGE* by Zane Grey)

ACTION: SPEAK: Preston went on with a twinkle in his big gray eyes. (Source: *SUNSET PASS* by Zane Grey)

ACTION: SPEAK: She talked and smiled and laughed with all the dazzling play of lips and eyes that a beautiful, daring woman could summon to her purpose. (Source: *RIDERS OF THE PURPLE SAGE* by Zane Grey)

ACTION: SPEAK: She was able to offer employment for all the men and boys. No little shock was it, then, to have man after man tell her that he dare not accept her kind offer. "It won't do," said Carson, an intelligent man who had seen better days. "We've had our warning. Plain and to the point! Now there's Judkins. He packs guns, and he can use them, and so can the daredevil boys he's hired. But they've little responsibility. Can we risk having our homes burned in our absence?" Jane felt the stretching and chilling of the skin of her face as the blood left it. (Source: *RIDERS OF THE PURPLE SAGE* by Zane Grey)

ACTION: SPEAK: The effort it cost him to speak made him conscious of extreme lassitude following upon great exertion. It seemed that, when he lay down and drew his blanket over him, the action was the last before utter prostration. He stretched inert, wet, hot, his body one great strife of throbbing, stinging nerves and bursting veins. And there he lay for a long while before he felt that he had begun to rest. (Source: *RIDERS OF THE PURPLE SAGE* by Zane Grey)

ACTION: SPEAK: This slow, cool speech contrasted with Blake's hot, impulsive words. "You might have saved some of your breath. See here, Blake, cinch this in your mind. Lassiter has met some square Mormons!" (Source: *RIDERS OF THE PURPLE SAGE* by Zane Grey)

ACTION: SPEAK: Venters was speaking, somewhat haltingly, without his former frankness. He paused, and shifted his position and his gaze. He looked as if he wanted to say something that he found beyond him. Sorrow and pity and shame seemed to contend for mastery over him. (Source: *RIDERS OF THE PURPLE SAGE* by Zane Grey)

Speculate

ACTION: SPECULATE: All the anxious speculation, the worry wearing into dread, the sickening realization that she was growing strained, pale, the waiting suspense, an then this sudden release—all these in vain!. (Source: *SUNSET PASS* by Zane Grey)

Stand (2)

ACTION: STAND: Lassiter staggered to his feet—staggered to a huge, leaning rock that rested on a small pedestal. He put his hand on it—the hand that had been shot through—and Jane saw blood drip from the ragged hole. (Source: *RIDERS OF THE PURPLE SAGE* by Zane Grey)

ACTION: STAND: With his back against a stone, he faced the east, and, stick in hand and idle blade, he waited. (Source: *RIDERS OF THE PURPLE SAGE* by Zane Grey)

Stalk

ACTION: STALK: He was stalking to and fro like a hyena behind bars. (Source: *SUNSET PASS* by Zane Grey)

Stand

ACTION: STAND: Rock stood stiff and immovable as the pine tree by his side. (Source: *SUNSET PASS* by Zane Grey)

Stare (4)

ACTION: STARE: One glance had sufficed for the keen rider to read Bess's real sex, and for once his cool calm had deserted him. He stared till the white of Bess's cheeks flared into crimson. (Source: *RIDERS OF THE PURPLE SAGE* by Zane Grey)

ACTION: STARE: Quickly with a gasp she broke away [from his embrace] to stare a moment, as if some realization had stricken her, then she fled across the porch and into the house. (Source: *SUNSET PASS* by Zane Grey)

ACTION: STARE: Two young women came out of the waiting-room, and they shyly gazed after him. He returned the compliment. (Source: *SUNSET PASS* by Zane Grey)

ACTION: STARE: Venters, unable to speak for consternation and bewildered out of all sense of what he might or ought not do, simply stared. (Source: *RIDERS OF THE PURPLE SAGE* by Zane Grey)

Steady (2)

ACTION: STEADY: "Thank you, Jane," replied Venters, trying to steady his voice. (Source: *RIDERS OF THE PURPLE SAGE* by Zane Grey)

ACTION: STEADY: Venters gently put her from him and steadied her upon her feet, and all the while his blood raced wildly, and a thrilling tingle unsteadied his nerve, and something—that h had seen and felt in her, that he could not understand—seemed very close to him, warm and rich as a fragrant breath, sweet as nothing ever before been sweet to him. (Source: *RIDERS OF THE PURPLE SAGE* by Zane Grey)

Steal

ACTION: STEAL: Venters exercised his usual care in the matter of hiding tracks from the outlet, yet it took him scarcely an hour to reach the rustler's cattle. Here sight of many calves changed his original intention, and instead of packing out meat, he decided to take a calf out alive. He roped one, securely tied its feet, and sung it up over his shoulder. Here was an exceedingly heavy burden, but Venters was powerful—he could take up a sack of grain and with ease pitch it over a pack saddle—and he made long distance without resting. The hardest work came in the climb up to the outlet and on through to the valley. When he had accomplished it, he became fired with another idea that again changed his intention. E would not kill the calf, but keep it alive. He would go back to the [rustler's] herd and pack out more calves. Thereupon he secured the calf in the best available spot for the moment and turned to make a second trip. (Source: *RIDERS OF THE PURPLE SAGE* by Zane Grey)

Step

ACTION: STEP: "Wait ... listen." he whispered. "I hear a hoss." He rose noiselessly, with his ear to the breeze. Suddenly he pulled his sombrero down over his bandaged head, and, swinging his gun sheaths around in front, he stepped into the alcove. (Source: *RIDERS OF THE PURPLE SAGE* by Zane Grey)

Stir

ACTION: STIR: The boy showed signs of returning consciousness. He stirred; his lips moved; a small brown hand clenched in his blouse. (Source: *RIDERS OF THE PURPLE SAGE* by Zane Grey)

Stop (2)

ACTION: STOP: At last she slowed her step, hesitated, and halted uder the magnificent pine tree that made dark shade around her cabin.. (Source: *SUNSET PASS* by Zane Grey)

ACTION: STOP: She rushed to meet him. She had reached out for him when, suddenly, as she saw him clearly, something checked her, and as quickly all her joy fled and with it her color, leaving her pale and trembling.. (Source: *RIDERS OF THE PURPLE SAGE* by Zane Grey)

Strengthen

ACTION: STRENGTHEN: She was gasping at the truth, when suddenly there came, in toward constriction, a hardening of gentle forces within her breast. Like a steel bar it was, stiffening all that had been soft and weak in her. She felt a birth in her of something new and unintelligible. (Source: *RIDERS OF THE PURPLE SAGE* by Zane Grey)

Stroll

ACTION: STROLL: Truman strolled in the black shadows of the pines near his cabin. The night was pleasant, the wind was at its old task in the tree-tops, the frogs along the creek were croaking drowsily of midsummer. The dark Pass, obscure and dreaming, seemed pregnant with life.. (Source: *SUNSET PASS* by Zane Grey)

Stubborn

ACTION: STUBORN: ... there never was any other rich Mormon woman here on the border, let alone one thet's taken the bit between her teeth." (Source: *RIDERS OF THE PURPLE SAGE* by Zane Grey)

Study (6)

ACTION: STUDY: Above him, through a V-shaped cleft in the dark rim of the cliff, shone the lustrous stars that had been his lonely accusers for a long, long year. Tonight they were different.

He studied them. Larger, whiter, more radiant they seemed, but that was not the difference he meant. Gradually it came to him that the distinction was not one he saw, but one he felt. In this he divined as much of the baffling change as he thought, would be revealed to him then. As he lay there, with the singing of the cliff winds in his ears, the white stars above the dark, bold bent, the difference which he belt was that he was no longer alone. (Source: *RIDERS OF THE PURPLE SAGE* by Zane Grey)

ACTION: STUDY: Before proceeding farther he halted, studying the strange character of this slope and realizing that a moving black object could be seen far against such background. . (Source: *RIDERS OF THE PURPLE SAGE* by Zane Grey)

ACTION: STUDY: He could not be sure of anything except that he vowed to find out why Thiry's eyes hid a shadow in their gray depths. (Source: *SUNSET PASS* by Zane Grey)

ACTION: STUDY: He leaned and crouched a little, his eyes piercing. Suddenly he tightness of his face loosened into a convulsive smile. "True Rock!" he shouted, incredulously. (Source: *SUNSET PASS* by Zane Grey)

ACTION: STUDY: He studied the other man's mask-like face. (Source: *WEST OF THE PECOS* by Zane Grey)

ACTION: STUDY: Venters called Ring [the dog] and went to the edge of the terrace, and there halted to survey the valley. He was prepared to find it larger than his unstudied glasses had made it appear, for more than a casual idea of dimensions and a hasty conception of oval shape and singular beauty he had not had time. Again the felicity of the name he had given the valley struck him forcibly. Around the red perpendicular walls, except under the great arch of stone, ran a terrace fringed at the cliff base by silver spruces; below that first terrace sloped another wider one densely overgrown with aspens, and the center of the valley was a level circle of oaks and elders, with the glittering green line of willows and cottonwood dividing it in half. Venters saw a number and variety of birds flitting among the trees. To his left, facing the stone bridge, an enormous cavern opened in the wall, and low down, just above the tree tops, he made out a long shelf of cliff-dwellings, with little black, staring windows or doors. Source: *RIDERS OF THE PURPLE SAGE* by Zane Grey)

Surmount

ACTION: SURMOUNT: Finally he surmounted it [the climb up the rock ladder], surprised to find the walls still several hundred feet high, and a narrow gorge leading down on the other side. This was a divide between two inclines, about twenty yards wide. At one side stood an enormous rock. Venters gave it a second glance, because it rested on a pedestal. It attracted close attention. It was like a colossal pear of stone standing on its stem. Around the bottom were thousands of little nicks just distinguishable to the eye. These were marks of stone hatchets. The cliff-dwellers had chipped and chipped away at the boulder till it rested its tremendous bulk upon a mere pinpoint of its surface.. (Source: *RIDERS OF THE PURPLE SAGE* by Zane Grey)

Teach

ACTION: TEACH: It was Sambo who had taught Terrill to stick like a burr on a horse and to throw a lasso. (Source: *WEST OF THE PECOS* by Zane Grey)

Tease

ACTION: TEASE: Lassiter said, “In my day I’ve seen a sight of horses but never their like. Now, ma’am, if you was waitin’ to make a long an’ fast ride across the sage ... say to elope...” Lassiter ended there with dry humor. Jane blushed and made arch eyes at him. (Source: *RIDERS OF THE PURPLE SAGE* by Zane Grey)

Tell

ACTION: TELL: "I hated to tell you." "I tried yesterday, but you were so cold, I was afraid I couldn't keep it much longer." (Source: *RIDERS OF THE PURPLE SAGE* by Zane Grey)

Think (27)

ACTION: THINK: [Dyer, now a bishop, was the proselyter ...] Then for Jane Withersteen there was a spinning of her brain in darkness, and in what seemed an endless fall into whirling chaos she clung to consciousness, and reeled from this black, circling storm to find she clutched Lassiter as if she were drowning. As by a lightning stroke she sprang from her dull apathy into exquisite torture. (Source: *RIDERS OF THE PURPLE SAGE* by Zane Grey)

ACTION: THINK: [For] Jane came the spinning of her brain in darkness, and, as she whirled in endless chaos, she seemed to be falling at the feet of a luminous figure—a man—Lassiter, grandly chivalrous and heroic, who had save her from herself, who could not be changed, who would ruthlessly, rightfully slay. (Source: *RIDERS OF THE PURPLE SAGE* by Zane Grey)

ACTION: THINK: "... she was watching as if I were all she had left on earth ... she belongs to me." The thought was startlingly new. Like a blow it was in an unprepared moment. The cheery salutation he had ready for her died unborn. (Source: *RIDERS OF THE PURPLE SAGE* by Zane Grey)

ACTION: THINK: "I don't mind sayin' for myself that I think you're a good deal of a man." (Source: *RIDERS OF THE PURPLE SAGE* by Zane Grey)

ACTION: THINK: "I'm glad you were afraid." "Why?" she asked in slow surprise. "I'll tell you someday," he answered soberly. Then around the campfire and through the morning meal he was silent. Afterward he strolled thoughtfully off alone along the terrace. He climbed a great yellow rock raising its crest among the spruces, and there he sat down to face the valley and the west wind, and thoughts as fresh and sweet. (Source: *RIDERS OF THE PURPLE SAGE* by Zane Grey)

ACTION: THINK: A rider had just left her and it was his message that held her thoughtful and almost sad. (Source: *RIDERS OF THE PURPLE SAGE* by Zane Grey)

ACTION: THINK: Back in tht strange canyon, which Venters had found indeed a valley of surprises, the wounded girl's whispered appeal, almost a prayer, not to take her back to the rustlers crowned the events of the last few days with a confounding climax. That she should not want to return to them staggered Venters. Presently, as logical thought returned, her appeal confirmed his first impression—that she was more unfortunate than bad—and he experienced a sensation of gladness. (Source: *RIDERS OF THE PURPLE SAGE* by Zane Grey)

ACTION: THINK: But a dammed-up torrent of emotion at last burst its bounds and the hour that saw his release from immediate action was one that confounded him in the reaction of his spirit. He suffered without understanding why. He caught glimpses into himself, into unlit darkness of soul. The fire that had blistered him—the cold which had frozen him—now united in one, torturing possession of his mind and heart and like a fiery steed with ice-shot feet ranged his being, ran rioting through his blood, trampling the resurging good, dragging ever at the evil. Out of the subsiding chaos came a clear question: What had happened? He had left the valley to go to Cottonwoods. Why? It seemed that he had gone to kill a man—Oldring! The name pivoted his consciousness on the one man of all men on earth who he had wanted to meet. He had met the rustler. Venters recalled the smoky haze of the saloon, the dark-visaged men, the huge Oldring. He saw him step out of the door, a splendid specimen o manhood, a handsome giant with purple-black and sweeping beard. He remembered the inquisitive gaze of falcon eyes—and he felt himself jerk, and his ears throbbed at the thunder of a gun, and he saw the giant sink slowly to his knees. Was that only the vitality of him—that awful light in the eyes—only the hard-dying life of a tremendously powerful brute as Oldring plunged face forward ... dead. (Source: *RIDERS OF THE PURPLE SAGE* by Zane Grey)

ACTION: THINK: Dark thoughts slunk deeply into the innermost recesses of his mind and, like dogs clinking their chains, lay down in slumber. (Source: *RIDERS OF THE PURPLE SAGE* by Zane Grey)

ACTION: THINK: He thought of the woman who loved the birds and the green of the leaves and the murmur of water. (Source: *RIDERS OF THE PURPLE SAGE* by Zane Grey)

ACTION: THINK: He thought passionately, and he knew it was not his old self speaking. It was this softer, gentler man who had awakened to new thoughts in the quiet valley. Tenderness, masterful in him now, watched the absence of joy and blunted the knife edge of entering jealousy. Strong and passionate effort of will, surprising to him, held back the poison from piercing his soul. (Source: *RIDERS OF THE PURPLE SAGE* by Zane Grey)

ACTION: THINK: In the day that followed, he balanced perpetually in mind this haunting conception of innocence over against the cold and sickening fact of an unintentional yet actual gift. (Source: *RIDERS OF THE PURPLE SAGE* by Zane Grey)

ACTION: THINK: In the whirling gulf of her thought there was yet one shining light to guide her, to sustain her in her hope, and it was that, despite her errors and her frailties and her blindness, she had one absolute and unfaltering hold on ultimate and supreme justice. That was love. Love your enemies as yourself was a divine word, entirely free from any church or creed. (Source: *RIDERS OF THE PURPLE SAGE* by Zane Grey)

ACTION: THINK: Lassiter's visit had a disquieting effect upon Bess, and Venters fancied that she entertained the same thought as to future seclusion. The breaking of their solitude, although by a well-meaning friend, had not only dispelled all the dream and much of its charm, but had instilled a canker of fear. Both had seen the footprint in the sand. (Source: *RIDERS OF THE PURPLE SAGE* by Zane Grey)

ACTION: THINK: No day passed but she prayed for all—and most fervently for her enemies. It troubled her that she had lost, or had never gained, the whole control of her mind. In some measure reason and wisdom and decision were locked in a chamber of her brain awaiting a key. Power to think of some things was taken from her. Meanwhile—abiding a day of judgement—she fought ceaselessly to den he bitter drops in her cup, to rear back the slow—the intangibly slow growth of a hot, corrosive lichen eating into her heart. (Source: *RIDERS OF THE PURPLE SAGE* by Zane Grey)

ACTION: THINK: Occasionally he tried to piece together the several stages of strange experience and to make a whole. He had shot a masked outlaw the very sight of whom had been ill omen to riders; he had carried off a wounded woman whose bloody lips quivered in prayer; he had nursed what seemed a frail, shrunken boy, now he watched a girl whose face had become strangely sweet, whose dark blue eyes ere ever upon him without boldness, without shyness, but with a steady, grave and growing light. (Source: *RIDERS OF THE PURPLE SAGE* by Zane Grey)

ACTION: THINK: One flashing thought tore in hot temptation through his mind—why not climb up into the gorge, roll Balancing Rock down the trail, and close forever the outlet to Deception Pass. (Source: *RIDERS OF THE PURPLE SAGE* by Zane Grey)

ACTION: THINK: Rest came to him that night, but o sleep. Sleep he did not want. The hours of strained effort were now as if they had never been, and he wanted to think. Earlier in the day he had dismissed an inexplicable feeling of change, but now there was no longer demand on his cunning and strength and he had time to think, he could not catch the elusive thing that had sadly perplexed as well as elevated his spirit. (Source: *RIDERS OF THE PURPLE SAGE* by Zane Grey)

ACTION: THINK: The resurging reality of the present, as if in irony of his wish, steeped him instantly in contending thought. (Source: *RIDERS OF THE PURPLE SAGE* by Zane Grey)

ACTION: THINK: the thought made his heart sink like cold lead. (Source: *SUNSET PASS* by Zane Grey)

ACTION: THINK: The thought seemed to cut fiercely into Rock's inner flesh. (Source: *SUNSET PASS* by Zane Grey)

ACTION: THINK: Then he set to deliberate thinking, and soon deduced from his own trouble the startling conviction that he must leave Surprise Valley and take Bess with him. . (Source: *RIDERS OF THE PURPLE SAGE* by Zane Grey)

ACTION: THINK: Then it was Venter's primitive, child-like mood, like a savage's seeing yet unthinking, gave way to the encroachment of civilized thought. The world had not been made for a single day's play or fancy or idle watching. The world was old. Nowhere could be gotten a better idea of its age than in this gigantic, silent tomb. The gray ashes in his hand had once been bone of a human being like himself. The pale gloom of the cave had shadowed people long ago. He saw that Bess had received the same shock—could not in moments such as his escape her feeling, living, thinking destiny. (Source: *RIDERS OF THE PURPLE SAGE* by Zane Grey)

ACTION: THINK: Then, with a quick spurt of warm blood along her veins, she thought of Black Star when he got the bit fast between his iron jaws and ran wildly in the sage. (Source: *RIDERS OF THE PURPLE SAGE* by Zane Grey)

ACTION: THINK: Venters thought of the eagles and their lofty nest in a niche under the arch. (Source: *RIDERS OF THE PURPLE SAGE* by Zane Grey)

ACTION: THINK: Venters went his way with busy, gloomy mind, revolving events of the day, trying to reckon those brooding in the night. His thoughts overwhelmed him. (Source: *RIDERS OF THE PURPLE SAGE* by Zane Grey)

ACTION: THINK: What a cold-blooded brute, thought Venters, and felt in him a love for the horse he had never given to any other. (Source: *RIDERS OF THE PURPLE SAGE* by Zane Grey)

Thirsty

ACTION: THIRSTY: The first intimation hat he had of her being aroused from sleep or lethargy was a low call for water. He hurried down into the ravine with his canteen. It was a shallow, grass-green place with aspens growing up everywhere. To his delight he found a tiny brook of swift-running water. Its faint tinge of amber reminded him of the spring at Cottonwoods, and the thought gave him a little shock. The water was so cold it made his fingers tingle as he dipped the canteen. Having returned to the cave, he was glad to see the girl drink thirstily. This time he noted that she could raise her head slightly without his help. (Source: *RIDERS OF THE PURPLE SAGE* by Zane Grey)

Thought

ACTION: THOUGHT: Then came a startling thought, like a lightning flash in the night. She wanted him to find out she was a woman. (Source: *WEST OF THE PECOS* by Zane Grey)

Touch (3)

ACTION: TOUCH: Gently he touched her arm an turned her to face the others, and then outspread his great hand to disclose a shiny, battered gold locket. (Source: *RIDERS OF THE PURPLE SAGE* by Zane Grey)

ACTION: TOUCH: he accidentally touched her bare hand with his. The soft contact shot a thrilling current through him. (Source: *SUNSET PASS* by Zane Grey)

ACTION: TOUCH: Venters felt a touch on his elbow. Jane stood beside him with a hand on his arm. She was smiling. Something radiated from her, and like an electric current accelerated the motion of his blood. (Source: *RIDERS OF THE PURPLE SAGE* by Zane Grey)

Track (2)

ACTION: TRACK: "I tracked him an' part of the trail was the hardest I ever talked. Mebbe there's a rustler or somebody in this country who's as good at trackin' as I am. It that's so, Venters ain't safe.' (Source: *RIDERS OF THE PURPLE SAGE* by Zane Grey)

ACTION: TRACK: "I trailed you. I wanted to know where you was, if you had a safe place. So I trailed you" "Trailed me!" cried Venters blankly. "I reckon. It was some of a job after I got to them smooth rocks. I was all day trackin' you up to them little cut steps in the rock. The rest was easy." (Source: *RIDERS OF THE PURPLE SAGE* by Zane Grey)

Trail

ACTION: TRAIL: Ranchers and settlers would trail water like wolves on a scent. (Source: *WEST OF THE PECOS* by Zane Grey)

Trust

ACTION: TRUST: Birds and squirrels and rabbits soon trusted her. Finding in her nothing to fear, the came close and pleased her with their soft-hued beauty and saucy barking and nibbling at the grass. (Source: *WEST OF THE PECOS* by Zane Grey)

Turn

ACTION: TURN: Lassiter turned his hat around and abound, as was his way, and took his time in replying. (Source: *RIDERS OF THE PURPLE SAGE* by Zane Grey)

Twist

ACTION: TWIST: Ash wheeled on his heel, as on an oiled pivot, and without answer strode back into the cabin, to slam the door. (Source: *SUNSET PASS* by Zane Grey)

Uncertain

ACTION: UNCERTAIN: "It's uncertainty that makes me a coward. The day grows, and with it doubts, fears, and that black-bat hate that bites hotter and hotter into my heart." (Source: *RIDERS OF THE PURPLE SAGE* by Zane Grey)

Understand

ACTION: UNDERSTAND: It was Lassiter, turning away his face and Black studying the stone flags at his feet, that brought Jane to the understanding of what she betrayed. She strove desperately, but she could not rise immediately from such a blow. (Source: *RIDERS OF THE PURPLE SAGE* by Zane Grey)

Unfriendly

ACTION: UNFRIENDLY: There cam a time when no words passed between Jane and her women. Silently they went about their household duties, and secretly they went about the underhand work to which they had been bidden. The gloom of the house and the gloom of its mistress, which darkened even the bight spirit of little Fay, did not pervade these women. Happiness was not among them, but hey were aloof from gloom. They spied and listened; they received and sent secret messages; they stole Jane's books and records, and finally the papers that were deeds of her possessions. Through it all they were silent rapt in a kind of trance. Then, one by one, without leave or explanation or farewell, they left , and never returned. (Source: *RIDERS OF THE PURPLE SAGE* by Zane Grey)

Uplift

ACTION: UPLIFT: At Jane's home the promise made to Mrs. Larkin to care for little Fay had begun to be fulfilled. Like a gleam of sunlight through the cottonwoods was the coming of the child to the gloomy house. The big, silent halls echoed with childish laughter. In the shady court, where Jane pent many of the hot July days, Fay's tiny feet pattered over the tone flags and splashed in the amber stream. She prattled incessantly. What difference Jane thought, a child in her home! It had never been a real home, she discovered. Even the tidiness and neatness she had so observed, and upon which she had insisted to her women, became in the light of Fay's smile, habits that now lost their importance. Fay littered the court with Jane' books and papers, and toys her fancy improvised, and many a strange craft went floating down the little brook. (Source: *RIDERS OF THE PURPLE SAGE* by Zane Grey)

Vanish

ACTION: VANISH: In the flux and reflux of the whirling torture of Jane's mind, that new, daring spirit of hers vanished in the old habitual order of life. (Source: *RIDERS OF THE PURPLE SAGE* by Zane Grey)

Verify

ACTION: VERIFY: "You were never really that rustler [Masked Rider], as we rider knew him? A thief ... a marauder ... a kidnapper of women ... a murderer of sleeping riders?" he said. "No, I never stole ... or harmed anyone ... in all my life, I only rode and rode ..." she replied. "But why ... ... why?" he burst out. "Tell me why?" "I never knew that," she answered in a low voice. Her drooping head straightened, and the large eyes, larger now and darker, met his with a clear, steadfast gaze in which he read the truth. It verified his own conviction. (Source: *RIDERS OF THE PURPLE SAGE* by Zane Grey)

Vibrate

ACTION: VIBRATE: The sheriff's frame vibrated as if it had been surcharged with a powerful current. (Source: *WEST OF THE PECOS* by Zane Grey)

Visit

ACTION: VISIT: He returned the next day, and the next, and upon the following day he came both at morning and at night. Upon the evening of the fourth day Jane seemed to feel the breaking of a brooding struggle in Lassiter. During all these visits he had scarcely a word to say, although he watched her, an played absent-mindedly with Fay. Jane had contented herself with silence. Soon Little Fay substituted "I like oo." With a warmer and more generous "I love oo." Thereafter, Lassiter came oftener to see Jane and her little protégée. (Source: *RIDERS OF THE PURPLE SAGE* by Zane Grey)

Vow

ACTION: VOW: He vowed to work like a beaver [to finish the job given to him]. (Source: *SUNSET PASS* by Zane Grey)

Wag

ACTION: WAG: "Trueman, your trail will sure be rough," returned Winter, wagging his grizzled head. (Source: *SUNSET PASS* by Zane Grey)

Wait

ACTION: WAIT: Before starting down, he waited to catch his breath. He had climbed far up tht wonderful, smooth slope and had almost reached the base of yellow cliff that rose skyward, a huge scarred and cracked bulk. It frowned down upon him as if to forbid further ascent. . (Source: *RIDERS OF THE PURPLE SAGE* by Zane Grey)

ACTION: WAIT: By and by Bess halted to wait for him, and he knew she had come to the trail. When he reached her, it was to smile at sight of her standing with arms around Black Star's neck. (Source: *RIDERS OF THE PURPLE SAGE* by Zane Grey)

ACTION: WAIT: Jane Withersteen, waiting in darkness of mind, remained faithful still. It was darkness that must soon be pierced by light. (Source: *RIDERS OF THE PURPLE SAGE* by Zane Grey)

Walk (24)

ACTION: WALK: ... sallied forth into the sunlight like a man possessed. (Source: *SUNSET PASS* by Zane Grey)

ACTION: WALK: Abruptly he arose, as if her words had been decision for him, and with a sharp command to the dogs he strode from the camp. (Source: *RIDERS OF THE PURPLE SAGE* by Zane Grey)

ACTION: WALK: Again he laid aside his rifle, and, removing boots and belt, he began to walk up the steps. Like a mountain goat, he was agile, sure-footed, and he mounted the first bench without bending to use his hands.. (Source: *RIDERS OF THE PURPLE SAGE* by Zane Grey)

ACTION: WALK: Ash strode over from his cabin, sullen, his face black and blue, and still swollen. (Source: *SUNSET PASS* by Zane Grey)

ACTION: WALK: Bess walked with Venters along the eastern terrace, up the long, weathered slope, under the great stone bridge. They entered the narrow gorge to climb around the fence long before built there by Venters. Farther than this she had never been. (Source: *RIDERS OF THE PURPLE SAGE* by Zane Grey)

ACTION: WALK: Bunches of scattered sage covered the center of the canyon, and among these he threaded his way with the step of an Indian. (Source: *RIDERS OF THE PURPLE SAGE* by Zane Grey)

ACTION: WALK: He casually walked around, looking at the bold pictures on the wall. He remembered some of them. Also he found what he was unostentatiously seeking—some bullet holes in the wall. (Source: *SUNSET PASS* by Zane Grey)

ACTION: WALK: He had not walked half a block before he came to another saloon, the familiar look of which, and the barely decipherable name—Happy Days—acted like a blow in his face. (Source: *SUNSET PASS* by Zane Grey)

ACTION: WALK: He hid his rifle in the sage, marking its exact location with extreme care. Then he faced down the lane and strode toward the center of the village. Men meeting him in the walk,

Gave him a wide berth. In front of Bern's stare a crowd melted apart for his passage and their faces and whispers were faces and whispers of a dream. He turned a corner to meet Tull face to face, eye to eye. As once before he had seen this man pale in a ghastly livid white, so again he saw the change. Tull stopped in his tracks with right hand raised and shaking. Suddenly it dropped, and he seemed to glide aside, to pass out of Venter's sight. Next he saw many horses with bridles down—all clean-limbed, dark bays or blacks—rustlers' horses! (Source: *RIDERS OF THE PURPLE SAGE* by Zane Grey)

ACTION: WALK: He quickened his step, then reacting to his characteristic spirit, he deliberately turned back to enter the saloon. The same place, the same bar, stained mirror, and faded paintings, the same pool tables. Except for a barkeeper, the room was deserted. (Source: *SUNSET PASS* by Zane Grey)

ACTION: WALK: He reined the horse to a walk, halted now and then to listen, and then proceeded cautiously with shifting and alert gaze.. (Source: *RIDERS OF THE PURPLE SAGE* by Zane Grey)

ACTION: WALK: He walked down the platform, passing station-men and others now moving about, without meeting anyone who took more than a casual glance at him. (Source: *SUNSET PASS* by Zane Grey)

ACTION: WALK: He walked the three racers [horses] down the broad, green-bordered village road. He heard the murmur of running water from Amber Spring. Bitter waters for Jane! Men and women stopped to gaze at him and the horses. All knew him; all knew the blacks and the bay. As well as if it had been spoken, Venters read in the faces of men the intelligence that Jane's Arabians had been known to have been stolen. (Source: *RIDERS OF THE PURPLE SAGE* by Zane Grey)

ACTION: WALK: Pale, rigid as a statue, the rider4 stood, not in listening, searching posture, but in one of doomed certainty. Suddenly he grasped Jane with an iron hand, and, turning his face from her gaze, he strode with her down the knoll. (Source: *RIDERS OF THE PURPLE SAGE* by Zane Grey)

ACTION: WALK: Scattered here and there upon this shelf were clumps of aspens, and he walked through them into a glade that surpassed, in beauty and adaptability for a wild home, any place he had ever seen. (Source: *RIDERS OF THE PURPLE SAGE* by Zane Grey)

ACTION: WALK: She led the way, with the bridle of his horse over her arm. They entered a grove, and walked down a wide path shaded by great, low-branching cottonwoods. (Source: *RIDERS OF THE PURPLE SAGE* by Zane Grey)

ACTION: WALK: She walked beside him, slender, light-stepping, with her profile showing clear-cut and cold in the moonlight. (Source: *SUNSET PASS* by Zane Grey)

ACTION: WALK: Soon Jane left the trail and rode into the sage, and presently she dismounted and threw her bridle. The men did likewise. Then, on foot, they followed her, coming out at length on the rim of a low escarpment. She passed by several little ridges of earth to halt before a faintly defined mound. It lay in the shade of a sweeping sagebrush close to the edge of the promontory, and a rider could have jumped his horse over it without recognizing a grave. A grave in the sage [was the] lonely resting place of Milly Erne. The cottonwoods or the alfalfa fields were not in sight, nor was there any rock or ridge or cedar to lend contrast to the monotony. Gray slopes, tingeing the purple, barren and wild, with the wind waving the sage, swept away to the dim horizon.. (Source: *RIDERS OF THE PURPLE SAGE* by Zane Grey)

ACTION: WALK: The burros obediently wheeled and started own the break with little, cautious steps, but Lassiter had to leash the whining dogs and lead them. Like an automaton, Jane followed Lassiter down the steep trail of dust and bits of weathered stone, and, when the little slides moved with her or piled around her knees, she experienced no alarm. Vague relief came to her in the sense of being enclosed between dark, stone walls, deeply hidden from the glare of sun, from the glistening sage.. (Source: *RIDERS OF THE PURPLE SAGE* by Zane Grey)

ACTION: WALK: They passed closely under shady, bulging shelves of cliff, through patches of grass and sage and thicket, and groves of slender trees, and over white, pebbly washes, and around masses of broken rock. The burros trotted tirelessly, the dogs, once more free, pattered tirelessly, and Lassiter led on with never a stop. (Source: *RIDERS OF THE PURPLE SAGE* by Zane Grey)

ACTION: WALK: Venters felt sure that he was the only white man who had ever walked under the shadow of the wonderful stone bridge, down into that wonderful valley with its circle of caves and its terraced rings of silver spruce and aspens. (Source: *RIDERS OF THE PURPLE SAGE* by Zane Grey)

ACTION: WALK: Venters went on and entered the thicket. Here he had to feel his way in pitch blackness and to wedge his progress between the close saplings. Time meant little to him now that he had started, and he edged along with slow ide movement till he got clear of the thicket. [The dogs] Ring and Whitie stood waiting for him. Taking to the open aisles and patches of the sage, he walked guardedly, careful not to stumble or step in dust or strike against spreading sage branches. (Source: *RIDERS OF THE PURPLE SAGE* by Zane Grey)

ACTION: WALK: Without a fear or a tremor or a slip or a touch of Lassiter's hand Jane walked up that ladder of but steps. He pushed her around the corner of wall. Fay lay with wide, staring eyes in the shade of a gloomy wall.. (Source: *RIDERS OF THE PURPLE SAGE* by Zane Grey)

ACTION: WALK: Without further speech Lassiter started off, walking his horse, and Venters followed with his dogs. Half a mile down the slope they entered a luxuriant growth of willows, and soon they came into an open space carpeted with grass like deep green velvet. (Source: *RIDERS OF THE PURPLE SAGE* by Zane Grey)

Wash

ACTION: WASH: As he began to wash the bloodstains from her breast and carefully re-bandage the wound, he was vaguely conscious of a strange, grave happiness in the thought that she might live. (Source: *RIDERS OF THE PURPLE SAGE* by Zane Grey)

Watch (15)

ACTION: WATCH: "Jane you're watched. There's no single move of yours except when you're hid in your house, that ain't seen by sharp eyes. The cottonwood grove's full of creepin', crawlin' men. Like Indians in the grass. When you rode, the sage was full of sneakin' men. At night they crawl under your windows, into the court, an' I reckon into the house. This here grove's hummin' beehive of mysterious happinin's. (Source: *RIDERS OF THE PURPLE SAGE* by Zane Grey)

ACTION: WATCH: After looking to his rifle and ascertaining that it was in working order, he watched, and, as he watched, slowly the force of bitter fierceness, long dormant, gathered, and ready to flame into life. If those riders were not rustlers, he had forgotten how rustlers looked and rode. On they came, a small group, so compact and dark that he could not tell their number. Their horses did not see [his horse], owing to the speed with which they were traveling. They moved at a swift canter, more affected by rustlers than by riders. He grew concerned over the possibility that these horsemen would actually ride down on him before he had a chance to tell what to expect. (Source: *RIDERS OF THE PURPLE SAGE* by Zane Grey)

ACTION: WATCH: As he stepped forward with a half-formed thought that she was absorbed in watching for his return, she turned her head and saw him. A swift start, a change rather than rush of blood under her white cheeks, a flashing of big eyes that fixed their glance upon him, transformed her face in that single instant of turning, and he knew she had been watching for him, that his return was the one thing in her mind. (Source: *RIDERS OF THE PURPLE SAGE* by Zane Grey)

ACTION: WATCH: He strolled up and down, listening to the wild night sounds, watching the moon slide down to the opposite wall of the canyon, peering into the river gap, slowly surrendering to the emotion dammed up within him. (Source: *WEST OF THE PECOS* by Zane Grey)

ACTION: WATCH: he watched with a thrilling eagerness. Straight at the waterfall the rustlers drove the burros, and straight through the middle, where the water spread into a fleecy, thin film like dissolving smoke. Following closely, the rustlers rode into this white mist, showing in bold black relief for an instant, and then they vanished. Venters drew a full breath, that rushed out in brief and sudden utterance. "Good heaven! Of all the holes for a rustler! There's a cavern under that waterfall, and a passage way leading out to a canyon beyond.. (Source: *RIDERS OF THE PURPLE SAGE* by Zane Grey)

ACTION: WATCH: His dancing gold-flecked eyes never oscillated a fraction from Sawtell. (Source: *WEST OF THE PECOS* by Zane Grey)

ACTION: WATCH: Often, in these hours of dreams, he watched the girl, and asked himself—of what was she dreaming? For the changing light of the valley reflected its gleam and its color and its meaning in the changing light of her eyes. He saw in them infinitely more than he saw in his dreams. He saw thought and soul and nature—strong vision of life. All tidings the west wind blew from distance and he found, deep in those dark blue depths, and found them mysteries solved. (Source: *RIDERS OF THE PURPLE SAGE* by Zane Grey)

ACTION: WATCH: She watched the shadows lengthen down the slope, and she wondered at low, yellow clouds sailing swiftly over her and beyond.. (Source: *RIDERS OF THE PURPLE SAGE* by Zane Grey)

ACTION: WATCH: Then he unsaddled the white, and hobbled both horses and watched them thump out in search of grass. (Source: *WEST OF THE PECOS* by Zane Grey)

ACTION: WATCH: Venters did not close his eyes. He watched the stars and the morning shadows, and always his glance returned to the girl's dimply pale face, and he remembered how white and still it had once looked in the starlight. (Source: *RIDERS OF THE PURPLE SAGE* by Zane Grey)

ACTION: WATCH: Venters kept a steady gaze in the northwest direction hoping to see from what canyon they rode. A quarter of an hour went by. Reward for his vigilance came when he descried three more mounted men, far over to the north. But out of what canyon they had ridden it was too late to tell. He watched the three riders across the oval and round the jutting red corner where the others had gone. (Source: *RIDERS OF THE PURPLE SAGE* by Zane Grey)

ACTION: WATCH: Venters walked with Bess, once more in a dream, and watched he lights change on the walls, and faced the wind from our of the west.. (Source: *RIDERS OF THE PURPLE SAGE* by Zane Grey)

ACTION: WATCH: Venters watched her in joy too deep for words. That moment, when she seemed to be lifted by some spiritual transfiguration, was the most beautiful moment of his life. (Source: *RIDERS OF THE PURPLE SAGE* by Zane Grey)

ACTION: WATCH: Venters watched the immovable white face, and, as he watched hour by hour, waiting for death, the infamy of her passed from his mind. He thought only of the sadness, the truth of the moment. Whoever she was—whatever she had done—she was young and she was dying. (Source: *RIDERS OF THE PURPLE SAGE* by Zane Grey)

ACTION: WATCH: With downcast eyes Jane watched the swift flow of the amber water. She saw it and tried to think of it—of the stones—of the ferns—but, like her body, her mind was in a leaden vise. Only the bishop's voice could release her. Seemingly there was silence of longer duration than all her former life. (Source: *RIDERS OF THE PURPLE SAGE* by Zane Grey)

Wave

ACTION: WAVE: He waved his hand in an imperative gesture of command. The red once more leaped to his face, and in his steel blue eyes glinted a pinpoint of fiery curiosity. (Source: *RIDERS OF THE PURPLE SAGE* by Zane Grey)

Whisper

ACTION: WHISPER: "Listen," she whispered, turning her ear to the south. Had she only imagined that she heard something?. (Source: *WEST OF THE PECOS* by Zane Grey)

Whistle

ACTION: WHISTLE: Presently a low jumble of rocks loomed up darkly somewhat to his right, and, turning that way, he whistled softly Out of the rocks glided a dog that leaped and whined about him. (Source: *RIDERS OF THE PURPLE SAGE* by Zane Grey)

ACTION: WHISTLE: Venters whistled for the dogs, and, they came trotting to him.. (Source: *RIDERS OF THE PURPLE SAGE* by Zane Grey)

Wipe

ACTION: WIPE: Then with the wet scarf he had used to bathe her face, he wiped the blood from the stone flags, and, picking up the gun, he threw it upon a couch. With that he began to pace the court, and his silver spurs jangled musically, and the great gun sheaths softly brushed against his leather chaps. (Source: *RIDERS OF THE PURPLE SAGE* by Zane Grey)

Work (2)

ACTION: WORK: His repair activity was indefatigable, and he made Sambo's red tongue hang out like that of a driven calf in the brakes [canyons]. (Source: *WEST OF THE PECOS* by Zane Grey)

ACTION: WORK: Pecos worked relentlessly. He was indefatigable, and he made Sambo's red tongue hand out like that of a driven calf in the brakes. (Source: *WEST OF THE PECOS* by Zane Grey)

PEOPLE- OTHER

IN THIS SECTION

Ears

EAR: "Wal, I only shot his ear off." Drawled Smith. "It stuck out like a jack rabbit's..." (Source: *WEST OF THE PECOS* by Zane Grey)

Eyes (20)

EYES: "Things crowd into my mind," she went on, and the wistful light in her eyes told him the truth of her thoughts. (Source: *RIDERS OF THE PURPLE SAGE* by Zane Grey)

EYES: ... with just a hint of mischief in her gray eyes. (Source: *SUNSET PASS* by Zane Grey)

EYES: He had a look in his eyes, and a hard set to his jaw. (Source: *INHERITANCE* by Nora Roberts)

EYES: Her eyed were large, wide apart and gray in color. (Source: *SUNSET PASS* by Zane Grey)

EYES: Her eyes [were] the color of the sky in early July when it was warm and still and so clear it made you weep. (Source: *WARRIOR'S SONG* by Catherine Coulter)

EYES: Her eyes reflected the transformation of her soul. Dark, brooding, hopeless beliefs—clouds of gloom—drifted, paled, vanished in glorious light. (Source: *RIDERS OF THE PURPLE SAGE* by Zane Grey)

EYES: Her eyes were unusually expressive, and they regarded him steadily. (Source: *RIDERS OF THE PURPLE SAGE* by Zane Grey)

EYES: Her eyes were widening, darkening with thought, and, whenever they did so, the steady, watchful, seeing gaze gave place to the wistful light. In the former she saw as the primitive woman without thought; in the latter she looked inward, and her gaze was the reflection of a troubled mind. (Source: *RIDERS OF THE PURPLE SAGE* by Zane Grey)

EYES: His eyes took on a dark flash, burning out a sadness that had gloomed there. (Source: *WEST OF THE PECOS* by Zane Grey)

EYES: Joy radiated out of summer-blue eyes. (Source: *INHERITANCE* by Nora Roberts)

EYES: "She has crazy eyes. I don't think I quite captured that." (Source: *INHERITANCE* by Nora Roberts)

EYES: she murmured, her grave eyes piercing him. (Source: *SUNSET PASS* by Zane Grey)

EYES: She suddenly opened eyes that transfixed Venters. They were fathomless, blue. Consciousness of death was there, a blended terror and pin, but no consciousness of sight. She did not see Venters. She stared into the unknown. (Source: *RIDERS OF THE PURPLE SAGE* by Zane Grey)

EYES: Sonya rolled her eyes toward Trey. "Don't encourage her." (Source: *INHERITANCE* by Nora Roberts)

EYES: The changing light of the valley reflected its gleam and its color and its meaning in the changing light of her eyes. He saw in them infinitely more than he saw in his dreams. He saw thought and soul and nature—strong vision of life. He found, deep in those dark blue depths, mysteries solved. (Source: *RIDERS OF THE PURPLE SAGE* by Zane Grey)

EYES: Then he appeared with the money belt clutched in his hands. There was a radiance about him, but it appeared far from beautiful. His eyes emitted a wolfish hunger. (Source: *WEST OF THE PECOS* by Zane Grey)

EYES: There was in Bess's eyes a slow-dawning consciousness that seemed about to break out in glorious radiance . (Source: *RIDERS OF THE PURPLE SAGE* by Zane Grey)

EYES: This one had eyes too terrible for her to look into. (Source: *WEST OF THE PECOS* by Zane Grey)

EYES: This was her closest contact with one of these tawny stalwart Texans. And this one had eyes too terrible for her to look into. A smile softened the set of his lean hard face, but did not change those light piercing eyes. (Source: *WEST OF THE PECOS* by Zane Grey)

EYES: This was her closest contact with one of these tawny stalwart Texans. And this one had eyes too terrible for her to look into. A smile softened the set of his lean hard face, but did not change those light piercing eyes. (Source: *WEST OF THE PECOS* by Zane Grey)

Face (14)

FACE Dark red mantled the clear tan of temple and cheek and neck. Her eyes were of shame upheld a long moment by intense, straining search for the verification of her fear. Suddenly they [her eyes] drooped, her head fell to her knees, her hands flew to her hot cheeks. (Source: *RIDERS OF THE PURPLE SAGE* by Zane Grey)

FACE: [His] brown face turned exceedingly pale (Source: *RIDERS OF THE PURPLE SAGE* by Zane Grey)

FACE: {His face} had all the characteristics of the range rider's—the leanness, the red burn of the sun, and the set changelessness that came from years of silence and solitude. The intensity of his gaze [showed] a strained weariness, a piercing wistfulness of keen, gray sight, as if the man was forever looking for that which he never found. (Source: *RIDERS OF THE PURPLE SAGE* by Zane Grey)

FACE: An exquisite rose flush—a glow—shone from her face. (Source: *RIDERS OF THE PURPLE SAGE* by Zane Grey)

FACE: he replied with his face lighting up.. (Source: *RIDERS OF THE PURPLE SAGE* by Zane Grey)

FACE: Her face flashed and flushed with the glow of a leaping joy, but like the vanishing of a gleam it disappeared to leave her as he had never beheld her—cold and hard. (Source: *RIDERS OF THE PURPLE SAGE* by Zane Grey)

FACE: her whole face seemed sad, particularly the deep gray eyes that had begun to regard him somewhat doubtfully. (Source: *SUNSET PASS* by Zane Grey)

FACE: His agitated face grew coldly set and he bronze changed to gray. (Source: *RIDERS OF THE PURPLE SAGE* by Zane Grey)

FACE: His face turned pearl gray, and such a blaze of purple fire flashed that he was surprised. (Source: *WEST OF THE PECOS* by Zane Grey)

FACE: His face turned pearl gray, and such a blaze of purple fire flashed that he was surprised. (Source: *WEST OF THE PECOS* by Zane Grey)

FACE: Lassiter sat down, put his head in his hands, and remained for a few moments in what appeared to be deep and painful thought. When he lifted his face, it was haggard, lined, cold as sculptured marble. . (Source: *RIDERS OF THE PURPLE SAGE* by Zane Grey)

FACE: She did not weep, but the sweet bloom and life died out of her face. She looked haggard and sad, all at once stunted. (Source: *RIDERS OF THE PURPLE SAGE* by Zane Grey)

FACE: The rider's sunburned face turned white. A few times Jane had seen Lassiter's cool calm broken—when he had met little Fay, when he had learned how and why he had come to love both the child and mistress, when he had stood beside Milly Erne's grave. But one and all they could not be considered in the light of his present agitation. (Source: *RIDERS OF THE PURPLE SAGE* by Zane Grey)

FACE: When he reached her side again, he was pale, and his lips were set in a hard line, and his gray eyes glittered coldly. (Source: *RIDERS OF THE PURPLE SAGE* by Zane Grey)

Hair

HAIR: he feasted his eyes on the little stray locks of fair hair that peeped from under her bonnet, on the small well-shaped ear, on the nape of her neck, beautiful and white, and upon the contour of cheek.. (Source: *SUNSET PASS* by Zane Grey)

Hands (2)

HANDS: He stole a glance at her ... hand. What a strong, shapely hand, neither too large, nor too small, nor red and rough like that of most ranchers' daughters. (Source: *SUNSET PASS* by Zane Grey)

HANDS: Lassiter spread wide his hands, as if to signify he could do no more, and his face clouded. (Source: *RIDERS OF THE PURPLE SAGE* by Zane Grey)

Lips (2)

LIPS: A terrible bitterness darkened her eyes, and her lips quivered. (Source: *RIDERS OF THE PURPLE SAGE* by Zane Grey)

LIPS: her lips were sweet and full and red, and ... curved into a little questioning smile. (Source: *SUNSET PASS* by Zane Grey)

FEEL

IN THIS SECTION

Afraid

FEEL: AFRAID: "Well, it's trouble. Every summer I get scared to death, and hid somewhere in the dark. Storms up on the sage are bad, but nothing to what they are down in the canyons. And in this little valley ...why echoes can rap back and forth so quick they'll split our ears." (Source: *RIDERS OF THE PURPLE SAGE* by Zane Grey)

Angry (5)

FEEL: ANGRY: He fell into a rage and stamped up and down, cursing. He was a passionate and headstrong man, evidently determined upon a certain line of conduct, and he meant to stick to it. (Source: *WEST OF THE PECOS* by Zane Grey)

FEEL: ANGRY: His hard jaw protruded and rioting blood corded the veins of his neck. (Source: *RIDERS OF THE PURPLE SAGE* by Zane Grey)

FEEL: ANGRY: Such was Venter's passion. The meeting with the rustlers, the unpresaged attack upon him, the spilling of blood, the recognition of Jerry Card and the horses, the rage, and that last plunge of mad Wrangle [over the cliff]—all these things, fuel on fuel to the smoldering fire, had kindled and swelled and leaped into living flame. His wrongs—Jane's wrongs—Bess's wrongs—all fire, consuming fire! His mind was a seething hell. (Source: *RIDERS OF THE PURPLE SAGE* by Zane Grey)

FEEL: ANGRY: This blasting passion, like fire at white heat, consumer itself in little time. Heer physical strength failed, and still her spirit attempted to go on in magnificent denunciation of those who had wronged her. (Source: *RIDERS OF THE PURPLE SAGE* by Zane Grey)

FEEL: ANGRY: White as chalk, with eyes like lightning, she rolled out on his head her terrible wrath and scathing scorn. (Source: *RIDERS OF THE PURPLE SAGE* by Zane Grey)

Ashamed

FEEL: ASHAMED: Like some delicate thing suddenly exposed to blasting heat, the girl wilted; her head dropped, and into her white, wasted cheeks crept the red of shame. (Source: *RIDERS OF THE PURPLE SAGE* by Zane Grey)

Bitter

FEEL: BITTER: So bitter certainty claimed her at last and trust fled forever. The women who owed much to Jane changed not in love for her, nor in devotion to their household work, but they poisoned both by a thousand acts of stealth and cunning and duplicity. Jane broke out once and caught them in strange, stone-faced, unhesitating falsehood. Thereafter, she broke out no more. What terrible thing bound them and locked their lips, when they showed neither consciousness of guilt toward their benefactress nor distress at the slow wearing apart f long-established and dear ties? (Source: *RIDERS OF THE PURPLE SAGE* by Zane Grey)

Cold

FEEL: COLD: Cold and intangible were all things in earth and heaven. Colder and tighter stretched the skin over his face; colder and harder grew the polished butts of his guns; colder and steadier became his hands, as he wiped the clammy sweat from his face or reached low to his gun sheaths. Men meeting him in the walk, Gave him a wide berth. (Source: *RIDERS OF THE PURPLE SAGE* by Zane Grey)

Elated

FEEL: ELATED: ... felt that he was soaring to the blue sky. (Source: *SUNSET PASS* by Zane Grey)

Excited

FEEL: EXCITED: her breast heaving like a plate of jelly. (Source: *WEST OF THE PECOS* by Zane Grey)

Exhausted

FEEL: EXHAUSTED: The effort it cost him to speak made him conscious of extreme lassitude following upon great exertion. It seemed, when he lay down and drew his blanket over him, the action was the last before utter prostration [complete physical exhaustion]. He stretched inert, wet, hot, his body one great strife of throbbing, stinging nerves and bursting veins. And there he lay for a long while before he felt that he had begun to rest. (Source: *RIDERS OF THE PURPLE SAGE* by Zane Grey)

Hate

FEEL: HATE: there was hate in the set glare of his deep gray eyes. (Source: *SUNSET PASS* by Zane Grey)

Lonely (3)

FEEL: LONELY: As a rider guarding the herd he had never thought of the night's wildness and loneliness, as an outcast now, when the full silence set in and the deep darkness, and trains of radiant stars shone cold and calm, he lay with an ache in his heart. (Source: *RIDERS OF THE PURPLE SAGE* by Zane Grey)

FEEL: LONELY: For a year he had lived as a black fox, driven from his kind. He longed for the sound of a voice, the touch of a hand. In the daytime there was riding from place to place, and the gun practice to which something drove him, and other tasks that at least necessitated action. At night, before he won sleep, there was strife in his soul. He yearned to leave the endless sage slopes, the wilderness of canyons, and it was in the lonely night that this yearning grew unbearable. It was then that he reached forth to feel Ring or Whitie, immeasurably grateful for the love and companionship of two dogs. On this night the same old loneliness beset Venters, the old habit of sad thought and burning unquiet had its way. (Source: *RIDERS OF THE PURPLE SAGE* by Zane Grey)

FEEL: LONELY: That day the vastness of Texas and the meaning of loneliness grow fixed in [her] heart forever. (Source: *WEST OF THE PECOS* by Zane Grey)

Pain

FEEL: PAIN: When strong and gentle hands lifted the injured man into the buckboard, he knew agony. Then when the swift wheels ran over a bump or a rut in the road, it was like a rending of flesh and bone. He set his teeth and endured. (Source: *SUNSET PASS* by Zane Grey)

Sad (2)

FEEL: SAD: Another day went by, in which he worked less and pondered more, and all the time covertly watched Bess. Her wistfulness had deepened into downright unhappiness, and that made his task to tell her [about leaving] all the harder. He kept the secret another day, hoping by some chance she might grow less moody, and to his exceeding anxiety she fell into far deeper gloom. (Source: *RIDERS OF THE PURPLE SAGE* by Zane Grey)

FEEL: SAD: Bess reverted to a wistful sadness that he had not observed in her since her recovery. His attempt to cheer her out of it resulted in dismal failure, and consequently in darkening of his own mood. (Source: *RIDERS OF THE PURPLE SAGE* by Zane Grey)

Safe (2)

FEEL: SAFE: Upon his descent back into the valley, Venters' emotion, roused to stirring pitch by the recital of his love story, quieted gradually and in its place came a sober, thoughtful mood. All at one he ascertained that he was serious because he would never more regain his sense of security while in the valley. What Lassiter could do, another skillful tracker might duplicate. (Source: *RIDERS OF THE PURPLE SAGE* by Zane Grey)

FEEL: SAFE: When his soft steps, clinked into the hall, and his tall, black-garbed form filled the door, she felt an inexpressible sense of immediate safety. (Source: *RIDERS OF THE PURPLE SAGE* by Zane Grey)

Sense (2)

FEEL: SENSE: ... the same sensation recurred. But it was different in that he felt cold-frozen—mechanical—incapable of free thought, and all about him seemed unreal, aloof, [and] remote. (Source: *RIDERS OF THE PURPLE SAGE* by Zane Grey)

FEEL: SENSE: Once long before, he had experienced the strangeness of faculties singularly, tinglingly acute. (Source: *RIDERS OF THE PURPLE SAGE* by Zane Grey)

Sullen

FEEL: SULLEN: The first flush—the raging of his wrath—passed to leave him in sullen, almost cold possession of his will. It was a deadly mood, utterly foreign to his nature, engendered, fostered, and released by the wild passions of wild men in a wild country. (Source: *RIDERS OF THE PURPLE SAGE* by Zane Grey)

Thankful

FEEL: THANKFUL: Then Venters found himself thankful that she was absent, for he meant that race to end in Jerry Card's death. (Source: *RIDERS OF THE PURPLE SAGE* by Zane Grey)

Wind

FEEL: WIND: [As she rode] she felt the cool west wind sweeping by from the rear. (Source: *RIDERS OF THE PURPLE SAGE* by Zane Grey)

PLACE

Descriptive Words, Phrases and Expressions

IN THIS SECTION

Prairie
Ranch (4)
River (19)
Road
Rock Walls
Room
Spring
Store (2)
Stream
Town (4)
Town Hall (2)
Trail (9)
Valley (11)
Village
Waterfall (2)
Wilderness
Yard

Barn

BUILDING: BARN: The barn was stuffed full of hay and fodder, some of it, freshly cut. A huge bin showed a reserve of last year's corn. Wagons and harnesses were new; a row of saddles hung opposite a dozen stalls. A long fenced lane ran down to pastures where there were horses whistling, cows mooing, and calves bawling. The whole environment reeked with the heady odor of stock, hay, and manure. (Source: *SUNSET PASS* by Zane Grey)

Brook

BROOK: Murmuring water drew their steps down into a shallow ravine where a brown brook brawled softly over mossy stones. Multitudes of strange gray frogs with white spots and black eyes lined the rocky bank and leaped only at close approach. (Source: *RIDERS OF THE PURPLE SAGE* by Zane Grey)

Cabin (9)

BUILDING: CABIN: A cabin was on the edge of a fringe of trees that faced the river. It sat fairly high on the bank and commanded a view across the river and down. It was long, with three doors opening out on the porch, and it had been crudely though strongly constructed of logs and poles, with sunbaked mud filing the chinks between. Several windows served equally for portholes. In the center the cabin had a low-peaked roof, which shelved down to cover the porch. (Source: *WEST OF THE PECOS* by Zane Grey)

BUILDING: CABIN: a little cabin, far over under the overhanging green slope and near a thin pile of white water falling from mossy rock. The largest of the pines marked this little cabin, and towered over it protectingly. (Source: *WEST OF THE PECOS* by Zane Grey)

BUILDING: CABIN: Just as twilight began to creep out of the larger canyon, gleaming cold on the steely river, a cabin appeared on the edge of the fringe of trees that faced the river. It was fairly high on the bank and commanded a view across the river and down. (Source: *WEST OF THE PECOS* by Zane Grey)

BUILDING: CABIN: Some of the cabins were weathered and gray, with green on the split shingles. They had wide eaves and sturdy gray chimneys built outside, and glass windows. (Source: *WEST OF THE PECOS* by Zane Grey)

BUILDING: CABIN: The cabin was long, with three doors opening out on the porch. It had been crudely though strongly constructed of logs and poles, with sunbaked mud filling the chinks between. The several windows served equally for portholes. In the center it had a low-peaked roof, which shelved down to cover the porch. It did not touch the side wall, thus leaving a considerable air space for the attic.. On the porch was a bench upon which stood a wooden pail and an iron dipper, a basin and soap, and above, hanging on pegs, clean, white towels. (Source: *WEST OF THE PECOS* by Zane Grey)

BUILDING: CABIN: The deserted cabin was very old. Its roof had caved in, and its door and window were vacant—like black eyes. (Source: *SUNSET PASS* by Zane Grey)

BUILDING: CABIN: The interior of the cabin was dark, like all log cabins, except in the neighborhood of the open fire. Evidently this large apartment was living-room and kitchen combined. A door at the end led into another room.. (Source: *WEST OF THE PECOS* by Zane Grey)

BUILDING: CABIN: The next cabin, some distance away under the pines, was a double one of the picturesque kind, long, with wide eaves, a porch all around, and ample space between the two log cabins. Water ran down from the stream, in a chute hollowed from saplings. This cabin was one of the older ones, which had become weathered with its roof greened over with moss. Both cabins had large stone chimneys. Deer and elk antlers, saddles and skins, hung on the walls between the cabins. (Source: *SUNSET PASS* by Zane Grey)

Cottage (2)

BUILDING: COTTAGE: Beyond the great lawn a line of dilapidated old cottages faced the road, vacant-eyed and melancholy. From only a few rose the thin columns of blue smoke that denoted habitation. He happy, dancing, singing slaves were gone, and heir whitewashed homes were falling to ruin.. (Source: *WEST OF THE PECOS* by Zane Grey)

BUILDING: COTTAGE: Beyond the great lawn a line of dilapidated old cottages faced the road, vacant-eyed and melancholy. From only a few rose the thin columns of blue smoke that denoted habitation. The happy, dancing, singing slaves were gone, and their whitewashed homes were falling to ruin. (Source: *WEST OF THE PECOS* by Zane Grey)

Camp

CAMP: For his camp Venters chose a shady, grassy plot between the silver spruces and the cliff. Here, in the stone wall, had been wonderfully carved by wind or washed by water several deep caves above the level of the terrace. They were clean, dry, [and] roomy. (Source: *RIDERS OF THE PURPLE SAGE* by Zane Grey)

Campsite

CAMPSITE: For a camp site, the leader of the expedition chose a wooded bend in the river, where a cleared spot and pole uprights sowed that it had been used before. The leaves on the trees were half grown, the grass was green, flowers on long stems nodded gracefully, and under the bank the river murmured softly (Source: *WEST OF THE PECOS* by Zane Grey)

Canyon *(7)*

CANYON: An opening in the pinons warned him that he was nearing the height of slope. He gained it, and dropped low with a burst of astonishment. Before him stretched a short canyon with a rounded stone floor bare of grass or sage or tree and with curved, shelving walls. A broad, rippling stream flowed toward him, and at the back of the canyon, a waterfall burst from a wide rent in the cliff, and bounding down in two green steps, spread into a long white sheet. (Source: *RIDERS OF THE PURPLE SAGE* by Zane Grey)

CANYON: From where [he] stood the walls [of the canyon] spread and curved on each side, lofty and perpendicular, craggy and impassable along the rims, rock-splintered and densely-thicketed at the bases, perhaps half a mile apart at the extreme width of the curve, and thereafter gradually closing to the mouth, which however, was large enough to permit a lengthy view of the river and the rugged wall opposite. (Source: *WEST OF THE PECOS* by Zane Grey)

CANYON: He moved his camp, choosing a wild and almost inaccessible retreat some miles below. A dense thicket choked the mouth of the little side canyon, where it opened on the Pecos, and back of it there were water and grass in abundance. It could not be entered from the mouth, owing to the matted underbrush, and as there were no cattle or horse tracks leading into it there was little danger of pursuers bothering with the place.. (Source: *WEST OF THE PECOS* by Zane Grey)

CANYON: It followed he low bank of the wash, and keeping it in sight, Venters hugged the line of sage and thicket. Like the curves pf a serpent the canyon wound for a mile or more and then opened into a valley. Patches of red showed clearly against the purple of sage, and farther out on the level dotted strings of red led away to the wall of rock. "Ha, the red herd!" exclaimed Venters. (Source: *RIDERS OF THE PURPLE SAGE* by Zane Grey)

CANYON: The canyon was 100 rods wide; its yellow walls were perpendicular; it had abundant sage and a scant growth of oak and piñon. For five miles it held to a comparatively straight bearing, and then began a heightening of rugged walls and a deepening of the floor. Beyond this point of sudden change in the character of the canyon he had never explored, and here was the real door to the intricacies of Deception Pass. The canyon assumed proportions that dwarfed those of its first ten miles. (Source: *RIDERS OF THE PURPLE SAGE* by Zane Grey)

CANYON: The oval canyon was twice its breadth in length, remarkable in many ways, and strikingly so for a luxuriance of green along the lonely, gray-walled river. (Source: *WEST OF THE PECOS* by Zane Grey)

CANYON: The wide, bone-dry jaws of the canyon yawned beneath him, and stretched away with the green river into the distance. There was a white rapid close enough for him to hear its low roar. The river bottom held wide green ands of mesquite, salt cedar and "arrow-weeds," and from these the gray brush-spotted slopes [the land] rose gradually to the ragged cliffs. Above spread the land for leagues and leagues, with grass and stone prevailing far as the eye could see (Source: *WEST OF THE PECOS* by Zane Grey)

Country (14)

COUNTRY: A wintry sun shone fitfully through the dreary clouds and lighted the winding road down toward the river. Out of the gray blur showed dark-spotted hills and blank spaces and white streaks, all forbidding, all he menace of the area. (Source: *WEST OF THE PECOS* by Zane Grey)

COUNTRY: Back to the west and south mounted the naked ridges, noble and austere by reason of their tremendous size and reach, and between them gloomed the purple gorges, mysterious, forlorn, seemingly inaccessible for beast or man. No grassy pastureland—all that was not gray stone, gray earth, were mere specks of cactus, of greasewood on the boundless slopes. (Source: *WEST OF THE PECOS* by Zane Grey)

COUNTRY: Below him spread a white-and-green checkerboard of grass and cedar, leading with striking boldness up into leagues and leagues of black timber, mesas with crowned walls of gray limestone, cliffs of red rock, fringed by pine, all mere steps up to the mountain kingdom unto which the great gap of Sunset Pass yawned, purple and dim and forbidding.. (Source: *SUNSET PASS* by Zane Grey)

COUNTRY: Driven by wonder, he went out on the porch to sit in the dusk. How serene the canyon! The river moaned low out of the shadow. A coyote wailed from the heights. (Source: *WEST OF THE PECOS* by Zane Grey)

COUNTRY: Far to the south, across a belt of gray desert, rose the range country. It looked its reputation. It rolled away to east and west, far as eye could see, an empire for cattlemen, needing only water to make it a paradise. (Source: *SUNSET PASS* by Zane Grey)

COUNTRY: Far to the southward rose a dim outline of rugged country, hazed in purple. (Source: *SUNSET PASS* by Zane Grey)

COUNTRY: Folding down over the range at its southern line lay the purple broken highlands of rok and gorge and forest, and above these rose the black mountains, not peaked, but wave on wave of great flat domes limned against the blue. The scene caused [him] to draw a deep breath. (Source: *SUNSET PASS* by Zane Grey)

COUNTRY: He gazed over into country that deserved its repute. Wide and far away it flung defiance, menace, and call to the long-absent rider. (Source: *SUNSET PASS* by Zane Grey)

COUNTRY: The great wall of the canyon stood up, receiving the golden blast of sunset, and the canyon lay under a canopy of spreading rays and dropping veils. (Source: *WEST OF THE PECOS* by Zane Grey)

COUNTRY: The huge pines shaded boulders covered with green moss; open forest stretched away on each side of a babbling brown stream that came rushing down from the higher country above; deer grazed with the cattle; wild horses trooped up to whistle and look, and then race away with manes flying. (Source: *SUNSET PASS* by Zane Grey)

COUNTRY: The sun hazed over. There was a chill in the air and a wind rustled the brush. No living creature of the wild crossed his vision. The coyotes had ceased following the herd, and Pecos felt a slight restlessness, and they picked up Indian mustang tracks not too many days old. (Source: *WEST OF THE PECOS* by Zane Grey)

COUNTRY: The vast range must ever be lonely, gray, brooding, hot as a furnace in the summers, cold in winters, when the bitter northers blew, a barren land of scaly ridges for leagues and leagues, a grazing wilderness for numberless cattle, from which the coyote and the buzzard would never disappear. It was what this country was that chained him to it.. (Source: *WEST OF THE PECOS* by Zane Grey)

COUNTRY: The water hole was the next camp, reached late in the evening of a dark and dismal day. If a norther threatened, it did not materialize. (Source: *WEST OF THE PECOS* by Zane Grey)

COUNTRY: wild country with bare grass spots alternating with scale patches, greasewood and cactus contrasting with the gray of rocks, winding ridges and winding canyons all so monotonous and lonely, rolling endlessly down from the west to the river, rolling endlessly up toward the east, and on and on. (Source: *WEST OF THE PECOS* by Zane Grey)

Countryside (29)

COUNTRYSIDE: A gloomy canopy overhead fitted the strange, wild country, which every mile appeared to take on more of its peculiar characteristics. (Source: *WEST OF THE PECOS* by Zane Grey)

COUNTRYSIDE: A thirty-mile gulf yawned wide and shallow, a yellow-green sea of desert grass and sage, which sloped into ridge on ridge of cedar and white grass. The length of the valley, both east and west extended beyond the limit of vision, and here began the vast cattle range that made the town possible. It was a beautiful scene. The rough country commenced some fifteen miles farther on. Sunset Pass and its environs were not in view, not even the mountain ranges that were visible from the town. (Source: *WEST OF THE PECOS* by Zane Grey)

COUNTRYSIDE: All about him was ridge-like roll of wind-smoothed, rain-washed rock. Not a tuft of grass or a bunch of sage colored the dull rust-yellow. To the right, this uneven flow of stone ended in a blunt wall. Leftward, from the hollow that lay at his feet, mounted a gradual slow-swelling slope to a great height topped by leaning, cracked, and ruined crags. It was o less than a mountainside, glistening in the sun like polished granite, with cedar trees springing as if by magic out of the denuded surface. Winds had swept it clear of weathered shale and rains had washed it free of dust. Far up the curved slope its beautiful lines broke to meet the vertical rim wall, to lose its grace in a different order and color of rock, a stained yellow cliff of cracks and caved and seamed crags. Straight before him was a scene less striking but more significant to his keen survey. For beyond a mile of the bare, hummocky rock began the valley of sage, and the mouths of canyons, one of which surely was another gateway into the pass. (Source: *RIDERS OF THE PURPLE SAGE* by Zane Grey)

COUNTRYSIDE: Back to the west and south mounted the naked ridges, noble and austere by reason of their tremendous size and reach, and between them gloomed he purple gorges, mysterious, forlorn, seemingly inaccessible for beast or man. No grassy pasturelands such as had existed in her hopeful dreams! All that was not gray stone, gray earth, were mere specks of cactus, of greasewood on the boundless slopes. (Source: *WEST OF THE PECOS* by Zane Grey)

COUNTRYSIDE: Before him ascended a gradual swell of smooth stone. It was hard, polished, and full of pockets worn by centuries of eddying rain water. A hundred yards up began a line of grotesque cedar trees, and they extended along the slope clear to its most southerly end. (Source: *RIDERS OF THE PURPLE SAGE* by Zane Grey)

COUNTRYSIDE: Before him, to left, to right, waving, rolling, sinking, rising, like low swells of a purple sea, stretched the sage. (Source: *RIDERS OF THE PURPLE SAGE* by Zane Grey)

COUNTRYSIDE: Drawing away from the dry-farming levels and the wastes of cut-over land, the desert proper waved away to the southward, gray and yellow, with spots of green cedars and dotted groups of cattle, on and on to a beckoning horizon line. [It was] a lonely land. (Source: *WEST OF THE PECOS* by Zane Grey)

COUNTRYSIDE: Far across that wide waste began the slow lift of uplands through which Deception Pass cut its tortuous, many-canyoned way. (Source: *RIDERS OF THE PURPLE SAGE* by Zane Grey)

COUNTRYSIDE: Farther on, he came into a region where deep indentations marked the line of canyon walls. These were huge, cove-like blind pockets extending back to a sharp corner with a dense growth of underbrush and trees. (Source: *RIDERS OF THE PURPLE SAGE* by Zane Grey)

COUNTRYSIDE: For ten years, he had lived more or less in an atmosphere of strife. That was Texas. It had to grow worse before it ever could grow better. And this range west of the Pecos was bound to see stirring life as the cattle herds augmented. Ranchers and settlers would trail grass and water like wolves on a scent. (Source: *WEST OF THE PECOS* by Zane Grey)

COUNTRYSIDE: From the ranch the pass spread into a wider stretch of grassy knolls tipped by cedars, and grassy flats dotted by cedars, and grassy ridges slopping like hog-backs down from the walls of gray and green.. (Source: *SUNSET PASS* by Zane Grey)

COUNTRYSIDE: He could not abide the haunted ford of Horsehead Crossing. He would not even camp there, but pushed on into the wilderness of twisted, swelling, greasewood-spotted ridges and the shallow ravines that ran between canyons that were few along this somber reach of the river, there being only at long intervals a break in the lofty walls. At times, he could see the opposite side of the canyon, with its high rim wall, and part of the shaggy-brushed and rock-ribbed slope; at other times the road curved far west of the river. (Source: *WEST OF THE PECOS* by Zane Grey)

COUNTRYSIDE: He had climbed far up that wonderful, smooth slope and had almost reached the base of yellow cliff that rose skyward, a huge scarred and cracked bulk. It frowned down upon him as if to forbid further ascent. Venters bent over for his rifle, and, as he picked it up from where it leaned against the steeper grade, he saw several little nicks cut in the solid stone. They were only a few inches deep and about a foot apart. Venters began to count them—one—two—three—four—on up to sixteen. That number carried his glance to the top of this first bulging bench of cliff base. Above, after a more level offset, was still steeper slope, and the line of nicks kept on, to wind around a projecting corner of wall (Source: *RIDERS OF THE PURPLE SAGE* by Zane Grey)

COUNTRYSIDE: Her clear sight intensified the purple sage slope as it rolled before her. Low swells of prairie-like ground sloped up to the west. Dark, lonely cedar trees, few and far between, stood out strikingly, and at long distances ruins of red rocks. Farther on, up the gradual slope, rose a broken wall, a huge monument, looming dark purple and stretching its solitary mystic way, a wavering line that faded in the north. Here to the westward was the light and color and beauty. Northward the slope descended to a dim line of canyons from which rose an up-flinging of the earth, not mountains, but a vast heave of purple uplands, with ribbed and fan-shaped walls, castle-crowned cliffs, and gray escarpments. (Source: *RIDERS OF THE PURPLE SAGE* by Zane Grey)

COUNTRYSIDE: Hour after hour the wagon wheels left tracks in the rich soil [of the prairie], and the purple beckoning distance seemed ever the same. (Source: *WEST OF THE PECOS* by Zane Grey)

COUNTRYSIDE: In this terrain ragged black streaks and spots [of buffalo], and great patches stood out clearly in the morning sunlight. Only a few were visible on the north side of the river, southward from the very banks these significant and striking contrasts to the yellow and grey of plain extended as far as the eye could see, dimming in the purple obscurity of the horizon. (Source: *WEST OF THE PECOS* by Zane Grey)

COUNTRYSIDE: It was a rolling sea of bleached grass and gray sage, cedared ridges, green washes, with clumps of cattle colorfully dotting levels and slopes—an endless monotony that waved away to the black rough horizon. (Source: *SUNSET PASS* by Zane Grey)

COUNTRYSIDE: It was a short ride to the opening canyons. There was no reason for a choice of which one to enter. The one he rode into was a clear, sharp shaft in yellow stone 1,000 feet deep, with wonderful wind-worn caves low down and high above buttressed and turreted ramparts. (Source: *RIDERS OF THE PURPLE SAGE* by Zane Grey)

COUNTRYSIDE: On this side of the ranch the outlook was different from that on the other; the immediate foreground was rough and the age more rugged and less colorful; there were no dark blue lines of canyons to held the eye, nor any uprearing rock walls. It was a long roll and slope into gray obscurity. (Source: *RIDERS OF THE PURPLE SAGE* by Zane Grey)

COUNTRYSIDE: One morning she went as far as the sage. She had not seen the slope since the beginning of the rains, and now it bloomed a rich, deep purple. There was a high wind blowing, and the sage tossed and waved and colored beautifully from light to dark. Clouds scudded across the sky and their shadows sailed darkly down the sunny slope. (Source: *RIDERS OF THE PURPLE SAGE* by Zane Grey)

COUNTRYSIDE: Out of the grove of cottonwoods, a green patch on the purple [sage], gleamed the dull red of Jane's old stone house. From there extended the wide green of the village gardens and orchards marked by the graceful poplars, and farther down shown the deep, dark richness of the alfalfa fields. Numberless red and black and white dots speckled the sage, and these were cattle and horses. (Source: *RIDERS OF THE PURPLE SAGE* by Zane Grey)

COUNTRYSIDE: The canyon opened fan-shaped into a great oval of green and gray growths. It was the hub of an oblong wheel, and from it, at regular distances, like spokes, ran the outgoing canyons. Here a dull red color predominated over the fading yellow. The corners of wall bluntly rose, scarred and scrawled, to taper into towers and serrated peaks and pinnacled domes. (Source: *RIDERS OF THE PURPLE SAGE* by Zane Grey)

COUNTRYSIDE: The grove seemed dreamy and silent. Presently she found a grassy seat, and reclining there in the sun-flecked shade, with sweet fragrance all around and pale-blue flowers peeping up at her from the green, she felt the slow receding of excitement [and stress]. (Source: *WEST OF THE PECOS* by Zane Grey)

COUNTRYSIDE: The lane opened out upon the sage-enclosed alfalfa fields, and the last habitation, at the end of that lane of hovels was the meanest. Formerly it had been a shed; now it was a home. (Source: *RIDERS OF THE PURPLE SAGE* by Zane Grey)

COUNTRYSIDE: The opening into Deception Pass was one of the remarkable natural phenomena in a country remarkable for vast slopes of sage, uplands insulated by gigantic red walls, and deep canyons of mysterious source and outlet. Here the valley floor was level, and here opened a narrow chasm, a ragged vent in yellow walls of stone. (Source: *RIDERS OF THE PURPLE SAGE* by Zane Grey)

COUNTRYSIDE: This was wild Pecos country, bare grass spots alternating with scaly patches, greasewood and cactus contrasting with the gray of rocks, winding ridge and winding canyon all so monotonous and lonely, rolling endlessly down from the west to the river, rolling endlessly up toward the east, on and on, a vast wasteland apparently extending to infinitude . (Source: *WEST OF THE PECOS* by Zane Grey)

COUNTRYSIDE: To his left, facing the stone bridge, an enormous cavern opened in the [canyon] wall, and low down, just above the tree tops, he made out a long shelf of cliff-dwellings, with little black, staring windows or doors. Like eyes they were, and seemed to watch him. The few cliff-dwellings he had seen—all ruins—had left him with haunting memory of age and solitude and of something past. He had come, in a way, to be a cliff-dweller himself, and those silent eyes would look down upon him, as if in surprise that after thousands of years a man had invaded the valley. (Source: *RIDERS OF THE PURPLE SAGE* by Zane Grey)

COUNTRYSIDE: Toward the center of this oblong circle the sagebrush grew smaller and farther apart. (Source: *RIDERS OF THE PURPLE SAGE* by Zane Grey)

COUNTRYSIDE: When the dust blew away, the plain ahead appeared clear. Behind and to the south rolled the slow dust cloud, soon settling so that the stringy, black horde [of buffalo] once more showed distinct against the gray.. (Source: *WEST OF THE PECOS* by Zane Grey)

Forest

FOREST: All around the forest enclosed them, standing and fallen timber, sapling pines and sturdy junipers, patches of aspen, white-stemmed with dead gold foliage, quaking as with a tremor of their roots. (Source: *SUNSET PASS* by Zane Grey)

Garden

GARDEN: a small enclosed garden, flowering wildly now in middle August, roses interlaced with bougainvillea and hydrangeas, the colors vivid reds and pinks and yellows. One old sessile oak tree was so thick, its heavy leafed branches covered one entire corner of the garden, and its trunk was wrapped round and round with ivy. Blue agrion damselflies hovered over the ivy making it appear to shimmer and shift in the lazy sunlight. [He] heard the croak of a bush cricket. (Source: *THE NIGHTINGALE LEGACY* by Catherine Coulter)

Gorge (3)

GORGE: The draw wound lazily down, turning back upon itself, keeping its narrow width, but heightening its rock walls. From an appreciable descent it fell off to jumps where the men had to dismount and lead the horses. It remained a gorge, however, never widening to the dignity of a canyon. Water certainly poured down here in floods at certain seasons, but the bed of the gorge continued dry as a bleached bone in the sun. (Source: *WEST OF THE PECOS* by Zane Grey)

GORGE: They entered the gorge, and he closed the willow gate. From rosy, golden morning light they passed into cool, dense gloom. The burros pattered up the trail with little, hollow-cracking steps. The gorge widened to narrow outlet and the gloom lightened to gray [as they exited]. (Source: *RIDERS OF THE PURPLE SAGE* by Zane Grey)

GORGE: Water certainly poured down here in floods at certain seasons, but the bed of the gorge continued dry as a bleached bone in the sun. (Source: *WEST OF THE PECOS* by Zane Grey)

Grove

GROVE: A golden glamour seemed to float over that grove of trees and to enrich all objects under the aspens, the fallen poles, the rocks and grass, the camp equipment, and the men themselves. It was cast by the golden sunlight falling through the dense aspen foliage, [and every quivering] leaf [burned] pure gold. Even when there was no wind, the leaves fluttered, as if endowed with life that was trembling, dying. (Source: *SUNSET PASS* by Zane Grey)

Hill

HILL: the hills slumbered in blue haze.. (Source: *SUNSET PASS* by Zane Grey)

Hotel

BUILDING: HOTEL: The hotel where he engaged rooms at an exorbitant figure hummed like a beehive. Its patrons appeared to be the same as the surging crowds in the street. (Source: *WEST OF THE PECOS* by Zane Grey)

House (4)

HOUSE: The big house where they lived was old, solid, picturesque, the lower part built of logs, the upper of rough clapboards, with vines growing up the outside stone chimneys. There were many wooden-shuttered windows, and one pretentious window of glass, proudly curtained in white. (Source: *RIDERS OF THE PURPLE SAGE* by Zane Grey)

HOUSE: The broad leaves of a wide-spreading cottonwood sheltered the sunken roof of weathered boards. Like an Indian hut, it had one floor. Around it were a few scanty rows of vegetables, such as the hand of a weak woman had time and strength to cultivate. This little dwelling place was just outside the village limits, and the widow who lived there had to carry her water from the nearest irrigation ditch.. (Source: *RIDERS OF THE PURPLE SAGE* by Zane Grey)

HOUSE: The home stood in a circle of cottonwoods and was a flat, long, red-stone structure with a covered court in the center through which flowed a lively stream of amber-colored water. The massive blocks of stone and heavy timbers and solid doors and shutters showed the hand of a man who had built against pillage and time, and the flowers and mosses lining the stone-bedded stream, the bright colors of rugs and blankets on the court floor, and the cozy corner with hammock and books and the clean-linen tablecloth, showed the grace of a daughter who lived for happiness and the day at hand. (Source: *RIDERS OF THE PURPLE SAGE* by Zane Grey)

BUILDING: HOUSE: Venters reined in and halted before Dyer's residence. It was a low, long, stone structure, resembling Withersteen House. The gracious front yard was green and luxuriant with grass and flowers; a gravel walk led to the huge porch, a well-trimmed hedge of purple sage separated the yard from the church grounds; birds sang in the trees; water flowed musically along the walks; there were glad, careless shouts of children. For Venters, the beauty of this home, and the serenity, and its apparent happiness all turned red and black. For Venters a shade overspread the lawn, the flowers, the old, vine-clad, stone house. (Source: *RIDERS OF THE PURPLE SAGE* by Zane Grey)

Living Room

BUILDING: LIVING ROOM: Pecos followed Sambo in. The living-room was full of sunlight now. Pecos, sitting at table, gazed from the flushed Terrill around upon the walls, at the crude cupboard, at the pots and pans on the coals, at the homemade furniture, the skins and horns over the rude mantel, at the old Henry rifles—and his mental reservation was that the Lambeths had the spirit of the pioneer, but not the resourcefulness.. (Source: *WEST OF THE PECOS* by Zane Grey)

Mansion (3)

BUILDING: MANSION: so they rode away from the gray, dim mansion, out under the huge live oaks with their long streamers of Spanish moss swaying in the breeze, and into the yellow road that stretched away along the green canal.. (Source: *WEST OF THE PECOS* by Zane Grey)

BUILDING: MANSION: the grove of stately moss-curtained oaks surrounded the worn and weathered Colonial mansion. (Source: *WEST OF THE PECOS* by Zane Grey)

BUILDING: MANSION: The morning of their departure, Terrill walked along the old road between the canal and the grove of stately moss-curtained oaks that surrounded the worn and weathered Colonial mansion. This was her last walk along the beloved old canal with its water-lily pads floating on the still surface. (Source: *WEST OF THE PECOS* by Zane Grey)

Meadow (2)

MEADOW: It was the most beautiful meadow and pasture land in the west! Dots and strings and bunches of cattle gave life to the scene. (Source: *SUNSET PASS* by Zane Grey)

MEADOW: The shaking of the high grass [in the meadow] told him of the running of animals, what species he could not tell, but from the dog's manifest desire to have a chase they were evidently some kind wilder than rabbits. (Source: *RIDERS OF THE PURPLE SAGE* by Zane Grey)

Mountain (3)

MOUNTAIN: For days on end dim blue hills had led her gaze on to dimmer and bluer mountains, like ghosts above the hazy horizon. These mountains were the Guadaloupes. They lay across the Pecos, and these blue hills were the brakes of the Pecos. (Source: *WEST OF THE PECOS* by Zane Grey)

MOUNTAIN: The blue hills they had sighted from a distance were the rock-and-idge region through which the Pecos cut its solitary way. (Source: *WEST OF THE PECOS* by Zane Grey)

MOUNTAIN: The high hunting-grounds were up in the mountains back of the Pass, about a day's climb on horseback, eight thousand feet above the low country. Up there early fall had set in and the foliage was one gorgeous array of color. The camp lay in a mountain meadow, at the edge of a magnificent grove of quaking asps. Behind on a gentler slope stood scattered silver spruces and yellow pines, growing larger as they climbed, until on the ridge above they massed in the deep timber line, which like a green-black belt circled the mountain under the gray grisly weathered and splintered peak. (Source: *SUNSET PASS* by Zane Grey)

Mountain Pass (5)

MOUNTAIN PASS: Beyond and above the foothills yawned the western end of the Pass—the grand gap that split the mountain range and gave the felicitous name to this beautiful rent in the crust of the earth. (Source: *SUNSET PASS* by Zane Grey)

MOUNTAIN PASS: Beyond the grassy levels and mounds the pass changed to a verdant floor, only here and there showing a glint of open parks, like lakes of gold set in a forest. The walls leaned away, less rugged and rocky. From the league-wide forested floor, then, the pass restricted to one-third that width and began its magnificent step by step, up and up, to open into the golden foothill country.. (Source: *SUNSET PASS* by Zane Grey)

MOUNTAIN PASS: He entered the cedars, climbed the ridge, and descended to a grassy open meadow, only to mount another cedared ridge. From the divide he could see willows and cottonwoods lining the brown brook; jackrabbits were numerous; hawks sailed over the open country and blue jays screeched from the slope (Source: *SUNSET PASS* by Zane Grey)

MOUNTAIN PASS: He entered the wide portal of Sunset Pass, and had a clear view of its magnificent reach and bold wild beauty. The winding Sunset Creek came down like a broken ribbon, bright here and dark there, to crawl at last into a gorge of his left. The sentinel pines seemed to greet him. They stood first one, isolated and stately, then another, and next two, and again one, and so on that way until at the height of the Pass they grew in numbers, yet apart, lording it over the few cedars on the level bench. (Source: *WEST OF THE PECOS* by Zane Grey)

MOUNTAIN PASS: Over the western wall, between its end and the foothills, now mystic and dim poured a medium like transparent lilac water. It moved. It flashed and glinted, as if falling stars shot through it down to the depths of amethyst. And every second there was change, until the blazing sun slid below the notch [of the pass], and as swiftly the color and beauty and glory faded, to show Sunset Pass only a wild, broken defile, shading to gray and black. (Source: *SUNSET PASS* by Zane Grey)

Park

PARK: The Park was naturally beautiful, level, with white grass surrounding the patches of brown mats of needles under the pines. The road cut through the center and went down the other side. He glimpsed gardens, corrals, field, and then the purple pass threaded with winding white. There were no rocks, no brush, no fallen logs or dead timber. The few cedars and piñons and pines stood far apart, as if distributed by a mighty landscape artist. (Source: *WEST OF THE PECOS* by Zane Grey)

Passage

PASSAGE: The passage narrowed as he went up [climbed]; it became a slant, hard for him to stick on; it was smooth as marble. (Source: *RIDERS OF THE PURPLE SAGE* by Zane Grey)

Prairie

PRAIRIE: The place was desolate, gray, and lonely, an utter solitude, uninhabited even by beasts of the hills or fowls of the air. It stretched away to infinitude. (Source: *WEST OF THE PECOS* by Zane Grey)

Ranch (4)

RANCH: About noon, Rock came to a stone cabin belonging to his old friend and employer, Jess Slagle. Rock rode into what was a sorry excuse for a yard, where fences were down and dilapidated wagons, long out of use, stood around amid a litter of stones and wood, and all kids of debris characteristic of a run-down range. The corral in the back was a makeshift, and the log barn would have shamed a poor homesteader. (Source: *SUNSET PASS* by Zane Grey)

RANCH: Below the largest lake were corrals and a wide stone barn and open sheds and coops and pens. Here were clouds of dust, and cracking sounds of hoofs, and romping colts and hee-hawing burros. Neighing horses trampled to the corral fences. From the little windows of the barn projected bobbing heads of bays and blacks nd sorrels. (Source: *RIDERS OF THE PURPLE SAGE* by Zane Grey)

RANCH: The grassy divide sloped gradually to the west, and down below the level, where cedars grew thicker and the pines thinned out, were the corrals and barns and open sheds, substantial and well built. A log chute brought running water from the hill above. (Source: *SUNSET PASS* by Zane Grey)

RANCH: The ranch presented a beautiful spectacle for that arid and rocky region. The gray rock walls never changed. They were immutable in their drab insulation, though the sunrise and sunset took fleeting colorful liberties with them. But at their base a yellow-and-gold hue vied with the green, and circled the whole oval canyon, a warm fringe that had no regularity. In the notch of the walls, where the gulch opened, there were clinging vines with hints of cerise among the brown and bronze leaves. Across the green canyon floor were lines and patches of goldenrod. (Source: *WEST OF THE PECOS* by Zane Grey)

River (19)

RIVER: From his range, up and down the Pecos for miles, the strange river had worn a deep channel through dull red soil, and the places where cattle could get down [to its bank] to drink were not many. (Source: *WEST OF THE PECOS* by Zane Grey)

RIVER: From the highest point, he gazed back at the river. It appeared the same as from the other side. The river crossing gleamed pale and steely under the wintry sun. There was no evidence of life. The white skulls of steers stood out distinctly, striking the deadly note of the place. It brooded there in its loneliness. (Source: *WEST OF THE PECOS* by Zane Grey)

RIVER: He gazed down from a height just [when] pale sunlight filtered through the drab clouds, to shine upon a winding silver river that formed a bend like the shape of a horse's head. It flowed out of gray and green wilderness, and probably came through a gap in the distant stone bluff. (Source: *WEST OF THE PECOS* by Zane Grey)

RIVER: Just on the moment pale sunlight filtered through the drab clouds to shine upon a winding silver river that formed a bend like the shape of a horse's head. It flowed out of gray and green wilderness and probably came through a gap in the distant stone bluff. (Source: *WEST OF THE PECOS* by Zane Grey)

RIVER: Most of the river bottoms had openness, color, life and beauty. But this Rio Pecos, with its pale silver gleam, its borders of white and green—it seemed cold, treacherous, aloof, winding its desolate way down into the desolate unknown. (Source: *WEST OF THE PECOS* by Zane Grey)

RIVER: Other river bottoms had openness, color, life, beauty. But this Rio Pecos, for all its pale silver gleam, its borders of white and green, seemed cold, treacherous, aloof, winding its desolate way down into the desolate unknown. (Source: *WEST OF THE PECOS* by Zane Grey)

RIVER: The Colorado River from the far eastern ridge top resembled a green snake with a shining line down he center of its back, crawling over rolling, yellow plains. (Source: *WEST OF THE PECOS* by Zane Grey)

RIVER: The course of the river appeared only as a dark meandering line, its walls hidden, its presence sometimes mysteriously vanished. (Source: *WEST OF THE PECOS* by Zane Grey)

RIVER: The part of the river he was now to explore proved to be the wildest and most dangerous reaches along its whole length. Nothing marked the course of the river. The cedar trees that grew sparsely were all down in the narrow deep-walled winding canyon. Cattle tracks led to the few breaks where it was possible to get down to water. (Source: *WEST OF THE PECOS* by Zane Grey)

RIVER: The river appeared black-streaked gold instead of green. But it struck him that the sinking of the sun over the rim could scarcely account for the changed color. Suddenly his heart leaped, as his quick eye registered the muddy hue of the water, and his ear caught a low, sullen, chafing murmur. A flood had some down causing the roily water in the early morning. (Source: *WEST OF THE PECOS* by Zane Grey)

RIVER: The river changed its course with Horsehead Crossing, but soon veered back to its main trend southward. It dominated that savagely monotonous and magnificent scene. Miles were nothing in this endless expanse. The green and gray along the river were but delusions. (Source: *WEST OF THE PECOS* by Zane Grey)

RIVER: The river from the far eastern ridge top resembled a green snake with a shining line down the center of its back, crawling over rolling, yellow plains.. (Source: *WEST OF THE PECOS* by Zane Grey)

RIVER: The river gloomed as the sun set, a winding purple band with silver edges. (Source: *WEST OF THE PECOS* by Zane Grey)

RIVER: The river slid on like a ribbon of red and gold. (Source: *WEST OF THE PECOS* by Zane Grey)

RIVER: The well-remembered river-sweep was in the shape of a horse's head. It gleamed dark in the old morning light. It meandered out of gray obscurity into the wide open break of the valley and meandered on into the gray confines. That river had a treacherous soul. It seemed to know that this ford was the only sure one for hundreds of miles, that in itself, and the few fountains it drained out of the stony earth, there hid the only allaying of thirst for beast and man in all tht aloof and inscrutable country. (Source: *WEST OF THE PECOS* by Zane Grey)

RIVER: There were gold and red ripples on the river, under a gentle wind. And ducks were winging flight upstream. (Source: *WEST OF THE PECOS* by Zane Grey)

RIVER: They traveled in a northwesterly direction, along a stream where beautiful pecan trees lined the banks. (Source: *WEST OF THE PECOS* by Zane Grey)

RIVER: This side of the river, at least as far up as he could see, differed considerably from the west shore. Rough wooded steps and benches rose up to the rim wall, which was insurmountable though only one-tenth the height of the sheer cliff in other places. They rode up along the edge of the water until halted by natural barriers. (Source: *WEST OF THE PECOS* by Zane Grey)

RIVER: When he halted to look at the river his excitement was augmented by dismay. The channel had wholly changed. It had been fairly swift when low, but now it was swollen and fast, with swirls and eddies, and ridges of current. Logs and sticks and patches of debris floated down. It reflected a strange black-and-gold sky, where broken clouds were taking on stormy colors of sunset. The whole scene, river, sky, walls seemed strangely unreal and full of menace. (Source: *WEST OF THE PECOS* by Zane Grey)

Road

ROAD: The road [across the prairie] penetrated deeper into this wilderness of stone and cactus, greasewood and gray earth.. (Source: *WEST OF THE PECOS* by Zane Grey)

Rock Walls

ROCK WALLS: From where he stood the walls spread and curved on each side, lofty and perpendicular, craggy and impassable along the rims, rock-splintered and densely-thicketed at the bases, perhaps half a mile apart at the extreme width of the curve, and thereafter gradually closing to the mouth of the oval canyon, which was large enough to permit a lengthy view of the river and the rugged wall opposite. (Source: *WEST OF THE PECOS* by Zane Grey)

Room

ROOM: BEDROOM: She passed through a huge low-ceiled chamber, like the inside of a fort, and into a smaller one where a bright wood fire blazed in an open fireplace, and from this into her own bedroom. It had the same comfort as was manifested in the home-like outer court; moreover, it was warm and rich in soft hues. (Source: *RIDERS OF THE PURPLE SAGE* by Zane Grey)

Spring

SPRING: The spring gushed forth water in a swirling torrent and leaped down joyously to make its swift way along a willow-skirted channel. Moss and ferns and lilies overhung its green banks. Except for the rough-hewn stones that held and directed the water, this willow thicket and glade had been left as nature had made it. Below were artificial lakes, three in number, one above the other in banks of raised earth, and around them rose the lofty, green-foliaged shafts of poplar trees. It was all in strange contrast to the endless slopes of lonely sage and the wild rock environs beyond. (Source: *RIDERS OF THE PURPLE SAGE* by Zane Grey)

Store (2)

BUILDING: STORE: Indians lounged around on the stone steps [of the trading post store] , sullen, greasy, painted savages supposed to be peaceful. They were not Comanche, but all the same Pecos would not have trusted some of them out on the range. (Source: *WEST OF THE PECOS* by Zane Grey)

BUILDING: STORE: The store had been enlarged since his last visit. A more complete stock of merchandise filled shelves and cluttered up the place so that there was scarcely room to move about.. (Source: *WEST OF THE PECOS* by Zane Grey)

Stream

WATER: STREAM: When he passed some dead water, he noted was held by a beaver dam, there was a current in the stream, and it flowed west. Following its course, he soon entered the oak forest again, and passed through to find himself before massed and jumbled ruins of cliff wall. The stream disappeared in a split at the base of immense rocks over which he could not climb. (Source: *RIDERS OF THE PURPLE SAGE* by Zane Grey)

Town (4)

TOWN: In the public square, in the center of town, stood the hall, crowded with noisy youngsters, scattered groups of men and women, many Mexicans of both sexes, lounging Indians, whose colored raiment vied with the others, and a host of cowboys in their range clothes. (Source: *SUNSET PASS* by Zane Grey)

TOWN: Rockport appeared to be surrounded on the sides by bawling cattle and on the other by the noisy water of the gulf. There was a main street upon which to ride or drive or walk at any hour of the day and far into the night, but to do so was a most strenuous and uncomfortable undertaking. (Source: *WEST OF THE PECOS* by Zane Grey)

TOWN: HAMLET: The little hamlet, Glaze, a white-and-green patch in the vast waste of purple, lay miles down a slope much like the Cottonwoods slope, only this descended to the west, and miles farther west a faint green spot marked the location of Stone Bridge. (Source: *RIDERS OF THE PURPLE SAGE* by Zane Grey)

TOWN: The town was filling up for the Fourth of July celebration. Rock saw that the town hall had been gayly decorated in red, white and blue. Flags were showing. Youngsters were already setting off firecrackers. The hitching-rails were lined with saddle-horses. Down the long main street, wagons came toiling in from the desert. Cowboys, Mexicans, Indians were numerous, mostly in the vicinity of the saloon.. The outside had been draped with flags and bunting in celebration of the national holiday. (Source: *SUNSET PASS* by Zane Grey)

Town Hall (2)

BUILDING: TOWN HALL: The new town hall was the finest structure in town, and the civic authorities, who happened to be mostly members of the Cattle Association, were proud of it and its expression of a progressive and prosperous community. (Source: *SUNSET PASS* by Zane Grey)

BUILDING: TOWN HALL: The town hall was of Spanish design, low, rambling, many arched and aisled, painted white, with red tiled roof. Whoever designed it must have had in mind a place for public functions as well as business. The outside had been draped with flags and bunting in celebration of the national holiday. Two aisles with arched walls formed the outside of a large patio. Here and everywhere gay many-colored Chinese lanterns gung, single from the tops of the arches, and in strings across from wall to wall. Flowers and desert shrubbery lined the walks and circled the fountain, where water tinkled musically. Many chairs had that day been added to the few benches up and down the aisles, in the vine-bowered corners, and along the walls. The large hall, which was to answer many purposes for the townspeople had been cleared and cleaned, its floor polished, and its ceiling rendered bewilderingly colored with endless streams of bunting. It was empty except for straight chairs set against the wall, on all sides, except at one end, where the platform had obviously been arranged for an orchestra. Flags and sage and evergreen furnished the interior decoration, very simply and attractively. (Source: *SUNSET PASS* by Zane Grey)

Trail (9)

TRAIL: A knotty point for Venters was the fact that the cattle tracks all pointed west. The broad trail came from the direction of the canyon into which the rustlers had ridden, and undoubtedly the cattle had been driven out of it across the oval. There were no tracks pointing the other way. It had been in his mind that they had driven the red herd toward the rendezvous, and not from it. Where did that broad trail come down into the pass, and where did it lead? For many years [the rustler's] mysterious entrance and exit to Deception Pass had ben all-absorbing topics to sage riders. (Source: *RIDERS OF THE PURPLE SAGE* by Zane Grey)

TRAIL: A wide, white trail wound away down the slope. (Source: *RIDERS OF THE PURPLE SAGE* by Zane Grey)

TRAIL: All along this trail, surely once a traveled road, lay skulls and bones of animals. Horses, cattle—a line of bones! From a rock stuck up the ghastly skull and weirdly long horns of a Texas steer—fit guideposts for that crossing.. (Source: *WEST OF THE PECOS* by Zane Grey)

TRAIL: An old grass-grown trail followed the course of a shallow wash where flowed a thin stream of water. (Source: *RIDERS OF THE PURPLE SAGE* by Zane Grey)

TRAIL: He was about to sheer off to his right, where thickets and jumbles of fallen rock would afford him cover, when he ran right upon a broad cattle trail. Like a road it was, more than a trail, and the cattle tracks were fresh, What surprised him more, they [the tracks]were wet! It had not rained. The only solution to this puzzle was that the cattle had been driven through water, and water deep enough to wet their legs. (Source: *RIDERS OF THE PURPLE SAGE* by Zane Grey)

TRAIL: No wheel had ever rolled along that trail, nor had a herd of cattle ever tramped its rocky, cactus-bordered course. At infrequent intervals cattle tracks crossed it, but [there was] no other trail for miles. (Source: *WEST OF THE PECOS* by Zane Grey)

TRAIL: The cattle trail wound for miles and miles down the slope. (Source: *RIDERS OF THE PURPLE SAGE* by Zane Grey)

TRAIL: The trail down the 500 feet of sheer depth always tested [his] nerve. It was bad going for even a burro. But Wrangle, as he led him [the horse] snorted defiance or disgust rather than fear, and, like a hobbled horse on the jump, lifted his ponderous iron-shod fore hoofs and crashed own over the first rough step. Venters warmed to greater admiration of the sorrel, and, giving him a loose bridle, he stepped down foot by foot. Oftentimes the stones and shale started by the horse buried Venters to his knees, again he was hard put to it to dodge a rolling boulder, there were times when he could not see Wrangle for dust, and once he and the horse rode a sliding shelf of yellow, weathered cliff. It was a trail on which there could be no stops, and therefore, if perilous, it was at least one that did not take long in the descent. Venters breathed lighter when that was over, and felt a sudden assurance in the success of his enterprise. (Source: *RIDERS OF THE PURPLE SAGE* by Zane Grey)

TRAIL: Venters marked the smooth gait of [the riders ahead] and understood it when his horse galloped out of the sage into the broad cattle trail down which he had once tracked the red herd. This hard-packed trail, from years of use, was as clean and smooth as a road. (Source: *RIDERS OF THE PURPLE SAGE* by Zane Grey)

Valley (11)

VALLEY: Above Venters loomed a wonderful arch of stone bridging the canyon rims. , and through the enormous round portal gleamed and glistened a beautiful valley shining under sunset gold reflected by surrounding cliffs. He gave a start of surprise. The valley was a cove a mile long, half that wide, and its enclosing walls were smooth and stained and curved inward, forming great caves. (Source: *RIDERS OF THE PURPLE SAGE* by Zane Grey)

VALLEY: He decided that its [the valley's] floor was far higher than the level of Deception Pass and the intersecting canyons. No purple sage colored this valley floor. Instead, there were the white of aspens, streaks of branch and slender trunk glistening from the green of leaves, and the darker green of oaks, and through the middle of this forest, from wall to wall, ran a winding line of brilliant green which marked the course of cottonwoods and willows. (Source: *RIDERS OF THE PURPLE SAGE* by Zane Grey)

VALLEY: PASS: he was not easy in mind and could not occupy himself with plans of moving the girl and his outfit until he had descended to the notch. There he rested a moment and looked about him. The pass was darkening with the approach of night. At the corner of the wall, where the stone steps tuned, he saw a spur of rock that would serve to hold the noose of a lasso. He needed no more aid to scale that place. So, taking several small stones with him, he stepped and slid down to the edge of the slope where he had left his rifle and boots. Here he placed the stones some yards apart. He left the rabbit lying upon the bench where the steps began. Then he addressed a keen-sighted, remembering gaze to the rim wall above. It was serrated, and between two spears of rock, directly in line with his position, showed a zigzag crack that at night would let through the gleam of sky. (Source: *RIDERS OF THE PURPLE SAGE* by Zane Grey)

VALLEY: The tremendous arch of stone curved, clear and sharp, in outline against the morning sky, and through it streaked the golden shaft [of sunlight]. The valley seemed one enchanted circle of glorious veils of gold and wraiths of white and silver haze and dim blue, moving shade—beautiful and wild and unreal as a dream. (Source: *RIDERS OF THE PURPLE SAGE* by Zane Grey)

VALLEY: The valley lay drenched and bathed, a burnished oval of glittering green. The rain-washed walls glistened in the morning light. Waterfalls of many forms poured over the rims, One, a broad lacy sheet, thin as smoke, slid over the western notch and struck a ledge in its downward fall, to bound into broader leap, to burst far below—into white and gold and rosy mist. (Source: *RIDERS OF THE PURPLE SAGE* by Zane Grey)

VALLEY: The valley smoked with the thick amber light of the warm June day. (Source: *WEST OF THE PECOS* by Zane Grey)

VALLEY: The valley swam in thick, transparent haze, golden at dawn, warm and white at noon, purple in the twilight. At the end of every storm a rainbow curbed down into the leaf-bright forest to shine and fade, and leave lingeringly some faint essence of its rosy iris in the air. (Source: *RIDERS OF THE PURPLE SAGE* by Zane Grey)

VALLEY: The valley was a golden, sunlit world. It was silent. The sighing wind, and the twittering quail, and the singing birds, even the rare and seldom recurring hollow crack of a sliding, weathered stone, only thickened and deepened that insulated silence. (Source: *RIDERS OF THE PURPLE SAGE* by Zane Grey)

VALLEY: The valley was miles long, several wide, and enclosed by unscalable walls. But it was the background of this valley that so forcibly struck him. Across the sage flat rose a strange up-flinging of yellow rocks. He could not tell which were close and which were distant. Scrawled mounds of stone, like mountain waves, seemed to roll up to steep bare slopes and towers. (Source: *RIDERS OF THE PURPLE SAGE* by Zane Grey)

VALLEY: Under the wistful shadows [of the valley] he softened, and in the softening felt himself grow a sudden and wiser, and better man. (Source: *RIDERS OF THE PURPLE SAGE* by Zane Grey)

VALLEY: Venters ran down the declivity to enter a zone of light shade streaked with sunshine. The oak trees were slender, none more than half a foot thick, and they grew close together, intermingling their branches. There were fluttering of wings among the branches and quick bird notes, and rustling of dead leaves and rapid patterings. Venters crossed well-worn trails marked with fresh tracks, and when he had stolen on a little farther, he saw many birds and running quail, and more rabbits than he could count. He had not penetrated the forest of oaks for a hundred yards, had not approached anywhere near the line of willows and cottonwoods that he grew along a stream. But he had seen enough to know that Surprise Valley was the home of many wild creatures. (Source: *RIDERS OF THE PURPLE SAGE* by Zane Grey)

Village

VILLAGE: Between the trees twinkled lights of cottage candles, and far down flared bright windows of the village stores. (Source: *RIDERS OF THE PURPLE SAGE* by Zane Grey)

Waterfall (2)

WATERFALL: He was now looking east at an immense, round, boxed corner of canyon down which tumbled a thin, white veil of water, scarcely twenty yards wide. (Source: *RIDERS OF THE PURPLE SAGE* by Zane Grey)

WATERFALL: The white stream fell and paused and fell and paused again, as if loath to plunge into the purple gorges below. (Source: *SUNSET PASS* by Zane Grey)

Wilderness

WILDERNESS: It was a wilderness of twisted, swelling, greasewood-spotted ridges wit shallow ravines that ran between. Canyons were few along this somber reach of the Pecos, there being only at long intervals a break in the lofty wall. At times he could see the opposite side of the canyon, with its high rim wall, and part of the shaggy-brushed and rock-ribbed slope . (Source: *WEST OF THE PECOS* by Zane Grey)

Yard

YARD: Jane turned into one of the wide lane leading from the main street and entered a huge, shady yard. Here were sweet-smelling clover, alfalfa, flowers, and vegetables. Like these fresh things were the dozens of babies, tots, toddlers, noisy urchins, laughing girls, a whole multitude of children of one family. For Collier Brandt, the father of all this numerous progeny, was a Mormon with four wives. (Source: *RIDERS OF THE PURPLE SAGE* by Zane Grey)

THING

Descriptive Words, Phrases and Expressions

IN THIS SECTION

Rock (6)
Season - Fall (8)
Season - Spring
Season - Summer (2)
Shot (3)
Smell – Air (3)
Smell – Animal (2)
Smell - Barn
Smell - Death
Smell - Desert
Smell – Dust (2)
Smell - Pine
Smell - Rain
Smell – Sage (2)
Smell - Slaughterhouse
Smell – Smoke (3)
Smell - Water
Solitude
Sound - Avalanche
Sound - Animal - Bird (17)
Sound - Animal - Cattle (3)
Sound - Animal - Coyote (7)
Sound - Animal - Deer
Sound - Animal – Dog (2)
Sound - Animal - Eagle
Sound - Animal - Elk
Sound - Animal - Horse (21)

Sound - Animal - Mice
Sound - Owl
Sound - Animal - Squirrel (2)
Sound – Animal - Turkey
Sound - Animal – Wolf (2)
Sound - Boom
Sound - Call
Sound - Flood
Sound - Hammering
Sound - Footsteps (2)
Sound - Gunshot (5)
Sound – Howl (2)
Sound - Insect - General (5)
Sound - Insect - Bees (3)
Sound – Jingling (2)
Sound - Leaves
Sound - Outdoors
Sound - Pounding
Sound - Riders (2)
Sound - Ring
Sound - Roar (3)
Sound - Rumble
Sound - Rustling (3)
Sound - Saloon
Sound - Scream
Sound - Silence
Sound - Steps

Sound - Storm (4)

Sound - Thud (2)

Sound – Thunder (2)

Sound - Tinkling

Animal - Beaver (2)

ANIMAL: BEAVER: A dam of brush and logs and mud and stones backed the stream into a little lake. The round, rough beaver houses projected from the water. Like the rabbits the beaver had become shy. Gradually, however, as Venters and Bess knelt low, holding the dogs, the beaver emerged to swim with logs and gnaw at cottonwoods and pat mud walls with their paddle-like tails, and, glossy and shiny in the sun, to go on with their persistent industry. They were the builders. The lake was a mud hole, and the immediate environment a scarred and dead region, but it was a wonderful home of wonderful animals. (Source: *RIDERS OF THE PURPLE SAGE* by Zane Grey)

ANIMAL: BEAVER: Venters approached the willow and cottonwood belt that he had observed from the height of the slope. He penetrated it to find considerable stream of water and great, half-submerged mounds of brush and sticks, and all about him were old and new gnawed circles at the base of the cottonwoods. "Beaver!" he exclaimed. (Source: *RIDERS OF THE PURPLE SAGE* by Zane Grey)

Animal - Bird (12)

ANIMAL: BIRD: A blue heron stood motionless on a water gate [from the lake]. (Source: *RIDERS OF THE PURPLE SAGE* by Zane Grey)

ANIMAL: BIRD: A brown bird fluttered, crying, from a bush. Bess peeped into the leaves. "Look, a nest and four little birds. They're not afraid of us. See how they open their mouths. They're hungry." (Source: *RIDERS OF THE PURPLE SAGE* by Zane Grey)

ANIMAL: BIRD: A white hawk sailed above. (Source: *RIDERS OF THE PURPLE SAGE* by Zane Grey)

ANIMAL: BIRD: DUCK: Flocks of ducks got up with a splashing start and winged swift flight up the canyon. (Source: *WEST OF THE PECOS* by Zane Grey)

ANIMAL: BIRD: Ducks dotted the glassy surface of the lakes. (Source: *RIDERS OF THE PURPLE SAGE* by Zane Grey)

ANIMAL: BIRD: From the trees and shrubs came the song of robins and catbirds. (Source: *RIDERS OF THE PURPLE SAGE* by Zane Grey)

ANIMAL: BIRD: It was the season when birds and ducks halted there on their southern migration. And there were splashes upon the blue lake and in the silver-colored river, and flashes of myriads of wings, and music of many songsters. (Source: *WEST OF THE PECOS* by Zane Grey)

ANIMAL: BIRD: It was the season when birds and ducks halted there on their southern migration. And there were splashes upon the blue lake and in the silver river, and flashes of myriads of wings, and music of many songsters. (Source: *WEST OF THE PECOS* by Zane Grey)

ANIMAL: BIRD: Kingfishers darted with shrieking flight along the shady banks [of the stream]. (Source: *RIDERS OF THE PURPLE SAGE* by Zane Grey)

ANIMAL: BIRD: Little darts of purple, that were running quail, crossed the glades, and a plaintive, sweet peeping came from the coverts. (Source: *RIDERS OF THE PURPLE SAGE* by Zane Grey)

ANIMAL: BIRD: The salt-cedar trees were full of singing birds while buzzards soared overhead. (Source: *WEST OF THE PECOS* by Zane Grey)

ANIMAL: BIRD: Twittering quail darted across the path. (Source: *RIDERS OF THE PURPLE SAGE* by Zane Grey)

Animal - Buffalo (7)

ANIMAL: BUFFALO: In this terrain ragged black streaks and spots, and great patches stood out clearly in the morning sunshine. These black patches were buffalo. There were thousands in the scattered head of the herd, and in that plain-wide mass far to the south there were millions. The annual spring migration north was well on its way. (Source: *WEST OF THE PECOS* by Zane Grey)

ANIMAL: BUFFALO: Terrill became aware that the teams were no longer keeping up with the buffalo. That lumbering lope had increased to a gallop, and the space between the closing lines of buffalo had narrowed to half what it had been. She saw with distended eyes those shaggy walls converging. There was no gap behind the wagon—only a dense, gaining, hairy mass. Sambo's eyes rolled till the whites stood out. He was yellowing to his horses, but Terrill could not hear a word. (Source: *WEST OF THE PECOS* by Zane Grey)

ANIMAL: BUFFALO: The black bobbing sea of stampeding [buffalo] backs swallowed up the open ground till Terrill could have tossed her sombrero upon the shaggy humps. She saw no more flying legs and hoofs. The change from a tame lope to a wild gallop, the hurtling of the blind horde, meant a stampede. (Source: *WEST OF THE PECOS* by Zane Grey)

ANIMAL: BUFFALO: The buffalo herd split a couple of hundred paces below the wagons and the two streams flowed by. The gentle trampling roar went on uneventfully. Dust filled the air and a strong odor prevailed. (Source: *WEST OF THE PECOS* by Zane Grey)

ANIMAL: BUFFALO: The herd spit a couple of hundred paces below and wagons and the two streams [of buffalo] flowed by. Terrill could not help shuddering at the prospect of a stampede. But the gentle trampling roar went on uneventfully. Dust filled the air and a strong odor prevailed. (Source: *WEST OF THE PECOS* by Zane Grey)

ANIMAL: BUFFALO: The horses, the wagons, were keeping pace with the stampede. He horse, Dixie, leaped frantically, sometimes narrowly missing the wagon. Just outside the wheels, rubbing them, swept huge, hairy, horned monsters that surely kept him running straight. (Source: *WEST OF THE PECOS* by Zane Grey)

ANIMAL: BUFFALO: The streams of buffalo had closed in solid and were now scarcely a hundred yards from the wagons. The black and tawny beasts appeared to bob up and down in unison. Dust rolled up yellow and thick, obscuring farther view. Behind, the gap was filling up with a sea of lifting hoofs and shaggy heads. (Source: *WEST OF THE PECOS* by Zane Grey)

Animal - Burro

ANIMAL: BURRO: Hour by hour the tireless burro kept to his faithful, steady trot. Venters guided the burro nearer to the trail so that he could see its white line from the ridges, and rode on through the hours.. (Source: *RIDERS OF THE PURPLE SAGE* by Zane Grey)

Animal - Cattle (9)

ANIMAL: CATTLE: "... the white herd [cattle]. It's on the slope now, not ten miles out ... three thousand head, an' all steers. They're wild an' likely to stampede at the pop of a jack rabbit's ears. (Source: *RIDERS OF THE PURPLE SAGE* by Zane Grey)

ANIMAL: CATTLE: "I knew how you'd take it. But if anythin', that makes it harder to tell. You see, a feller wants to do so much for you, an' I'd got fond of my job. We had the herd a ways off to the north of the break in the valley. There was a big level an' pool of water an' tip-to browse. But the cattle was in a high nervous condition. Wild ... But wild as antelope! You see, they'd been so scared they never slept. I ain't a-goin' to tell you of the many tricks that were pulled off out there in the sage. But there wasn't a day fer weeks that the herd didn't get started to run. We allus managed to ride 'em close an' drive 'em back an' keep 'em bunched. Honest, them steers was thin. They was thin when water and grass was everywhere. Thin at this season ... that'll tell you how your steers was pestered. For instance, one night a strange streak of fire run right through the herd. That streak was a coyote ... with an oiled an' blazin' tail! Fer I shot it an' found out. We hed hell with the herd that night, an' if the sage hedn't ben wet ... we, hosses, steers, an' all would hev' burned up. When the stampede did come, it was from natural cause ... jest a whirlin' devil of dust. An' this wasn't no big whirl, fer the dust was mostly settled. It had dried out in a little swale, an' ordinarily no steer would ever hev' run fer it. But the herd was nervous an' wild. An' when that bunch of white steers got to movin' they was as bad as buffalo. I've seen some buffalo stampedes back in Nebraska, an' this bolt of the steers was the same kind. I tried to mill the herd, but I wasn't equal to it. I don't believe the rider still lives who could hev' turned that herd. (Source: *RIDERS OF THE PURPLE SAGE* by Zane Grey)

ANIMAL: CATTLE: Cattle made a great bustle to climb out of sight or disappear in one of the brakes. (Source: *WEST OF THE PECOS* by Zane Grey)

ANIMAL: CATTLE: Movement went on in the outer circle [of cattle], and that, too, gradually stilled. The white herd had come to a stop, and the pall of yellow dust bean to drift away on the wind. (Source: *RIDERS OF THE PURPLE SAGE* by Zane Grey)

ANIMAL: CATTLE: The cattle trail headed out. If he could be sure of anything, it was of the careful scrutiny had had given that cattle track, every hoof mark of which headed straight west. (Source: *RIDERS OF THE PURPLE SAGE* by Zane Grey)

ANIMAL: CATTLE: The enormously wide-spreading, bow–shaped horns of the Texas long-horn steer had inspired the name of this Mexican breed, and they quite dwarfed the other characteristics of the animal. (Source: *WEST OF THE PECOS* by Zane Grey)

ANIMAL: CATTLE: The foremost cattle had reached the water. It had been the scent of water that had stampeded them and they raced toward the gleaming white sandbars. (Source: *WEST OF THE PECOS* by Zane Grey)

ANIMAL: CATTLE: The long, white, bobbing line of steers streaked swiftly through the sage, and a funnel-shaped dust cloud arose at a low angle. A dull rumbling filled Jane's ears. (Source: *RIDERS OF THE PURPLE SAGE* by Zane Grey)

ANIMAL: CATTLE: The white herd was now strung out in a line two miles long. The dull rumble of thousands of hoofs deepened into continuous low thunder, and, as the steers swept swiftly closer, the thunder became a heavy roll. (Source: *RIDERS OF THE PURPLE SAGE* by Zane Grey)

Animal - Dog (6)

ANIMAL: DOG: All at once the dog put an end to Venter's pondering. Ring sniffed the air, turned slowly in his tracks with a whine, and then growled. (Source: *RIDERS OF THE PURPLE SAGE* by Zane Grey)

ANIMAL: DOG: He talked to his dogs. He called them Ring and Whitie. They were sheep dogs, half collie, half deer hound, superb in build, perfectly trained. It seemed that in his fallen fortunes these dogs understood the nature of their value to him an governed their affection and faithfulness accordingly. Whitie watched him with somber eyes of love, kept tireless guard. When the sun rose, the white dog took the place of the other, and Ring went to sleep at his master's feet. (Source: *RIDERS OF THE PURPLE SAGE* by Zane Grey)

ANIMAL: DOG: Ring growled and sniffed the keen air, and bristled. <u>Whitie sometimes made a mistake—Ring never</u>. (Source: *RIDERS OF THE PURPLE SAGE* by Zane Grey)

ANIMAL: DOG: The dog growled and rushed into the forest. [It] came running back with a rabbit in his mouth. (Source: *RIDERS OF THE PURPLE SAGE* by Zane Grey)

ANIMAL: DOG: Venters ... was somewhat concerned because Whitie appeared to have succumbed to temptation and, while carrying the rabbit, was also chewing on it. Ring evidently regarded this as an injury to himself, especially as he had carried the heavier load. Presently he snapped at one end of the rabbit and refused to let go. But his action prevented Whitie from further misdoing, and then the two dogs pattered down, carrying the rabbit between them. (Source: *RIDERS OF THE PURPLE SAGE* by Zane Grey)

Animal - Horse (29)

ANIMAL: HORSE: [The horse] recognized him, but was too wild to stand still. He ran up the glade, and on into the narrow lane between the walls. This favored Venters's speedy capture of the horse, so coiling his noose ready to throw he hurried on. [The horse] let Venters get to within 100 feet, and then he broke. As he plunged by, rapidly getting into his stride, Venters made a perfect throw with the rope. He had time to brace himself for the shock; nevertheless, [The horse] threw him and dragged him several yards before halting. [The horse] yielded to the lasso, and then to Venters's strong hand. He was as shaggy and wild-looking as a horse left to roam free in the sage. He dropped his long ears and stood readily to be saddled and bridled, but he was exceedingly sensitive and quivered at every touch and sound. (Source: *RIDERS OF THE PURPLE SAGE* by Zane Grey)

ANIMAL: HORSE: [The horse] stood in the center of [the enclosure] with his head up, and he appeared black and of gigantic proportions in the dim light. Venters whistled softly, began a slow approach, and then called. The horse snorted, and plunging away with dull, heavy sound of hoofs, he disappeared in the gloom. (Source: *RIDERS OF THE PURPLE SAGE* by Zane Grey)

ANIMAL: HORSE: [The horse] whistled his pleasure at the smell of the sage. (Source: *RIDERS OF THE PURPLE SAGE* by Zane Grey)

ANIMAL: HORSE: [The horse's] long, swinging canter was a wonderful ground gainer. His stride was almost twice that of an ordinary horse, and his endurance was equally remarkable. (Source: *RIDERS OF THE PURPLE SAGE* by Zane Grey)

ANIMAL: HORSE: "Come!" called Jane, holding out her hands. Only two came to her, those she called Night and Black Star. The first was soft dead black, the other glittering black, and they were perfectly matched in size, both being high and long-bodied, wide through the shoulders, with lithe, powerful legs.. (Source: *RIDERS OF THE PURPLE SAGE* by Zane Grey)

ANIMAL: HORSE: "Wrangle don't get enough work," he said as the big saddle went on. "He's unruly when he's corralled an' wants to run. Wait till he smells the sage! This horse is an iron-jawed devil. I never straddled him but once. He's swift as wind." (Source: *RIDERS OF THE PURPLE SAGE* by Zane Grey)

ANIMAL: HORSE: As Venters ran back to Black Star, he saw he horse stagger on shaking legs into the sage and go down in a heap. Upon reaching him, Venters removed the saddle and bridle. Black Star had been killed on his legs. He had no hope for the stricken horse. Black Star lay flat, covered with bloody froth, mouth wide, tongue hanging, eyes glaring, and all his beautiful body in convulsions.. (Source: *RIDERS OF THE PURPLE SAGE* by Zane Grey)

ANIMAL: HORSE: At his low whistle the black horse whinnied, and carefully picked is blind way out of the grove. The rider did not bridle him, but walked beside him, leading him by touch of hand, and together they passed slowly into the shade of the cottonwoods. (Source: *RIDERS OF THE PURPLE SAGE* by Zane Grey)

ANIMAL: HORSE: Black Star and Night, answering to spur, swept swiftly westward along the white, slow-rising, sage-bordered trail. The blacks settled into their fleet, long-striding gallop. They slowed from gallop to canter, then to trot. The fresh and eager horses did not like the check. (Source: *RIDERS OF THE PURPLE SAGE* by Zane Grey)

ANIMAL: HORSE: Black Star came pounding into the court, dragging Jerd half off his feet, and he whistled at Lassiter's black. But at sight of Jane all his defiant lines seemed to soften, and with tosses of his beautiful head he whipped his bridle. (Source: *RIDERS OF THE PURPLE SAGE* by Zane Grey)

ANIMAL: HORSE: Black Star stamped his iron-shod hoofs, and tossed his beautiful head and eyed her with knowing eyes. [Then] Black Star bent his graceful neck and bowed his noble head and sagged his broad shoulders as he knelt for Jane to mount. (Source: *RIDERS OF THE PURPLE SAGE* by Zane Grey)

ANIMAL: HORSE: By and by Venters forced himself to go over to where Black Star lay, expecting to find him dead. Instead, he found the racer partially, if not wholly recovered. There was recognition, even fire, in his big black eyes. Venters was overjoyed. He sat by the black for a long time. Black Star presently labored to his feet with a heave and a groan, shook himself, and snorted for water. Venters repaired to the little pool he had found, filled his sombrero, and gave the racer a drink. Black Star gulped it at one draft, as if it were but a drop, pushed his nose into the hat and snorted for more. Venters now led Night down to drink, and after a further time Black Star, also. Then the blacks began to graze. (Source: *RIDERS OF THE PURPLE SAGE* by Zane Grey)

ANIMAL: HORSE: Darkness soon emboldened and lent him greater speed. It occurred to him, as he glided into the grassy glade near camp and heard the whinny of a horse, that he had forgotten Wrangle. The big sorrel could not be gotten into Surprise Valley. He would hve to be left here [by camp]. Venters determined at once to lead the other horses out through the thicket and turn them loose. The farther they wandered from this canyon, the better it would suit him. He easily descried Wrangle through the gloom, cut the others were not in sight. It soon developed that the horses had wandered away. (Source: *RIDERS OF THE PURPLE SAGE* by Zane Grey)

ANIMAL: HORSE: He dropped his head, and, slowly lengthening, he bent one foreleg, then the other, and sank to his knees. Jane slipped her left foot in the stirrup, swung lightly into the saddle, and Black Star rose with a ringing stamp(Source: *RIDERS OF THE PURPLE SAGE* by Zane Grey)

ANIMAL: HORSE: He had proceeded for perhaps a couple of miles when [the horse] stopped with a suddenness that threw him heavily against the pommel. "What's wrong, old boy?" called Venters, looking down for a loose shoe, or a snake, or a hoof lamed by a picked-up stone. (Source: *RIDERS OF THE PURPLE SAGE* by Zane Grey)

ANIMAL: HORSE: It was not easy for Jane to hold him to a canter through the grove, and like the wind he broke when he saw the sage. Jane let him have a couple of miles of free running on the open trail, and then she coaxed him in. (Source: *RIDERS OF THE PURPLE SAGE* by Zane Grey)

ANIMAL: HORSE: Near at hand he found Wrangle, and to his surprise the horse came to him. Wrangle was one of the horses that left his viciousness in the home corral. What he wanted was to be free of mules and burros and steers, to roll in dust patches and then to run down the wide, open, windy sage plains, and at night browse and sleep in the cool wet grass of a spring hole. (Source: *RIDERS OF THE PURPLE SAGE* by Zane Grey)

ANIMAL: HORSE: One of her safe racers was a dark bay, and she called him Bells because of the way he struck his iron shoes on the stones. (Source: *RIDERS OF THE PURPLE SAGE* by Zane Grey)

ANIMAL: HORSE: Only 100 yards now stretched between Black Star and Wrangle. The great sorrel thundered on—and on. In every yard he gained a foot. He was whistling through his nostrils, wringing wet, flying lather, and as hot as fire. Savage as ever—strong as ever—fast as ever—but each tremendous stride almost jarred Venters out of the saddle! Wrangle's power and spirit and momentum had begun to run him off his legs. Wrangle's great race was nearly won—and run. Wrangle thundered on—on—on! Venters felt the increase in quivering, straining shock after every leap. Lather flew into Venters eyes burning him, making him see all the sage as red. Wrangle thundered on to change his pace with a violent break. Then Venters pulled him hard. From run to gallop—gallop to canter—canter to trot—trot to walk—and walk to stop, the great sorrel ended his race. (Source: *RIDERS OF THE PURPLE SAGE* by Zane Grey)

ANIMAL: HORSE: The first stall—Bell's stall—was empty. All the stalls were empty. No racer whinnied and stamped greeting to her. Night was gone! Black Star was gone! (Source: *RIDERS OF THE PURPLE SAGE* by Zane Grey)

ANIMAL: HORSE: The huge pines shaded boulders covered with green moss; open forest stretched away on each side of a babbling brown stream that came rushing down from the higher country above; deer grazed with the cattle; wild horses trooped up to whistle and look, and then race away with manes flying. (Source: *SUNSET PASS* by Zane Grey)

ANIMAL: HORSE: The sorrel had wandered off down the sage between the trail and the canyon. Once or twice he disappeared in little swales. Finally Venters concluded Wrangle had grazed far enough, and taking his lasso, he went to fetch him back. In crossing from one ridge to another he saw where the horse had made muddy a pool of water. It occurred to Venters then that Wrangle had drunk his fill, and did not seem the worse for it, and might be anything but easy to catch. And true enough, he could not come within roping reach of the sorrel. He tried for an hour and gave up in disgust. Wrangle did not seem so wild as simply perverse. In a quandary,

Venters returned to the other horses, hoping much, yet doubting more that when Wrangle had grazed to suit himself, he might be caught. (Source: *RIDERS OF THE PURPLE SAGE* by Zane Grey)

ANIMAL: HORSE: The sound of dropping bars inside the barn was the signal for the horses to jerk their heads in the windows, to snort and stamp. Then they came pounding out of the door, a file of thoroughbreds, to plunge about the barnyard, heads and tails up, manes flying. They halted far off, squared away to look, came slowly forward with whinnies for their mistress, and doubtful snorts for the strangers and their horses. (Source: *RIDERS OF THE PURPLE SAGE* by Zane Grey)

ANIMAL: HORSE: The white horse took Rock's mount easily, pranced and champed a little, and tossed his head. (Source: *SUNSET PASS* by Zane Grey)

ANIMAL: HORSE: Venters cunningly sank, slowly trying to merge into the sagebrush. But the first horse detected him. It stopped short, snorted, and shot up his ears. . (Source: *RIDERS OF THE PURPLE SAGE* by Zane Grey)

ANIMAL: HORSE: When Venters' boot touched the stirrup, the sorrel bolted, giving him the rider's flying mount. The swing of this fiery horse recalled to Venters days that were not really long past, when he rode into the sage as the leader of Jane's rides. [His horse] Wrangle pulled hard on a tight rein. He galloped out of the lane, down the shady border of the grove, and hauled up at the watering trough, where he pranced and champed his bit.. (Source: *RIDERS OF THE PURPLE SAGE* by Zane Grey)

ANIMAL: HORSE: Whether that run was of moments or hours she could not tell. Lassiter's horse covered her with froth that blew back in white streams. Both horses ran their limit, were allowed to slow down in time to save them, and went on, dripping, heaving, staggering. The horses walked—trotted—galloped—ran—to fall again to walk. Hours sped or dragged. Time was an instant—an eternity. A last, breaking run across the sage brought Lassiter's horse to a walk. "He's done," said the rider. (Source: *RIDERS OF THE PURPLE SAGE* by Zane Grey)

ANIMAL: HORSE: Wrangle whinnied and thumped the ground as Venters passed by him with the dogs. The sorrel knew he was being left behind, and was not sure whether he liked it or not. (Source: *RIDERS OF THE PURPLE SAGE* by Zane Grey)

ANIMAL: HORSE: WRANGLE: A tight band closed around her breast as she saw the giant sorrel flit in reddish-brown flashes across the openings in the green. Then he was pounding down the lane—thundering into the court—crashing his great, iron-shod hoofs on the stone flags. Wrangle was shaggy and wild-eyed and sage-streaked, with dust-caked lather staining his flanks. E reared and crashed down and plunged. (Source: *RIDERS OF THE PURPLE SAGE* by Zane Grey)

Animal - Lizard

ANIMAL: LIZARD: Her soft step disturbed a sleeping lizard that scampered away over the leaves. She gave chase and caught it, a slim creature of nameless color, but of exquisite beauty. (Source: *RIDERS OF THE PURPLE SAGE* by Zane Grey)

Animal - Rabbit (3)

ANIMAL: RABBIT: A jack-rabbit went bobbing by. (Source: *SUNSET PASS* by Zane Grey)

ANIMAL: RABBIT: From one of these shady holes [in the rock] a rabbit hopped out and squatted down, laying his ears flat. (Source: *RIDERS OF THE PURPLE SAGE* by Zane Grey)

ANIMAL: RABBIT: Rabbits rustled the dead brush and pattered away. (Source: *RIDERS OF THE PURPLE SAGE* by Zane Grey)

Animal – Snake

ANIMAL: SNAKE: Then Venter's eye descried a very thin, very long, green snake coiled around a sapling. They drew closer and closer till they could have touched it. The snake had no fear and watched them with scintillating eyes. (Source: *RIDERS OF THE PURPLE SAGE* by Zane Grey)

Animal - Turkey (2)

ANIMAL: TURKEY: A gobbler stood up straight, head high, his purple-and-black breast puffed, his beard hanging low. (Source: *SUNSET PASS* by Zane Grey)

ANIMAL: TURKEY: Presently she espied a huge gobbler, bronzed and flecked, with a purple beard and red comb. How stately he strutted! Then he stopped under a tree to scratch in the leaves and grass. (Source: *WEST OF THE PECOS* by Zane Grey)

(end Animal section)

Avalanche

AVALANCHE: The miniature avalanche cracked and roared and rattled itself into an inertness at the base of the incline. Yellow dust, like the gloom of the cave, but not so changeless, drifted away on the wind; the roar clapped an echo from the cliffs—returned—went back, and came again to die in hollowness. (Source: *RIDERS OF THE PURPLE SAGE* by Zane Grey)

Campfire

CAMPFIRE: ... the campfire blazed and burned down to red embers. (Source: *RIDERS OF THE PURPLE SAGE* by Zane Grey)

Cattle Tracks

CATTLE TRACKS: A knotty point for Venters was the fact that the cattle tracks all pointed west. The broad trail came from the direction of the canyon into which the rustlers had ridden, and undoubtedly the cattle had been driven out of it across the oval. There were no tracks pointing the other way. It had been in his mind that they had driven the red herd toward the rendezvous, and not from it. Where did that broad trail come down into the pass, and where did it lead? For many years [the rustler's] mysterious entrance and exit to Deception Pass had ben all-absorbing topics to sage riders. (Source: *RIDERS OF THE PURPLE SAGE* by Zane Grey)

Culvert

CULVERT: The culvert was not the handiwork of masons. The aperture was large, to take care of a considerable flow of water during the wet season. Crude walls of heavy stone had been laid about ten feet high, and the same distance apart. Logs and brush had been placed across the top. Above this a heavy layer of earth formed the road above. (Source: *SUNSET PASS* by Zane Grey)

Dewdrops

DEWDROPS: dewdrops like diamonds sparkled on the grass. (Source: *WEST OF THE PECOS* by Zane Grey)

Dust (2)

DUST: Clouds of yellow dust drifted from under the cottonwoods out over the sage. (Source: *RIDERS OF THE PURPLE SAGE* by Zane Grey)

DUST: Dust rolled up yellow and thick [by the buffalo herd], obscuring farther view. (Source: *WEST OF THE PECOS* by Zane Grey)

Flash Flood

FLASH FLOOD: The river [looked] black-streaked gold instead of green. Suddenly his heart leaped, as his quick eye registered the muddy hue change in color of the water, and his ear caught a low, sullen chafing murmur. A flood was coming and that explained the roily water in the early morning. "Jump on [your horse] and ride!" he yelled. "The river! Look at it!" In a few minutes of perilous riding Pecos got off the lowest bench to the sandy shore. Already the water had half covered it. When he looked back at the river, [he saw] the channel had wholly changed. It had been fairly swift when low, but now it was swollen and fast, with swirls and eddies, and ridges of current. Logs and sticks and patches of debris were floating down. Close at hand the low sullen roar had a growing ominous sound. It reflected a strange black-and-gold sky, where broken clouds were taking on stormy colors of sunset. The whole scene, river, sky, [canyon] walls, seemed strangely unreal and full of menace. To Pecos, he found that the water was fully two feet higher than normal and so swift and thick that the horses slipped and rolled. (Source: *WEST OF THE PECOS* by Zane Grey)

Giant Rock

GIANT ROCK: Venters divined its [the balancing rock] significance. It had been meant for defense. The cliff-dwellers, driven by dreaded enemies to this last stand, had cunningly cut the rock until it balanced perfectly, ready to be dislodged by strong hands. Just below it leaned a tottering crag that would have toppled, starting an avalanche on an acclivity where [that] no sliding mass could stop. Crags and pinnacles, splintered cliffs, and leaning shafts and monuments would have thundered down to block forever the outlet to Deception Pass. (Source: *RIDERS OF THE PURPLE SAGE* by Zane Grey)

Grass (2)

GRASS: Grass grew plentifully over the scaly ridges, but so scattered in little patches that stock had to range far to get enough [to eat]. (Source: *WEST OF THE PECOS* by Zane Grey)

GRASS: The grass was deep and rich, welcome contrast to sage-tired eyes. (Source: *RIDERS OF THE PURPLE SAGE* by Zane Grey)

Letter (2)

LETTER: "An' I found there was one thing still precious to him, an' it was a little drawer where he kept his papers. This was in the room where he slept. An' it 'peared he seldom slept. But after being' patient, I got the contents of that drawer an' found his letters from Milly. One was a long letter written a few months after her disappearance. She had been bound an' gagged an' dragged away from her home by three men, an' she named them, Hurd, Metzger,

Slack. They was strangers to her. She was taken to the little town where I found trace of her two years after. But she didn't send the letter from that town. Outside that town, she was penned in a cave, an' she was black an' blue from beatin', and she was tied even while her baby was bein' born. 'Peared that the proselyter, who had, of course, come on the scene was not runnin' any risks of losin' her. She went on to say that for a time she was out of her head, an', when she got right again, all that kept her alive was the baby. It was a beautiful baby, she said, an' all she thought an' dreamed of was somehow to get the baby back home and be with Frank, to forget forever the man with the gold beard who was the father, an' the letter ended abrupt, in the middle of a sentence, an' it wasn't signed." (Source: *RIDERS OF THE PURPLE SAGE* by Zane Grey)

LETTER: "The second letter was written more than two years after the first. It was from Salt Lake City. It simply said that Milly had heard her brother was on her trail. She asked Frank to tell her brother to give up the search because, if he didn't, she would suffer in a way too horrible to tell. She didn't beg, she just stated a fact, an' made the simple request. An' she ended that letter by sayin' she would soon leave Salt Lake with the man she had come to love, an' would never be heard of again." "I recognized Milly's handwritin', an' I recognized her way of puttin' things. But that second letter told me of some great change in her. Ponderin' over it, I felt at last she'd either come to love that feller with the gold beard an' his religion, or some terrible fear had made her lie an' say so. I couldn't be sure which. But, of course, I meant to find out. I'll say here, if I'd known Mormons then as I do now, I'd've left Milly to her fate. For mebbe she was right about what she'd suffer if I kept on her trail. But I was young an' wild them days." (Source: *RIDERS OF THE PURPLE SAGE* by Zane Grey)

Money Belt

MONEY BELT: The heavy money belt lay over her like a caressing arm. (Source: *WEST OF THE PECOS* by Zane Grey)

Plant (6)

PLANT: FLOWER: flowers on long stems nodded gracefully. (Source: *WEST OF THE PECOS* by Zane Grey)

PLANT: FLOWER: Wildflowers sprang up everywhere, swaying with the lengthening grass on the terraces, smiling wanly from shady nooks, peeping wondrously from year-dry crevices of the walls. The valley bloomed into a paradise. Every single moment, from the breaking of the gold bar [sunlight] through the bridge at dawn on to the reddening of rays over the western wall, was one of colorful change. (Source: *RIDERS OF THE PURPLE SAGE* by Zane Grey)

PLANT: SAGE: [As he followed the path the herd took], the crushed sage resembled the path of a monster snake. (Source: *RIDERS OF THE PURPLE SAGE* by Zane Grey)

PLANT: SAGE: Always the graceful, purple wave of sage remained wide and lonely, a clear, un-dotted waste. (Source: *RIDERS OF THE PURPLE SAGE* by Zane Grey)

PLANT: SAGE: The sage about him was breast-high to his horse, oversweet with its warm, fragrant breath, gray where it waved to the light, darker where the wind left it still, and beyond the wonderful haze-purple lent by distance. (Source: *RIDERS OF THE PURPLE SAGE* by Zane Grey)

PLANT: TUMBLEWEED Out on the dusty, windswept plains of West Texas, tumbleweeds the size of young buffalo skitter across the highway, framed with endless rows of cotton plants their thistly bolls bursting open spreading seed. From the air, this flat land appears as if rough burlap bags were stitched together by a child's hand. (Source: *CONTRY CHRONICLES* 10 October 2025)

Rock (6)

ROCK: "Look at this rock. It's balanced here ... balanced perfectly. You know I told you the cliff-dwellers cut the rock ... ad why. But they're gone and the rock waits. I moved it once, and I'll never dare again. A strong heave would start it. Then it could fall and bang and smash that crag, and jar the walls, and close forever the outlet to Deception Pass." (Source: *RIDERS OF THE PURPLE SAGE* by Zane Grey)

ROCK: ARCH: Venters then descended, passing through the arch, looking up at its tremendous height and sweep. It spanned the opening to Surprise Valley, stretching in almost perfect curve from rim to rim. Even in his hurry and concern Venters could not but feel its majesty, and the thought came to him that the cliff-dwellers must have regarded it as an object of worship. (Source: *RIDERS OF THE PURPLE SAGE* by Zane Grey)

ROCK: BOULDER: Balancing Rock loomed huge, cold in the gray light of dawn, a thing without life, yet it spoke silently to Venters. (Source: *RIDERS OF THE PURPLE SAGE* by Zane Grey)

ROCK: DENTS: A casual look would have passed by these little dents [in the rock]. If Venters had not known what they signified, he would never have bestowed upon them a second glance. But he knew they had been cut there by hand, and, although age-worn, he recognized them as steps cut in the rock by cliff-dwellers.. (Source: *RIDERS OF THE PURPLE SAGE* by Zane Grey)

ROCK: LADDER It would be a foolhardy man who risked his life under the leaning, waiting avalanches of rock in that gigantic split. Yet how many years had they leaned [over] there without falling! At the bottom of the incline was an immense heap of weathered sandstone all crumbling to dust, but there were no huge rocks as large as houses, such as rested so lightly and frightfully above, waiting patiently and inevitably to crash down. Slowly split from the parent rock by the weathering process, and carved and sculptured by ages of wind and rain, they waited their moment. (Source: *RIDERS OF THE PURPLE SAGE* by Zane Grey)

ROCK: LADDER: Venters had a moment's notice of the rock, which was of the same smoothness and hardness as the slope below, before his gaze went irresistibly upward to the precipitous walls of this wide ladder of granite. These were ruined walls of yellow sandstone and so split and splintered, so over-hanging with great sections of balancing rim, as impending with tremendous, crumbling crags, that Venters caught his breath sharply, and appalled, he instinctively recoiled as if a step upward might jar the ponderous cliffs from their foundation. Indeed, it seemed that these ruined cliffs were but awaiting a breath of wind to collapse and come tumbling down. (Source: *RIDERS OF THE PURPLE SAGE* by Zane Grey)

SEASON

Season - Fall (8)

SEASON: AUTUMN: A very faint moan of wind floated down from the pines. From some lofty height an eagle whistled piercingly, and as if in reply, on the wooded ridge an elk bugled. Snowbirds were cheeping back in the grove, an on the wing somewhere wild canaries were twittering, both series of notes totally different, yet pregnant with the same portent—autumn was a hand. The wood behind the aspen grove gave forth familiar sounds of nature, the screech of jay, the chatter of squirrel, the crack of antler on dead wood, the rustle an tread and brush of denizens of the wilderness. (Source: *SUNSET PASS* by Zane Grey)

SEASON: AUTUMN: It was mid-November. Earl frost had severed yellow willow leaves from the branches, and seared the goldenrod and killed the scarlet of the vines on the rocks. The melancholy days had come. Birds and ducks had long bade farewell to the canyon; and the coyotes were sneaking down off the bleak range. Wary, they kept to the thickets and rocks until night, when they pierced the solitude with their wild barks. (Source: *WEST OF THE PECOS* by Zane Grey)

SEASON: AUTUMN: October waned. The sunny days were still hot, but no longer hit in comparison with those of midsummer. (Source: *WEST OF THE PECOS* by Zane Grey)

SEASON: AUTUMN: September came with colder nights and dawn, and with a nip in the air. (Source: *WEST OF THE PECOS* by Zane Grey)

SEASON: AUTUMN: September came. At least that was how Terrill calculated. And with it came cooler nights and dawn with a nip in the air. (Source: *WEST OF THE PECOS* by Zane Grey)

SEASON: AUTUMN: The melancholy fall season hung over the rangeland like a mantle. But it was invisible; it might have hidden in the smoky blue haze. Slopes and swales, leagues of level land, ridges fringed by cedars, round gray mounts and limitless stretches of green—all bare of cattle. (Source: *SUNSET PASS* by Zane Grey)

SEASON: AUTUMN: Then came Indian summer, that enchanting brief period of smoky warm, still days, and floating amber and purple haze in the air. The smoky haze, the purple veils, the warm, swimming air, so full of fragrance and dreamy languor, the riotous mosaic of autumn colors, the melancholy birds, the dim sun still high and red above the slope of the mountains held him in strong grip. (Source: *SUNSET PASS* by Zane Grey)

SEASON: AUTUMN: Through the autumn haze a magenta sun burned, but dully, so that he could look into it with his naked eye. And as he rode on the sun lowered so the faint magenta hue gained on the gray and green. (Source: *SUNSET PASS* by Zane Grey)

Season - Spring

SEASON: SPRING: It was early spring. The air was full of the sweet, fragrant languor of the South; mockingbirds were singling, full-throated and melodious; meadow larks and swamp blackbirds sang their farewell to the South for that season; the sky was blue and the sun shone warm; dewdrops like diamonds sparkled on the grass. (Source: *WEST OF THE PECOS* by Zane Grey)

Season - Summer (2)

SEASON: SUMMER: It was now near the end of June and the summer rains were due. This season, next to autumn, was the most beautiful for a rider in the open. The range needed rain. The grass was bleached white, the waterholes were dry or stagnant pools, the streams, even in the Pass, were getting low. (Source: *SUNSET PASS* by Zane Grey)

SEASON: SUMMER: Summer came, hot and drowsy, with its storms. (Source: *WEST OF THE PECOS* by Zane Grey)

Season - Winter

(end Season section)

Shot (3)

ACTION: SHOT: He saw the first horseman lean sidewise and fall. He saw another lurch in his saddle and heard a cry of pain. The band scattered so as not to afford such a broad mark for bullets. He heard a sharp report and caught the whiz of a leaden missile that would have hit him, but for [his horse's] sudden jump. A swift, hot wave, turning cold, passed over him. Deliberately he picked out the one rider with a carbine, and killed him. (Source: *RIDERS OF THE PURPLE SAGE* by Zane Grey)

ACTION: SHOT: He was qucker'n eyesight ... thet's all. But I seen the red spurtin' of his guns, an' heard the shots of the riders. An' when I turned, Wright an' Carter was down, an' Jengessen who's tough like a steer was pullin' the trigger of a wobblin' gun. But it was plain he was shot through, plumb center. An' sudden he fell with a crash, an' is gun clattered on the floor." "Then there was a hell of a silence. Nobody breathed. I didn't, anyway. I saw Lassiter slip a smokin' gun back in a belt. But he hadn't drawn either of the big black guns, an' I though thet strange. Then there come a scrapin' on the floor, an' Dyer got up, his face like lead. I wanted to watch Lassiter, but Dyer's face, oncet I seen it like thet, glued my eyes. I seen him go fer his gun. An' then there was a thunderin' shot from Lassiter, an it hit Dyer's right arm, an' his gun went off as it dropped. Like some cornered sage wolf he looked at Lassiter, an' sort of howled, an' reached down fer his gun. He'd jest picked it off the floor an' was raisin' it when another thunderin' shot almost tore that arm off. So it seemed to me. He gun dropped again, an' he went down on his knees, kind of flounderin' after it. It was some strange an' terrible to see his awful earnestness. Anyway, he got the gun with his left hand, an' was raisin' it, pullin' trigger in his weakness when the third thunderin' shot his his left arm, an' he dropped the gun again. But thet left arm wasn't useless yet, fer he grabbed up the gun, an' with a shakin' aim thet would hev' been pitiful to see ... he began to shoot. One wild bullet struck a man twenty feet from Lassiter. An' it killed thet man. Then come a bunch of thunderin' shots ... nine I calculated after, fer they come so quick. I couldn't count them ... an' I knew Lassiter had turned the black guns loose on Dyer. I remember distinctly it was the smell of gun-powder. The court had about adjourned fer thet judge. He was on his knees an' he wasn't prayin'. He was gaspin', and' trying' to press his big, floppin' cripple hands over his bowels. Lassiter had sent all those last, thunderin' shots through Dyer's bowels. An' he looked up at Lassiter. An' then he stared horrible at somethin' thet wasn't Lassiter, nor anyone there, nor the room, nor the branches of purple sage peepin' into the winder. Whatever he seen, it was with the look of a man who discovers somethin' too late. Thet's a terrible look. An' with a horrible understandin' cry he slid forrard on his face." (Source: *RIDERS OF THE PURPLE SAGE* by Zane Grey)

ACTION: SHOT: I seen him go fer his gun. An' then there was a thunderin' shot from Lassiter, an it hit Dyer's right arm, an' his gun went off as it dropped. Like some cornered sage wolf he looked at Lassiter, an' sort of howled, an' reached down fer his gun. He'd jest picked it off the floor an' was raisin' it when another thunderin' shot almost tore that arm off. So it seemed to me. He gun dropped again, an' he went down on his knees, kind of flounderin' after it. It was some strange an' terrible to see his awful earnestness. Anyway, he got the gun with his left hand, an' was raisin' it, pullin' trigger in his weakness when the third thunderin' shot his his left arm, an' he dropped the gun again. But thet left arm wasn't useless yet, fer he grabbed up the gun, an' with a shakin' aim thet would hev' been pitiful to see ... he began to shoot. One wild bullet struck a man twenty feet from Lassiter. An' it killed thet man. Then come a bunch of thunderin' shots ... nine I calculated after, fer they come so quick. I couldn't count them ... an' I knew Lassiter had turned the black guns loose on Dyer. The court had about adjourned fer thet judge. He was on his knees an' he wasn't prayin'. He was gaspin', and' trying' to press his big, floppin' cripple hands over his bowels. Lassiter had sent all those last, thunderin' shots through Dyer's bowels. An' he looked up at Lassiter. An' then he stared horrible at somethin' thet wasn't Lassiter, nor anyone there, nor the room, nor the branches of purple sage peepin' into the winder. Whatever he seen, it was with the look of a man who discovers somethin' too late. Thet's a terrible look. An' with a horrible understandin' cry he slid forrard on his face." (Source: *RIDERS OF THE PURPLE SAGE* by Zane Grey)

SMELL

Smell – Air (3)

SMELL: AIR: It smelled of dust and musty stone, or age and disuse. (Source: *RIDERS OF THE PURPLE SAGE* by Zane Grey)

SMELL: AIR: The air was full of the sweet, fragrant languor of the South. (Source: *WEST OF THE PECOS* by Zane Grey)

SMELL: AIR: The air was sultry, and smelled of brimstone and rain. Lightning had struck somewhere near the ranch that day. (Source: *SUNSET PASS* by Zane Grey)

Smell – Animal (2)

SMELL: ANIMAL: Dust filled the air and a strong odor [of buffalo] prevailed. (Source: *WEST OF THE PECOS* by Zane Grey)

SMELL: ANIMAL: the gentle trampling roar [of buffalo] went on uneventfully. Dust filled the air and a strong odor prevailed. (Source: *WEST OF THE PECOS* by Zane Grey)

Smell - Barn

SMELL: BARN: The whole place reeked with the heady odor of stock, hay, and manure. (Source: *SUNSET PASS* by Zane Grey)

Smell - Death

SMELL: DEATH: Then he smelled something faint, but raw, an odor that was tainted! It was dead and skinned cattle. (Source: *SUNSET PASS* by Zane Grey)

Smell - Desert

SMELL: DESERT: the wind ... brought the fragrant odors of the desert, spiced by a hint of sage; the hills slumbered in blue haze.. (Source: *SUNSET PASS* by Zane Grey)

Smell – Dust (2)

SMELL: DUST: He both smelled and saw dust in the ai. (Source: *SUNSET PASS* by Zane Grey)

SMELL: DUST: The odor of dust permeated the air with the rain, and the glistening sagebrush seemed conscious of refreshment. (Source: *SUNSET PASS* by Zane Grey)

Smell - Pine

SMELL: PINE: A thick rang of pine filled the air. (Source: *SUNSET PASS* by Zane Grey)

Smell - Rain

SMELL: RAIN: The night air bore the cool freshness of past rain, and the scents of a desert moistened and revived. (Source: *SUNSET PASS* by Zane Grey)

Smell – Sage (2)

SMELL: SAGE: A wind blew the scent of sage in his face. (Source: *RIDERS OF THE PURPLE SAGE* by Zane Grey)

SMELL: SAGE: The breath of sage blew strong, sweet, heavy on the breeze that came through from the west. (Source: *WEST OF THE PECOS* by Zane Grey)

Smell - Slaughterhouse

SMELL: SLAUGHTERHOUSE: It was not long until the sweet sage-wind suffered a change and became tainted. He rode up, the stench unmistakably heralded a slaughter-house. Cabins, corral, fences, barns and sheds, and even the trees bore ghastly evidence of the nature of what this old ranch had sunk to. Skins of cattle hung everywhere. (Source: *SUNSET PASS* by Zane Grey)

Smell – Smoke (3)

SMELL: SMOKE: His nose gave first and sure proof of people nearby. “Smoke! I shore smell smoke,” he whispered. (Source: *WEST OF THE PECOS* by Zane Grey)

SMELL: SMOKE: it was his nose that gave first and sure proof of hi sagacity. Smoke! “I shore smell smoke,” he whispered. (Source: *WEST OF THE PECOS* by Zane Grey)

SMELL: SMOKE: Thick, driving belts of smoke traveled by on the wind, and with it came a strong, pungent odor of burning wood. (Source: *RIDERS OF THE PURPLE SAGE* by Zane Grey)

Smell - Water

SMELL: WATER: Gradually the dry fragrance of the country failed, which fact came to his attention through the actions of the horses. They scented water, and presently he smelled it too, and felt in his face a warm, drowsy breath of air, moving, laden with sweet essence of greens and blossoms. (Source: *WEST OF THE PECOS* by Zane Grey)

(end Smell section)

Solitude

SOLITUDE: That day the vastness of Texas and the meaning of loneliness grew fixed in her heart forever. On all sides the prairie waved, on and on, in an endless solitude. The wild animals, the hawks and ravens, the black clouds of passenger pigeons that coursed by, the faint, dark lines behind in the valley,—all these only accentuated the solitude. (Source: *WEST OF THE PECOS* by Zane Grey)

SOUND

Sound - Avalanche

SOUND: AVALANCHE: The miniature avalanche cracked and roared and rattled itself into an inertness at the base of the incline. Yellow dust, like the gloom of the cave, but not so changeless, drifted away on the wind; the roar clapped an echo from the cliffs—returned—went back, and came again to die in hollowness. (Source: *RIDERS OF THE PURPLE SAGE* by Zane Grey)

Sound - Animal - Bird (17)

SOUND: BIRD: [He heard] the shrill call of a yellowhammer. (Source: *SUNSET PASS* by Zane Grey)

SOUND: BIRD: [He heard] the twittering of the quail. (Source: *RIDERS OF THE PURPLE SAGE* by Zane Grey)

SOUND: BIRD: ... the canyon bird whistled his melancholy notes. (Source: *RIDERS OF THE PURPLE SAGE* by Zane Grey)

SOUND: BIRD: A very faint moan of wind floated down from the pines. From some lofty height an eagle whistled piercingly, and as if in reply, on the wooded ridge an elk bugled. Snowbirds were cheeping back in the grove, an on the wing somewhere wild canaries were twittering, both series of notes totally different, yet pregnant with the same portent—autumn was a hand. The wood behind the aspen grove gave forth familiar sounds of nature, the screech of jay, the chatter of squirrel, the crack of antler on dead wood, the rustle an tread and brush of denizens of the wilderness. (Source: *SUNSET PASS* by Zane Grey

SOUND: BIRD: An owl hooted on the canyon side of the river, to be answered from a distance. (Source: *WEST OF THE PECOS* by Zane Grey)

SOUND: BIRD: Dusk shaded the grove where she walked; the birds ceased singing; the wind sighed through the leaves of the cottonwoods, and the running water murmured down its stone-bedded channel. (Source: *RIDERS OF THE PURPLE SAGE* by Zane Grey)

SOUND: BIRD: From a tree top a robin sang its evening song. (Source: *RIDERS OF THE PURPLE SAGE* by Zane Grey)

SOUND: BIRD: He awakened to the sound of melody that he imagined was only the haunting echo of dream music. In the lacy leafage fluttered a number of gray birds with black and white stripes and long tails. They were mockingbirds, and they were singing as it they wanted to burst their throats. One long, silver-tipped branch drooped almost to his cave, and upon it, within a few yards of him, sat one of the graceful birds. Venters saw the swelling and quivering of its throat in song. (Source: *RIDERS OF THE PURPLE SAGE* by Zane Grey)

SOUND: BIRD: He heard the mockingbirds singing in the trees. (Source: *RIDERS OF THE PURPLE SAGE* by Zane Grey)

SOUND: BIRD: In the morning he was awakened by the gobbling of turkeys. (Source: *SUNSET PASS* by Zane Grey)

SOUND: BIRD: Meadow larks and swamp blackbirds sang their farewell to the South for that season. (Source: *WEST OF THE PECOS* by Zane Grey)

SOUND: BIRD: Mockingbirds were singing, full-throated and melodious. (Source: *WEST OF THE PECOS* by Zane Grey)

SOUND: BIRD: She heard the chirp of awakening birds. (Source: *RIDERS OF THE PURPLE SAGE* by Zane Grey)

SOUND: BIRD: The day broke beautifully to the melody of a mockingbird in the mesquite. (Source: *WEST OF THE PECOS* by Zane Grey)

SOUND: BIRD: The melancholy note of a canyon bird broke clearly and lonely from the high cliffs. He had no name for this night singer, and he had never seen one, but the few notes, always pealing out just at darkness, were as familiar as the canyon silence. (Source: *RIDERS OF THE PURPLE SAGE* by Zane Grey)

SOUND: BIRD: The rushing of water and singing of birds filled their ears. (Source: *RIDERS OF THE PURPLE SAGE* by Zane Grey)

SOUND: BIRD: Venters awakened from sleep, and his ears rang with innumerable melodies from full-throated mockingbirds.. (Source: *RIDERS OF THE PURPLE SAGE* by Zane Grey)

Sound - Animal - Cattle (3)

SOUND: CATTLE: A faint roar of trampling hoofs came to Jane's ears. (Source: *RIDERS OF THE PURPLE SAGE* by Zane Grey)

SOUND: CATTLE: The dull rumble of thousands of hoofs deepened into continuous low thunder, and, as the steers swept swiftly closer, the thunder became a heavy roll. (Source: *RIDERS OF THE PURPLE SAGE* by Zane Grey)

SOUND: CATTLE: The long, white, bobbing line of steers streaked swiftly through the sage, and a funnel-shaped dust cloud arose at a low angle. A dull rumbling filled Jane's ears. (Source: *RIDERS OF THE PURPLE SAGE* by Zane Grey)

Sound - Animal - Coyote (7)

SOUND: COYOTE: ... the melancholy music a cowboy found inseparable from his lonely vigil—the staccato cry of coyotes. (Source: *WEST OF THE PECOS* by Zane Grey)

SOUND: COYOTE: Coyotes barked in the night. (Source: *SUNSET PASS* by Zane Grey)

SOUND: COYOTE: Coyotes mourned eerily. A deep-voiced hound bayed them in answer. (Source: *SUNSET PASS* by Zane Grey)

SOUND: COYOTE: Coyotes were barking at the far end of the swale, and a melancholy solitude enfolded the place. (Source: *WEST OF THE PECOS* by Zane Grey)

SOUND: COYOTE: Coyotes were sneaking down off the bleak range. Wary of the people, they kept to the thickets and rocks until night, when they pierced the solitude with their wild barks.. (Source: *WEST OF THE PECOS* by Zane Grey)

SOUND: COYOTE: Somewhere back on his trail a coyote yelped, splitting the dead silence. Venter's faculties seemed singularly acute. (Source: *RIDERS OF THE PURPLE SAGE* by Zane Grey)

SOUND: COYOTE: The sound of trotting horses had ceased, and there was silence broken only by a faint, dry pattering of cottonwood leaves in the soft night wind. Into this peace and calm suddenly broke the high-keyed yelp of a coyote, and from far off in the darkness came the faint answering note of a trailing mate. (Source: *RIDERS OF THE PURPLE SAGE* by Zane Grey)

Sound - Animal - Deer

SOUND: DEER: A very faint moan of wind floated down from the pines. From some lofty height an eagle whistled piercingly, and as if in reply, on the wooded ridge an elk bugled. Snowbirds were cheeping back in the grove, an on the wing somewhere wild canaries were twittering, both series of notes totally different, yet pregnant with the same portent—autumn was a hand. The wood behind the aspen grove gave forth familiar sounds of nature, the screech of jay, the chatter of squirrel, the crack of antler on dead wood, the rustle an tread and brush of denizens of the wilderness. (Source: *SUNSET PASS* by Zane Grey)

Sound - Animal – Dog (2)

SOUND: DOG: Just then a hound bayed, deep and hollow, announcing the advent of a stranger. (Source: *WEST OF THE PECOS* by Zane Grey)

SOUND: DOG: Suddenly Ring [the dog] growled low. (Source: *RIDERS OF THE PURPLE SAGE* by Zane Grey)

Sound - Animal - Eagle

SOUND: EAGLE: A very faint moan of wind floated down from the pines. From some lofty height an eagle whistled piercingly, and as if in reply, on the wooded ridge an elk bugled. Snowbirds were cheeping back in the grove, an on the wing somewhere wild canaries were twittering, both series of notes totally different, yet pregnant with the same portent—autumn was a hand. The wood behind the aspen grove gave forth familiar sounds of nature, the screech of jay, the chatter of squirrel, the crack of antler on dead wood, the rustle an tread and brush of denizens of the wilderness. (Source: *SUNSET PASS* by Zane Grey)

Sound - Animal - Elk

SOUND: ELK: A very faint moan of wind floated down from the pines. From some lofty height an eagle whistled piercingly, and as if in reply, on the wooded ridge an elk bugled. Snowbirds were cheeping back in the grove, an on the wing somewhere wild canaries were twittering, both series of notes totally different, yet pregnant with the same portent—autumn was a hand. The wood behind the aspen grove gave forth familiar sounds of nature, the screech of jay, the chatter of squirrel, the crack of antler on dead wood, the rustle an tread and brush of denizens of the wilderness. (Source: *SUNSET PASS* by Zane Grey)

Sound - Animal - Horse (21)

SOUND: HORSE: {The] clatter of hoofs distracted Fay and interrupted the scolding she was gleefully receiving from Jane. The sound was not the light-spirited trot that Bells made when Lassiter rode him into the outer court. This was slower and heavier, and Jane did not recognize in it any of her other horses. (Source: *RIDERS OF THE PURPLE SAGE* by Zane Grey)

SOUND: HORSE: ... a sudden start on Lassiter's part alarmed her. "I heard hosses ... hosses with muffled hoofs," he said, and he [stood[up guardedly. (Source: *RIDERS OF THE PURPLE SAGE* by Zane Grey)

SOUND: HORSE: A sharp clip-clop of iron-shod hoofs deadened and died away. (Source: *RIDERS OF THE PURPLE SAGE* by Zane Grey)

SOUND: HORSE: As he neared [the canyon] he thought he heard a distant neigh of a horse. (Source: *WEST OF THE PECOS* by Zane Grey)

SOUND: HORSE: As he was about to pass out of the street to sirt the grove, he once more slunk down at the sound of trotting horses. (Source: *RIDERS OF THE PURPLE SAGE* by Zane Grey)

SOUND: HORSE: From behind the grove came the clicking sound of horses in a rapid trot. (Source: *RIDERS OF THE PURPLE SAGE* by Zane Grey)

SOUND: HORSE: He heard a distant neigh of a horse. (Source: *WEST OF THE PECOS* by Zane Grey)

SOUND: HORSE: He heard the click of iron-shod hoofs on stone, the coarse laughter of men, and then voices gradually dying away. (Source: *RIDERS OF THE PURPLE SAGE* by Zane Grey)

SOUND: HORSE: he heard the clip-clop of trotting horses, and then a rattle of wheels as a big empty wagon appeared. (Source: *SUNSET PASS* by Zane Grey)

SOUND: HORSE: Her ears—that had been strained to breaking all these interminable hours—caught a low swift rhythmic patter of hoofs. (Source: *WEST OF THE PECOS* by Zane Grey)

SOUND: HORSE: It [the silence] was broken by a horrid, long-drawn scream of a horse, and the thudding of heavy hoofs.

Venters sprang erect and wheeled south. Along the canyon rim, near the edge, came Wrangle once more in thundering flight. (Source: *RIDERS OF THE PURPLE SAGE* by Zane Grey)

SOUND: HORSE: Jane heard the cracking of horses' hoofs on the stones, and the sound came nearer and nearer. (Source: *RIDERS OF THE PURPLE SAGE* by Zane Grey)

SOUND: HORSE: Jane's listening ear soon caught a faint, rapid, rhythmic beat of hoofs. It came from the sage. It gave her a thrill that she was at a loss to understand. The sound rose stronger, louder. Then came a clear, sharp difference when the horse passed from sage trail to the hard-packed ground o the grove. It became a ringing run, swift in its bell-like clatterings, yet singular in longer pause than usual between the hoof beats of a horse. (Source: *RIDERS OF THE PURPLE SAGE* by Zane Grey)

SOUND: HORSE: Lassiter led the swift flight across the wide apace, over washes, through sage, into a narrow canyon where the rapid clatter of hoofs rapped sharply from the walls. (Source: *RIDERS OF THE PURPLE SAGE* by Zane Grey)

SOUND: HORSE: Several times he went to the window to peer out. The clip-clop of hoofs drew him again to the window. Ash and Boots Preston were riding by, headed east.. (Source: *SUNSET PASS* by Zane Grey)

SOUND: HORSE: The bray of a lazy horse broke the afternoon quiet. (Source: *RIDERS OF THE PURPLE SAGE* by Zane Grey)

SOUND: HORSE: The clank of iron hoofs upon the stone courtyard drew her hurriedly from her retirement. (Source: *RIDERS OF THE PURPLE SAGE* by Zane Grey)

SOUND: HORSE: The dull thud of hoofs almost deprived him of power to turn and see from where disaster threatened. (Source: *RIDERS OF THE PURPLE SAGE* by Zane Grey)

SOUND: HORSE: The grove was long, and he had not reached the end when he heard something that brought him to a halt. Low padded thuds told him horses were coming his way. Much before he had expected, judging from sound, to his amazement, he descried horsemen near at hand. They were riding along the border of the sage, and instantly he knew the hoofs of the horses were muffled. (Source: *RIDERS OF THE PURPLE SAGE* by Zane Grey)

SOUND: HORSE: The huge pines shaded boulders covered with green moss; open forest stretched away on each side of a babbling brown stream that came rushing down from the higher country above; deer grazed with the cattle; wild horses trooped up to whistle and look, and then race away with manes flying. (Source: *SUNSET PASS* by Zane Grey)

SOUND: HORSE: The sound of trotting horses had ceased, and there was silence broken only by a faint, dry pattering of cottonwood leaves in the soft night wind. (Source: *RIDERS OF THE PURPLE SAGE* by Zane Grey)

Sound - Animal - Mice

SOUND: MICE: [She heard] the mice squeaking in the walls. (Source: *RIDERS OF THE PURPLE SAGE* by Zane Grey)

Sound - Owl

SOUND: OWL: An owl hooted in the gloom and insects kept up their low mournful hum. (Source: *WEST OF THE PECOS* by Zane Grey)

Sound - Animal - Squirrel (2)

SOUND: SQUIRREL: A black squirrel squalled from a silver spruce that towered over them. (Source: *SUNSET PASS* by Zane Grey)

SOUND: SQUIRREL: A very faint moan of wind floated down from the pines. From some lofty height an eagle whistled piercingly, and as if in reply, on the wooded ridge an elk bugled. Snowbirds were cheeping back in the grove, an on the wing somewhere wild canaries were twittering, both series of notes totally different, yet pregnant with the same portent—autumn was a hand.

The wood behind the aspen grove gave forth familiar sounds of nature, the screech of jay, the chatter of squirrel, the crack of antler on dead wood, the rustle and tread and brush of denizens of the wilderness. (Source: *SUNSET PASS* by Zane Grey)

Sound – Animal - Turkey

SOUND: TURKEY: She was distracted by a rustling of brush, a queer sound like put-put, put, put, put. Then she heard a gobble. Wild turkeys were near and approaching. (Source: *WEST OF THE PECOS* by Zane Grey)

Sound - Animal – Wolf (2)

SOUND: WOLF: Wolves mourned from the ridges above the restless herd. (Source: *WEST OF THE PECOS* by Zane Grey)

SOUND: WOLF: Wolves mourned in the night. (Source: *SUNSET PASS* by Zane Grey)

(end Sound Animal section)

Sound - Boom

SOUND: BOOM: The bank of clouds now swept hugely out of the western sky. Its front was purple and black with gray between, a bulging, mushrooming, vast thing instinct with storm. It had a dark, angry, threatening aspect. As if all the power of the winds were pushing and piling behind, it rolled ponderously across the sky. A red flare burned out instantaneously, flashed from west to east, and died. Then from the deepest black of the purple cloud burst a boom. It was like the bowling of a huge boulder along the crags and ramparts, and seemed to roll on and fall into the valley to bound and bang and boom from cliff to cliff. (Source: *RIDERS OF THE PURPLE SAGE* by Zane Grey)

Sound - Call

SOUND: CALL: The silence broke to a clear call from an incoming rider and, almost like the peal of a hunting horn, floated back the answer. (Source: *RIDERS OF THE PURPLE SAGE* by Zane Grey)

Sound - Flood

SOUND: FLOOD: Close at hand the sullen roar [of the flood] had a growing ominous sound. (Source: *WEST OF THE PECOS* by Zane Grey)

Sound - Hammering

SOUND: HAMMERING: Presently he heard the sound of hammer or ax blows on wood. (Source: *SUNSET PASS* by Zane Grey)

Sound - Footsteps (2)

SOUND: FOOTSTEPS: His step sounded in the hall—the familiar, soft silver-clinking step—and she heard it with thrilling new emotions.. (Source: *RIDERS OF THE PURPLE SAGE* by Zane Grey)

SOUND: FOOTSTEPS: Silence intervened until Lassiter's soft, jingling step assured her of his approach. (Source: *RIDERS OF THE PURPLE SAGE* by Zane Grey)

Sound - Gunshot (5)

SOUND: GUNSHOT: More rattling shots disturbed the noon-day quiet, She heard a sliding of weathered rock—a hoarse shout of warning—a yell of alarm—again the clear, sharp crack of the rifle-and another cry that was a cry of death. (Source: *RIDERS OF THE PURPLE SAGE* by Zane Grey)

SOUND: GUNSHOT: RIFLE: On the morning of the 10th of August, Jane, while waiting in the court for Lassiter, heard a clear, ringing report of a rifle. It came from the grove, somewhere out toward the corrals. Jane glanced out in alarm. A rifle report meant more [than revolver shots]. Riders seldom used rifles. . (Source: *RIDERS OF THE PURPLE SAGE* by Zane Grey)

SOUND: GUNSHOT: She heard a low, dull, distant gunshot. She had expected it, was waiting for it, nevertheless, and electric shock checked her heart, froze the very living fiber of her bones. The vise-like hold on her faculties did not relax for a long time. (Source: *RIDERS OF THE PURPLE SAGE* by Zane Grey)

SOUND: GUNSHOT: Suddenly from the mouth of the canyon just beyond her rang out a clear, sharp report of a rifle. Echoes clapped. Then followed a piercingly high yell of anguish, quickly breaking. Again echoes clapped in grim imitation. Dull revolver shots—hoarse yells—pound of hoofs—shrill neighs of horses—commingling of echoes—and again silence! (Source: *RIDERS OF THE PURPLE SAGE* by Zane Grey)

SOUND: GUNSHOT: Then rifle reports pierced a dull volley of revolver shots. Bullets whizzed over Jane's hiding place; one struck a stone, and whined away in the air. After that, for a time, succeeded desultory shots, an then they ceased under long, thundering fire from heavier guns. (Source: *RIDERS OF THE PURPLE SAGE* by Zane Grey)

Sound – Howl (2)

SOUND: HOWL: A low rustle of leaves and a tinkle of [river] water [was followed] by a howl that curdled her blood. The howl rose again, somehow different. It seemed like the bay of a hound, only infinitely deeper, wilder, stranger, and with a fierce mournful note. Answers came from above their camp [with] a chorus of chirping, shrieking barks of wolves and coyotes. (Source: *WEST OF THE PECOS* by Zane Grey)

SOUND: HOWL: Sometime later she awoke, an unusual thing for her. A noise had disturbed her rest. But the camp was dark and silent. A low rustle of leaves and a tinkle of water could scarcely have been guilty. Then from across the river [came] a howl that curdled her blood. She sat up quivering in every muscle. The howl rose again, somehow different. It seemed like the bay of a hound, only infinitely deeper, wilder, and stranger, with a fierce, mournful note. Answers came from above the camp, and then a chorus of chirping, shrieking barks. These sounds she at once associated with the wolves and coyotes that the hunters said followed the buffalo in packs. (Source: *WEST OF THE PECOS* by Zane Grey)

Sound - Insect - General (5)

SOUND: INSECTS: An owl hooted in the gloom and insects kept up their low mournful hum. (Source: *WEST OF THE PECOS* by Zane Grey)

SOUND: INSECTS: The canyon silence appeared full of the low, continuous hum of insects. (Source: *RIDERS OF THE PURPLE SAGE* by Zane Grey)

SOUND: INSECTS: The forest was full of a drowsy hum of insects. (Source: *RIDERS OF THE PURPLE SAGE* by Zane Grey)

SOUND: INSECTS: The silence [of the night] awoke to the low hum of insects. (Source: *RIDERS OF THE PURPLE SAGE* by Zane Grey)

SOUND: INSECTS: There was a brooding silence emphasized by the incessant hum of insects. (Source: *SUNSET PASS* by Zane Grey)

Sound - Insect - Bees (3)

SOUND: INSECTS: BEES: A murmuring of many bees, buzzing and humming in the foliage mingled with a soft sound of an unseen, falling stream. (Source: *WEST OF THE PECOS* by Zane Grey)

SOUND: INSECTS: BEES: Bees hummed by Pecos as he crouched among the rocks, listening. (Source: *WEST OF THE PECOS* by Zane Grey)

SOUND: INSECTS: BEES: He heard the hum of bees, melodious on the mellow summer air. (Source: *SUNSET PASS* by Zane Grey)

Sound – Jingling (2)

SOUND: JINGLING: On the morning of the second day after his recital, the soft jingling step of Lassiter gave her overwhelming relief, a feeling akin to joy. (Source: *RIDERS OF THE PURPLE SAGE* by Zane Grey)

SOUND: JINGLING: Preston retired within his cabin, and soon after the boys slouched away, their spurs jingling, their dark lank forms silhouetted against the moon-blanched grass. (Source: *SUNSET PASS* by Zane Grey)

Sound - Leaves

SOUND: LEAVES: The sound of trotting horses had ceased, and there was silence broken only by a faint, dry pattering of cottonwood leaves in the soft night wind. (Source: *RIDERS OF THE PURPLE SAGE* by Zane Grey)

Sound - Outdoors

SOUND: OUTDOORS: The leaves quivered and rustled; a lonesome cricket chirped in the grass; a bee hummed by. The silence of the waning afternoon breathed hateful portent. It terrified Jane. When had silence been so infernal? (Source: *RIDERS OF THE PURPLE SAGE* by Zane Grey)

Sound - Pounding

SOUND: POUNDING: On sudden he heard above the soft roar of the waterfall an unusual sound that he could not define. He dropped flat behind a stone and listened. From the direction he had come swelled something that resembled a strange, muffled pounding and splashing and ringing. The unnatural sound passed beyond him as he lay, gripping his rifle and fighting for coolness. Then from the open came the sound, now distinct and different. Venters recognized a hobble bell of a horse, the cracking of iron on submerged stones, and the hollow splash of hoofs in water. Curiosity prompted him to peep from behind the rock. In the middle of the stream waded a long string of packed burros driven by three superbly mounted men {whom he recognized as rustlers]. These men were packing in supplies from one of the northern villages. They were tired, and their horses were almost played out, and the burros plodded on, after the manner of their kind when exhausted, faithful and patient, but as if very weary, splashing, slipping step would be their last. (Source: *RIDERS OF THE PURPLE SAGE* by Zane Grey)

Sound - Riders (2)

SOUND: RIDERS: The dirty-booted and long-spurred riders clanked nosily into the grove of cottonwoods and disappeared in the shade. (Source: *RIDERS OF THE PURPLE SAGE* by Zane Grey)

SOUND: RIDERS: The rapid beat of hoofs recalled Jane to the question at hand. Group of riders cantered up the lane, dismounted, and threw their bridles [up onto their saddles].. (Source: *RIDERS OF THE PURPLE SAGE* by Zane Grey)

Sound - Ring

SOUND: RING: The ring of Sambo's ax chopping wood in the gray dawn was her signal to arise and begin the momentous day. (Source: *WEST OF THE PECOS* by Zane Grey)

Sound - Roar (3)

SOUND: ROAR: The roar bothered him, for he could hear nothing else. Likewise, however, no rustlers could hear him. Emboldened by his, and sure that nothing but a bird could see him, he arose from his hands and knees to hurry on. (Source: *RIDERS OF THE PURPLE SAGE* by Zane Grey)

SOUND: ROAR: The roar rolled on, diminishing to thunder, [and] then gradually lessening. The ground ceased to shake. In an hour, the stampede was again a low rumble in the distance. (Source: *WEST OF THE PECOS* by Zane Grey)

SOUND: ROAR: The trampling roar [of the buffalo herd] seemed engulfed in deafening thunder. (Source: *WEST OF THE PECOS* by Zane Grey)

Sound - Rumble

SOUND: RUMBLE: The rumble [of the buffalo herd] had grown appreciably louder, more consistent and deeper, with a menacing note. (Source: *WEST OF THE PECOS* by Zane Grey)

Sound - Rustling (3)

SOUND: RUSTLING: [He heard] a rustling of dry leaves of brush near at hand. (Source: *SUNSET PASS* by Zane Grey)

SOUND: RUSTLING: She saw only this sad, gray, passion-worn man, and she heard only the faint rustling of the leaves. (Source: *RIDERS OF THE PURPLE SAGE* by Zane Grey)

SOUND: RUSTLING: That moment a rustling of leaves attracted her attention, then the familiar clinking accompaniment of a slow, soft, measured step, and Lassiter walked into the court. (Source: *RIDERS OF THE PURPLE SAGE* by Zane Grey)

Sound - Saloon

SOUND: SALOON: Loud voices and boisterous laughter, rattle of dice and scrape of chair and clink of gold burst in mingled din from an open doorway. (Source: *RIDERS OF THE PURPLE SAGE* by Zane Grey)

Sound - Scream

SOUND: SCREAM: Upon the last of his trips, when he was some distance down the terrace and out of sight of camp, he heard a scream, and then the sharp barking of the dogs. (Source: *RIDERS OF THE PURPLE SAGE* by Zane Grey)

Sound - Silence

SOUND: SILENCE: Coyotes were barking at the far end of the swale, and a melancholy solitude enfolded the place. (Source: *WEST OF THE PECOS* by Zane Grey)

Sound - Steps

SOUND: STEPS: The burros pattered up the trail with little, hollow-cracking steps. (Source: *RIDERS OF THE PURPLE SAGE* by Zane Grey)

Sound - Storm (4)

SOUND: STORM: A blinding flash of lightning illumined the cave and all about him. He saw Bess's face, white now with dark, frightened eyes. He saw the dogs leap up, and he followed suit. The golden glare vanished—all was black—then came the splitting crack and the internal din of echoes.. (Source: *RIDERS OF THE PURPLE SAGE* by Zane Grey)

SOUND: STORM: A driving pall of rain, black as the clouds, came sweeping on to obscure the bridge, and the gleaming walls, and the shining valley. The lightning played incessantly, streaking down through opaque darkness of rain. The roar of the wind, with its strange knell, and the re-crashing echoes mingled with the roar of the flooding rain—and all seemingly were deadened and drowned in a world of sound. (Source: *RIDERS OF THE PURPLE SAGE* by Zane Grey)

SOUND: STORM: Then the storm burst with a succession of ropes and streaks and shafts of lightning, playing continuously, filling the valley with a broken radiance, and the cracking shots followed each other swiftly till the echoes blended in one fearful, deepening crash. (Source: *RIDERS OF THE PURPLE SAGE* by Zane Grey)

SOUND: STORM: Venters and Bess faced the open terrace, the valley, and the west to watch and await the approaching storm. It required keen vision to see any movement whatever in the purple clouds. By infinitesimal degrees the dark cloud line merged upward into the golden red haze of the afterglow of sunset. A shadow lengthened from under the western wall across the valley. As straight and rigid as steel rose the delicate, spear-pointed silver spruces; the aspen leaves, by nature pendant and quivering, hung, limp and heavy, no slender, leaning blade of grass moved. A gentle splashing of water came from the ravine. Then from out of the west [came] the low, dull, and rumbling roll of thunder. (Source: *RIDERS OF THE PURPLE SAGE* by Zane Grey)

Sound - Thud (2)

SOUND: THUD: She was dropping off to sleep when she heard a thud of soft feet outside on the porch. Pecos had jumped down from his loft. His steps sounded faintly, and after a considerable interval she heard a rapid beat of hoofs on the trail. Pecos had ridden away. (Source: *WEST OF THE PECOS* by Zane Grey)

SOUND: THUD: Then a clink of spurs, slow steps, and thuds of hoofs sounded behind Rock. (Source: *SUNSET PASS* by Zane Grey)

Sound – Thunder (2)

SOUND: THUNDER: The purple cloud bank darkened the lower edge of the setting sun, crept up and up, obscuring its fiery red heart, and finally passed over the last ruddy crescent of its upper rim. The intense, dead silence awakened to a long, low rumbling of thunder. (Source: *RIDERS OF THE PURPLE SAGE* by Zane Grey)

SOUND: THUNDER: The trampling roar seemed engulfed in deafening thunder. (Source: *WEST OF THE PECOS* by Zane Grey)

Sound - Tinkling

SOUND: TINKLING: ... were disturbed by Lassiter's soft, tinkling step in the court. Always he wore the clinking spurs! Always he was ready to ride! (Source: *RIDERS OF THE PURPLE SAGE* by Zane Grey)

Sound - Twang

SOUND: TWANG: Somewhere a guitar twanged low melody and a girl's sweet voice in Spanish accompanied it. (Source: *SUNSET PASS* by Zane Grey)

Sound - Voice (12)

SOUND: VOICE: [His] tone was wheedling. (Source: *WEST OF THE PECOS* by Zane Grey)

SOUND: VOICE: [His] voice cracked like steel on ice. (Source: *WEST OF THE PECOS* by Zane Grey)

SOUND: VOICE: "It was natural, of course for me to notice many of them packed guns. That's a way of mine, first noticin' them things. Venters spoke up, an' his voice sort of chilled an'cut, an' he told Tull he had a few things to say." (Source: *RIDERS OF THE PURPLE SAGE* by Zane Grey)

SOUND: VOICE: "Oldring," whispered Venters. His voice, as all fire and pulse within him, seemed to freeze. (Source: *RIDERS OF THE PURPLE SAGE* by Zane Grey)

SOUND: VOICE: ... heard his voice ringing high and sweet. (Source: *RIDERS OF THE PURPLE SAGE* by Zane Grey)

SOUND: VOICE: Her ringing voice sank into a broken, husky whisper. (Source: *RIDERS OF THE PURPLE SAGE* by Zane Grey)

SOUND: VOICE: His deep voice pealed from behind where he was rejoicing with his wife. (Source: *WEST OF THE PECOS* by Zane Grey)

SOUND: VOICE: Jane's dead-locked feeling, rent by his deep, quivering voice, leaped into an agony of sensitive life. (Source: *RIDERS OF THE PURPLE SAGE* by Zane Grey)

SOUND: VOICE: She heard a deep, muttering curse under his breath, and then she silvery tinkling of his spurs as he moved away. (Source: *RIDERS OF THE PURPLE SAGE* by Zane Grey)

SOUND: VOICE: The tone of his voice had undergone a change. A different man had spoken. Where, in addressing Jane, he had been mild and gentle, now with his first speech to Tull, he was dry, cool, biting. (Source: *RIDERS OF THE PURPLE SAGE* by Zane Grey)

SOUND: VOICE: When Bishop Dyer's voice cleave the silence, it was high, curiously shrill, and on the point of breaking. (Source: *RIDERS OF THE PURPLE SAGE* by Zane Grey)

SOUND: VOICE: With wonderful distinctness Jane heard her own, clear voice. She heard the water murmur at her feet, an flow on to the sea; she heard the rushing of all the waters in the world. They filled her ears with low unreal murmurings—these sounds that deadened her brain and yet could not break the long and terrible silence. (Source: *RIDERS OF THE PURPLE SAGE* by Zane Grey)

Sound - Water (16)

SOUND: WATER: A low soft murmur of running water came to him in the lulls of the wind. (Source: *SUNSET PASS* by Zane Grey)

SOUND: WATER: A murmuring of many bees, buzzing and humming in the foliage mingled with a soft sound of an unseen, falling stream. (Source: *WEST OF THE PECOS* by Zane Grey)

SOUND: WATER: By listening intently he caught a faint murmur of water chafing by [the] reedy shore. (Source: *WEST OF THE PECOS* by Zane Grey)

SOUND: WATER: By listening intently he caught a faint murmur of water chafing by a reedy shore. (Source: *WEST OF THE PECOS* by Zane Grey)

SOUND: WATER: Dusk shaded the grove where she walked; the birds ceased singing; the wind sighed through the leaves of the cottonwoods, and the running water murmured down its stone-bedded channel. (Source: *RIDERS OF THE PURPLE SAGE* by Zane Grey)

SOUND: WATER: He heard the continuous splash of falling water. (Source: *RIDERS OF THE PURPLE SAGE* by Zane Grey)

SOUND: WATER: He was relieved to hear a ripple of shallow water, denoting an easy ford on the morrow. (Source: *WEST OF THE PECOS* by Zane Grey)

SOUND: WATER: On the still air floated the freshness and murmur of flowing water. (Source: *RIDERS OF THE PURPLE SAGE* by Zane Grey)

SOUND: WATER: Pecos was relieved to hear a ripple of shallow water, denoting an easy ford. (Source: *WEST OF THE PECOS* by Zane Grey)

SOUND: WATER: Suddenly a low, dull murmur assailed his ears. At first he thought it was thunder, then the slipping of a weathered slope of rock. But it was incessant, and as he progressed, it filled out deeper and from a murmur changed into a dull roar. "Falling water," he said. "There's volume to that." (Source: *RIDERS OF THE PURPLE SAGE* by Zane Grey)

SOUND: WATER: The falling water tinkled in harmony with the soft strains of music from inside the hall. (Source: *SUNSET PASS* by Zane Grey)

SOUND: WATER: The mellow murmur of a stream came on the summer wind. Water was falling close under the right wall of the canyon, fringed by green that was turning to gold. (Source: *SUNSET PASS* by Zane Grey)

SOUND: WATER: The roar of the disappearing stream dinned in their ears. (Source: *RIDERS OF THE PURPLE SAGE* by Zane Grey)

SOUND: WATER: The rushing of water and singing of birds filled their ears. (Source: *RIDERS OF THE PURPLE SAGE* by Zane Grey)

SOUND: WATER: The water tinkled off in the darkness of night. (Source: *SUNSET PASS* by Zane Grey)

SOUND: WATER: under the bank the river murmured softly. (Source: *WEST OF THE PECOS* by Zane Grey)

Sound - Whistle

SOUND: WHISTLE: Watson whistled significantly, and no more was said. (Source: *WEST OF THE PECOS* by Zane Grey)

Sound - Wind (11)

SOUND: WIND: "When the wind blows a gale in the caves, it makes what the rustlers call Oldring's Knell. They believe it bodes his death. I think he believes so, too. It's not like any sound on earth. It's beginning." (Source: *RIDERS OF THE PURPLE SAGE* by Zane Grey)

SOUND: WIND: ... the wind sang softly in the cliffs. (Source: *RIDERS OF THE PURPLE SAGE* by Zane Grey)

SOUND: WIND: A wave, a ripple of light, a trembling and turning of the aspen leaves, like the approach of a breeze on the water, crossed the valley from the west, and the hill, and the deadly stillness, and the sultry air, passed away as a cool wind. The night bird of the canyon with his clear and melancholy notes announced the twilight, and from all along the cliffs rose the faint murmur and moan and mourn of the wind singing in the caves. (Source: *RIDERS OF THE PURPLE SAGE* by Zane Grey)

SOUND: WIND: from high up in the carved crevices of the arch, floated down the low, strange wail of wind—a knell, indeed, for all that had gone. (Source: *RIDERS OF THE PURPLE SAGE* by Zane Grey)

SOUND: WIND: It was only wind, thought Venters. Here sped and shrieked the sculptor that carved out the wonderful caves in the cliffs. It was only a gale, but as Venters listened, as his ears became accustomed to the fury and strife, out o it all, or through it or above it, pealed low and perfectly clear and persistently uniform a strange sound that had no counterpart in all the sounds of the elements. It was not of earth or life. It was the grief and agony of the gale. [It was] a knell to all upon whom it blew. (Source: *RIDERS OF THE PURPLE SAGE* by Zane Grey)

SOUND: WIND: Outside, the branches of a pine tree waved, and a soft sough of wind came strangely, like an accompaniment of something sad in the past. (Source: *SUNSET PASS* by Zane Grey)

SOUND: WIND: She heard the wind moaning in the cottonwoods. (Source: *RIDERS OF THE PURPLE SAGE* by Zane Grey)

SOUND: WIND: The gale swooped down with a hollow, unearthly howl. It yelled and pealed and shrilled and shrieked. It was made up of a thousand piercing cries. It was a rising and a moving sound. Beginning at the western break of the valley, it rushed along each gigantic cliff, whistling into the caves and cracks, to mount in power, to bellow a blast through the great stone bridge. Gone—as into an engulfing roar of surging waters—it seemed to shoot back, and begin all over again. (Source: *RIDERS OF THE PURPLE SAGE* by Zane Grey)

SOUND: WIND: The night wind sighed through the aspens, soughed in the pines, and roared low up on the mountain slope. (Source: *SUNSET PASS* by Zane Grey)

SOUND: WIND: The tips of the cottonwood and the oaks waved to the east, and the rings of aspens along the terraces twinkled their myriad of bright faces in fleet and glancing gleam. A low roar rose from the leaves of the forest, and the spruces swished in the rising wind. It came in gusts, with light breezes between. As it increased in strength, the hills shortened in length till there was a strong and steady blow, all the time, and violent puffs at intervals, and sudden whirling currents. The clouds spread over the valley, rolling swiftly, and low, and twilight faded into a sweeping darkness. Then the singing of the wind in the caves drowned the soft roar of rustling leaves; the song swelled to a mourning, moaning wail, then with the gathering power of the wind the wail changed to a shriek. Steadily the wind strengthened and constantly the sound changed. (Source: *RIDERS OF THE PURPLE SAGE* by Zane Grey)

SOUND: WIND: Then they [birds] ceased, and the rustle of leaves and the murmur of water hushed in a growing sound that he fancied were not of earth. Neither had he a name for this, only it was inexpressibly wild and sweet. The thought came that it might be a moan of the girl in her last outcry of life, and he felt a tremor shake him. But no! This sound was not human, although it was like despair. Then the sound swelled with the strengthening of the breeze, and he realized it was the singing of the wind in the cliffs. (Source: *RIDERS OF THE PURPLE SAGE* by Zane Grey)

(end Sound section)

Taste

TASTE: the dust tasted sweet. (Source: *SUNSET PASS* by Zane Grey)

Train

TRAIN: The dusty overland train pulled into Wagon-tongue about noon of a sultry June day. The dead station appeared slow in coming to life. Mexicans lounging in the shade of the platform did not move. (Source: *SUNSET PASS* by Zane Grey)

Tree (7)

TREE: ASPEN: Scattered here and there upon this shelf were clumps of aspens, and he walked through them into a glade that surpassed, in beauty and adaptability for a wild home, any place he had ever seen. (Source: *RIDERS OF THE PURPLE SAGE* by Zane Grey)

TREE: CEDAR: The trees were farther up than he had estimated, although he had from long habit made allowance for the deceiving nature of distances in this country. When he gained the cover of cedars, he paused to rest and look, and it was then he saw how the trees sprang from holes in the bare rock. Ages of rain had run down the slope, circling, eddying in depressions, wearing deep, round holes. There had been dry seasons, accumulations of dust, wind-blown seeds, and cedars rose wonderfully out of solid rock. But these were not beautiful cedars. They were gnarled, twisted into weird contortions, as if growth were torture, dead at the tops, shrunken, gray, and old. Theirs had been a bitter fight. This country was hard on trees—and men. (Source: *RIDERS OF THE PURPLE SAGE* by Zane Grey)

TREE: CEDAR: The weird cedars, like great demons and witches chained to the rock and writhing in silent anguish, loomed up with wide and twisting, naked arms. (Source: *RIDERS OF THE PURPLE SAGE* by Zane Grey)

TREE: LEAVES: The leaves of the cottonwoods drooped, as if they had foretold the doom of Withersteen House, and were now ready to die and drop and decay. Never had Jane seen such shade. (Source: *RIDERS OF THE PURPLE SAGE* by Zane Grey)

TREE: SPRUCE: Silver spruces bordered the base of a precipitous wall that rose loftily. (Source: *RIDERS OF THE PURPLE SAGE* by Zane Grey)

TREE: gray-sheathed [cedar] trees [were] fragrant. With their massed green foliage and grotesque dead branches—[they] seemed as much a part of a cowboy's life as grass or rocks or cactus. (Source: *WEST OF THE PECOS* by Zane Grey)

TREE: Piñon pines clustered in little clumps along the level floor of the pass. (Source: *RIDERS OF THE PURPLE SAGE* by Zane Grey)

Water

WATER: The water that flowed along the path at her feet and turned into each cottage yard to nourish garden and orchard, also was hers, no less her private property because she chose to give it freely.. (Source: *RIDERS OF THE PURPLE SAGE* by Zane Grey)

WEATHER

Weather - Afternoon

WEATHER: AFTERNOON: When they got back to camp, the afternoon was closing, and it was exceedingly sultry. Not a breath of air stirred the aspen leaves, and, when these did not quiver, the air was, indeed, still. The dark purple clouds moved almost imperceptibly out of the west. (Source: *RIDERS OF THE PURPLE SAGE* by Zane Grey)

Weather - Cloudy

WEATHER: CLOUDY: Each morning white clouds peeper up over the eastern gateway of the Pass, and then from all around they appeared to climb toward the zenith, gloriously white against the deep blue sky, swelling, darkening, mushrooming. But they had not yet brought the welcome rain. (Source: *SUNSET PASS* by Zane Grey)

Weather - Cold

WEATHER: COLD: A white frost glistened on the grass, ice had formed in the pans; the meat they had hung up was frozen stiff. (Source: *SUNSET PASS* by Zane Grey)

Weather - Dark

THING: WEATHER: DARK: Darkness was coming on and he welcomed it. Stars were blinking when he reached .... (Source: *RIDERS OF THE PURPLE SAGE* by Zane Grey)

Weather - Dawn

WEATHER: DAWN: Day had broken. It was a morning with good visibility, but no indication of sunshine. It was still too early for sunrise, though by this time there should have been a ruddy glow on the horizon. But the east was still black. (Source: *WEST OF THE PECOS* by Zane Grey)

Weather – Daylight (3)

WEATHER: DAYLIGHT: Broad daylight and a hint of sunshine high on the cliff rim to the west bought him to consideration of what he had better do. It would not be wise for him to remain long in his present hiding place. He had better make a move at once. (Source: *RIDERS OF THE PURPLE SAGE* by Zane Grey)

WEATHER: DAYLIGHT: The day at hand resembled many days gone before. (Source: *RIDERS OF THE PURPLE SAGE* by Zane Grey)

WEATHER: DAYLIGHT: The day broke beautifully to the melody of a mockingbird in the mesquite. (Source: *WEST OF THE PECOS* by Zane Grey)

Weather – Dusk (2)

WEATHER: DUSK: Dusk shaded the grove where she walked; the birds ceased singing; the wind sighed through the leaves of the cottonwoods, and the running water murmured down its stone-bedded channel. (Source: *RIDERS OF THE PURPLE SAGE* by Zane Grey)

WEATHER: DUSK: The sun sank and the long shadows lengthened down the slope. Moving veils of purple twilight crept out of the hollows and, mustering and forming on the levels, soon merged and shaded into night. (Source: *RIDERS OF THE PURPLE SAGE* by Zane Grey)

Weather - General

WEATHER: The weather stayed fine, cold at night, stinging at dawn, warm at midday. (Source: *WEST OF THE PECOS* by Zane

Weather – Moonlight (2)

WEATHER: MOONLIGHT: Across the canyon the moonlit line had grown to a broad white band creeping down, imperceptibly diminishing the darkness below. (Source: *WEST OF THE PECOS* by Zane Grey)

WEATHER: MOONLIGHT: The moon had long since topped the rim and had just then come out from behind the corner of the cabin, to shine in its silver radiance upon her. (Source: *WEST OF THE PECOS* by Zane Grey)

Weather – Morning (5)

WEATHER: MORNING: Gold and red ripples were on the river, under a gentle wind. Ducks ere winging flight upstream and cattle spotted the green banks. (Source: *WEST OF THE PECOS* by Zane Grey)

WEATHER: MORNING: In the morning when he descended the trail, he found the sun was pouring a golden stream of light through the arch of the great stone bridge. Surprise Valley, like a valley of dreams, lay mystically soft and beautiful, awakening to the golden flood that was rolling away its slumberous bands of mist, brightening the walled faces. (Source: *RIDERS OF THE PURPLE SAGE* by Zane Grey)

WEATHER: MORNING: The rosy sunrise found them on their way, headed toward the purple horizon. (Source: *WEST OF THE PECOS* by Zane Grey)

WEATHER: MORNING: Venters awakened from sleep, and his eyes opened wide upon the glorious, golden shaft of sunlight shining through the great stone bridge. The circle of cliffs surrounding the valley lay shrouded in morning mist, a dim blue, low down along the terraces, a creamy, moving cloud along the ramparts. The oak forest in the center was a plumed and tufted oval of gold. (Source: *RIDERS OF THE PURPLE SAGE* by Zane Grey)

WEATHER: MORNING: When his eyes unclosed, day had come again, and he saw the rim of the opposite wall tipped with the gold of sunrise. (Source: *RIDERS OF THE PURPLE SAGE* by Zane Grey)

Weather - Night (26)

WEATHER: NIGHT: A bright line tipped the opposite canyon rim. The moon was rising. (Source: *WEST OF THE PECOS* by Zane Grey)

WEATHER: NIGHT: a mellow warm summer night, with hum of insects and croak of frogs, and the melancholy music a cowboy found inseparable from his lonely vigil—the staccato cry of coyotes. (Source: *WEST OF THE PECOS* by Zane Grey)

WEATHER: NIGHT: Above the bold rim [of the canyon] blinked white stars, cold and austere in their message to him. (Source: *WEST OF THE PECOS* by Zane Grey)

WEATHER: NIGHT: It was a solemn black night, full of weird voices of the storm, fraught with the menace of the wild range. (Source: *WEST OF THE PECOS* by Zane Grey)

WEATHER: NIGHT: It was not going to be very dark, at least early in the evening, for a half-moon soared out from under the white fleecy clouds. (Source: *SUNSET PASS* by Zane Grey)

WEATHER: NIGHT: Night came on, swift as the fleet racers [horses], and stars peeped out to brighten and grow, and the huge, windy, eastern heave of sage paled under a rising moon and turned to silver. Blanched in moonlight the sage yet seemed to hold its line of purple and was infinitely more wild and lonely. So the night hours wore on. (Source: *RIDERS OF THE PURPLE SAGE* by Zane Grey)

WEATHER: NIGHT: Outside there were spaces of silver moonlight, and then streaks and bars of black shadow across the light. The night wind breathed in the huge spreading mass of foliage overhead. How supernaturally beautiful was the moment. (Source: *SUNSET PASS* by Zane Grey)

WEATHER: NIGHT: Suddenly the moon slipped up over the black rim above, and magically the darkness lightened. A silver radiance touched her hair and face. The night wind, sweet and balmy, was moving up from the Pass, roaring low in the tree-tops.. (Source: *SUNSET PASS* by Zane Grey)

WEATHER: NIGHT: Sunset and twilight gave way to night, and the canyon bird whistled his melancholy notes, and the wind sang softly in the cliffs, and the campfire blazed and burned down to red embers. (Source: *RIDERS OF THE PURPLE SAGE* by Zane Grey)

WEATHER: NIGHT: The early night blackness cleared to cold starlight. Hours passed. The white stars moved across the narrow strip of dark blue sky above. The after part of the night wore on interminably. The starlight failed and the gloom blackened to the darkest hour. (Source: *RIDERS OF THE PURPLE SAGE* by Zane Grey)

WEATHER: NIGHT: The first early blackness of night passed with the brightness of the stars. (Source: *RIDERS OF THE PURPLE SAGE* by Zane Grey)

WEATHER: NIGHT: The glimmer of the first star was like the peace and beauty of the night. Her faith welled up in her heart and said that all would soon be right in her little world. (Source: *RIDERS OF THE PURPLE SAGE* by Zane Grey)

WEATHER: NIGHT: The moon appeared long in rising and it came at last rising as silver radiance over the rim. (Source: *SUNSET PASS* by Zane Grey)

WEATHER: NIGHT: The moon roared white and grand above the pines and he night wind roared.. (Source: *SUNSET PASS* by Zane Grey)

WEATHER: NIGHT: The moon shone brighter as the clouds grew more open. There were moments of pale gloom, then a long interval of silver light. (Source: *SUNSET PASS* by Zane Grey)

WEATHER: NIGHT: The moon tipped the pines above the rim of the Pass, which was late in the early morning hours. (Source: *SUNSET PASS* by Zane Grey)

WEATHER: NIGHT: The night darkened, the air cooled, the camp fire flickered out. Rock crawled into his blankets under the widespread cedar. The soft feel of wool, the hard ground, the smell of cedar, the twinkle of a star through the branches, the moan of a rising night wind., the lonesome coyote bark, and the silence—how good they were and how they recalled other days!. (Source: *WEST OF THE PECOS* by Zane Grey)

WEATHER: NIGHT: The night threatened to be stormy. The stillness gave place to a moaning of the wind, and thunder rumbled nearer. The wind moaning overhead was like a knell. Drops of rain pattered on his bare head. The lightning flared brighter, showing the black mountains and the pass leading up to them. The weird flashes of lightning along the battlements of the horizon fitted the melancholy sound. (Source: *SUNSET PASS* by Zane Grey)

WEATHER: NIGHT: The night was exquisite, clear and cold, with blue velvet sky lighted by trains of stars, white sparks of fire across the zenith. (Source: *SUNSET PASS* by Zane Grey)

WEATHER: NIGHT: The night was pleasant, the wind was at its old task in the tree-tops, the frogs along the creek were croaking drowsily of midsummer. The dark Pass, obscure and dreaming, seemed pregnant with life... (Source: *SUNSET PASS* by Zane Grey)

WEATHER: NIGHT: The night was starry, almost cool, and the wind moved through the tree-tops. (Source: *SUNSET PASS* by Zane Grey)

WEATHER: NIGHT: The rest of that night seemed to Venters only a few moments of starlight, a dark overcasting of sky, an hour or so of grey gloom, and then the lighting of dawn. When he had bestirred himself ... it was clear daylight, although the sun had not tipped he yellow [canyon] wall in the east. (Source: *RIDERS OF THE PURPLE SAGE* by Zane Grey)

WEATHER: NIGHT: The sky darkened and stars began to show, at first pale and then bright. Sharp notches of the canyon rim wall [were] biting like teeth into the blue.. (Source: *RIDERS OF THE PURPLE SAGE* by Zane Grey)

WEATHER: NIGHT: The stars shone white and watchful through the foliage. (Source: *SUNSET PASS* by Zane Grey)

WEATHER: NIGHT: Then with the wind soon came a shade and a darkening, and suddenly he valley was gray. Night came there quickly after the sinking of the sun. (Source: *RIDERS OF THE PURPLE SAGE* by Zane Grey)

WEATHER: NIGHT: Twilight stole from some invisible source, and night followed, a mellow warm summer night, with hum of insects and croak of frogs, and the melancholy music a cowboy found inseparable from his lonely vigil—the staccato cry of coyotes. (Source: *WEST OF THE PECOS* by Zane Grey)

Weather - Rain (6)

WEATHER: RAIN: It rained every day, mostly summer showers, with rainbows bent from cloud to forest. The dry dusty brush grew green with renewed life; the pines and oaks were washed clean; the streams sang bank-full of amber water; the aspens began to take on a tinge of gold. (Source: *SUNSET PASS* by Zane Grey)

WEATHER: RAIN: Late in the afternoon he encountered the first rain of the summer. It was only a shower, and while the glistening drops pattered down, the sun continued to shine behind him. To the east, over the desert, a low far-spreading vivid rainbow stood out against a background of purple cloud. Soon the shower passed on. (Source: *SUNSET PASS* by Zane Grey)

WEATHER: RAIN: The following day [was] warm and muggy—threatening rain. (Source: *RIDERS OF THE PURPLE SAGE* by Zane Grey)

WEATHER: RAIN: The white clouds sailed up back of the rims to fill the blue vault above, and to thicken and change and darken, until a heavy black one would come trailing veils of rain across the ranch. (Source: *WEST OF THE PECOS* by Zane Grey)

WEATHER: RAIN: The white clouds sailed up back of the rims to fill the blue vault above, and to thicken and change and darken, until a heavy black one would come along trailing veils of rain across the ranch. (Source: *WEST OF THE PECOS* by Zane Grey)

WEATHER: RAIN: Toward the end of August the drought was broken by occasional rainstorms, most welcome to him. Even the well-watered canyon had begun to grow dusty and gray. But the rains worked magic. (Source: *WEST OF THE PECOS* by Zane Grey)

Weather - Sky

WEATHER: SKY: It was min-afternoon. The clouds had broken somewhat and already there were tinges of god and purple against the blue sky. (Source: *WEST OF THE PECOS* by Zane Grey)

Weather - Storm (24)

WEATHER: STORM: "Bess, I haven't seen that since last summer. Look," said Venters, pointing to the scalloped edge of rolling, purple clouds that peeped over the western wall. "We're in for a storm." (Source: *RIDERS OF THE PURPLE SAGE* by Zane Grey)

WEATHER: STORM: "Maybe I have a lot to learn, Bess. I'll lose my guess if this storm isn't bad enough. We're going to have heavy wind first ... then lightning and thunder, then the rain." (Source: *RIDERS OF THE PURPLE SAGE* by Zane Grey)

WEATHER: STORM: "We've had big black clouds before this without rain," said Venters. "But there's no doubt about that thunder. The storms are coming. I'm glad. Every rider on the sage will hear that thunder with glad ears.". (Source: *RIDERS OF THE PURPLE SAGE* by Zane Grey)

WEATHER: STORM: A blinding flash of lightning illumined the cave and all about him. He saw Bess's face, white now with dark, frightened eyes. He saw the dogs leap up, and he followed suit. The golden glare vanished—all was black—then came the splitting crack and the internal din of echoes.. (Source: *RIDERS OF THE PURPLE SAGE* by Zane Grey)

WEATHER: STORM: A driving pall of rain, black as the clouds, came sweeping on to obscure the bridge, and the gleaming walls, and the shining valley. The lightning played incessantly, streaking down through opaque darkness of rain. The roar of the wind, with its strange knell, and the re-crashing echoes mingled with the roar of the flooding rain—and all seemingly were deadened and drowned in a world of sound. (Source: *RIDERS OF THE PURPLE SAGE* by Zane Grey)

WEATHER: STORM: A norther was blowing, the first of the season, and the wind moaned up on the rims. Drab clouds scudded low toward the south and scattering rain pattered on the cabin roof. (Source: *WEST OF THE PECOS* by Zane Grey)

WEATHER: STORM: A wave, a ripple of light, a trembling and turning of the aspen leaves, like the approach of a breeze on the water, crossed the valley from the west, and the hill, and the deadly stillness, and the sultry air, passed away as a cool wind. The night bird of the canyon with his clear and melancholy notes announced the twilight, and from all along the cliffs rose the faint murmur and moan and mourn of the wind singing in the caves. (Source: *RIDERS OF THE PURPLE SAGE* by Zane Grey)

WEATHER: STORM: Bess shrank closer to him, and closer, found his hands and pressed them tightly over her ears, and dropped her face upon his shoulder, and hid her eyes. (Source: *RIDERS OF THE PURPLE SAGE* by Zane Grey)

WEATHER: STORM: Black night enfolded the valley. Venters could not see his companion, and knew of her presence only through the tightening hold of her hand on his arm. He felt the dogs huddle closer to him. Suddenly, the dense black vault overhead split [apart] to a blue-white, dazzling streak of lightning. The whole valley lay vividly clear and luminously bright in his sight. [Appearing] vast and magnificent, the stone bridge glimmered like some grand god of storm in the lightning's fire. Then all flashed black again—blacker than pitch—a thick, impenetrable, coal blackness. There came a ripping, cracking report. Instantly an echo resounded with clapping crash. The initial report was nothing to the echo. It was a terrible, living, reverberating, detonating crash. The walls threw the sound across and could have made no greater roar if it had slipped in avalanche. From cliff to cliff the echo went in crashing retort, and banged in lessening power, and boomed in thinner volume, and clapped weaker and weaker till a final clap could not reach across to waiting cliff. (Source: *RIDERS OF THE PURPLE SAGE* by Zane Grey)

WEATHER: STORM: Day after day the west wind blew across the valley. Day after day the clouds clustered gray and purple and black. The cliffs sang and the caves rang, and the lightning flashed, the thunder rolled, the echoes crashed and crashed, and the rains flooded the valley. (Source: *RIDERS OF THE PURPLE SAGE* by Zane Grey)

WEATHER: STORM: It was only wind, thought Venters. Here sped and shrieked the sculptor that carved out the wonderful caves in the cliffs. It was only a gale, but as Venters listened, as his ears became accustomed to the fury and strife, out o it all, or through it or above it, pealed low and perfectly clear and persistently uniform a strange sound that had no counterpart in all the sounds of the elements. It was not of earth or life. It was the grief and agony of the gale. [It was] a knell to all upon whom it blew. (Source: *RIDERS OF THE PURPLE SAGE* by Zane Grey)

WEATHER: STORM: The bank of clouds now swept hugely out of the western sky. Its front was purple and black with gray between, a bulging, mushrooming, vast thing instinct with storm. It had a dark, angry, threatening aspect. As if all the power of the winds were pushing and piling behind, it rolled ponderously across the sky.

A red flare burned out instantaneously, flashed from west to east, and died. Then from the deepest black of the purple cloud burst a boom. It was like the bowling of a huge boulder along the crags and ramparts, and seemed to roll on and fall into the valley to bound and bang and boom from cliff to cliff. (Source: *RIDERS OF THE PURPLE SAGE* by Zane Grey)

WEATHER: STORM: The dark spruces were tipped with glimmering lights; the aspens bent low in the winds; as waves in a tempest at sea the forest of oaks tossed wildly and shone with gleams of fire. Across the valley the huge cavern of the cliff-dwellers yawned in the glare, every little black window as clear as at noonday, but the night and the storm added to their tragedy. Flung arching to the black clouds, the great stone bridge seemed to bear the brunt of the storm. It caught the full fury of the rushing wind. It lifted its noble crown to meet the lightning. (Source: *RIDERS OF THE PURPLE SAGE* by Zane Grey)

WEATHER: STORM: The gale swooped down with a hollow, unearthly howl. It yelled and pealed and shrilled and shrieked. It was made up of a thousand piercing cries. It was a rising and a moving sound. Beginning at the western break of the valley, it rushed along each gigantic cliff, whistling into the caves and cracks, to mount in power, to bellow a blast through the great stone bridge. Gone—as into an engulfing roar of surging waters—it seemed to shoot back, and begin all over again. (Source: *RIDERS OF THE PURPLE SAGE* by Zane Grey)

WEATHER: STORM: The last bit of blue sky yielded to the on sweep of clouds. Like angry surf the pale gleams of gray amid the purple of that scudding front swept beyond the eastern rampart of the valley. The purple deepened to black. Broad sheets of lightning flared over the western wall. There were not yet any ropes or zigzag streaks darting down through the gathering darkness. The storm center was still beyond Surprise Valley. (Source: *RIDERS OF THE PURPLE SAGE* by Zane Grey)

WEATHER: STORM: The next day the norther blew out of a clear sky, and the sheltered sunny spots in the canyon were the desirable ones. (Source: *WEST OF THE PECOS* by Zane Grey)

WEATHER: STORM: The norther was a familiar thing, and she hated it, especially at night, when the conformation of the canyon and the structure of the cabin made sounding boards for the gale. It moaned and shrieked and roared by turns. After a while, however, this sound ceased and the cabin was silent. The next day, the norther blew out of a clear sky, and the sheltered sunny spots in the canyon were the desirable ones. (Source: *WEST OF THE PECOS* by Zane Grey)

WEATHER: STORM: The purple cloud bank darkened the lower edge of the setting sun, crept up and up, obscuring its fiery red heart, and finally passed over the last ruddy crescent of its upper rim. The intense, dead silence awakened to a long, low rumbling of thunder. (Source: *RIDERS OF THE PURPLE SAGE* by Zane Grey)

WEATHER: STORM: The tips of the cottonwood and the oaks waved to the east, and the rings of aspens along the terraces twinkled their myriad of bright faces in fleet and glancing gleam. A low roar rose from the leaves of the forest, and the spruces swished in the rising wind. It came in gusts, with light breezes between. As it increased in strength, the hills shortened in length till there was a strong and steady blow all the time, and violent puffs at intervals, and sudden whirling currents. The clouds spread over the valley, rolling swiftly and low, and twilight faded into a sweeping darkness. Then the singing of the wind in the caves drowned the soft roar of rustling leaves; the song swelled to a mourning, moaning wail, then with the gathering power of the wind the wail changed to a shriek. Steadily the wind strengthened and constantly the sound changed. (Source: *RIDERS OF THE PURPLE SAGE* by Zane Grey)

WEATHER: STORM: Then the storm burst with a succession of ropes and streaks and shafts of lightning, playing continuously, filling the valley with a broken radiance, and the cracking shots followed each other swiftly till the echoes blended in one fearful, deepening crash. (Source: *RIDERS OF THE PURPLE SAGE* by Zane Grey)

WEATHER: STORM: Venters and Bess faced the open terrace, the valley, and the west to watch and await the approaching storm. It required keen vision to see any movement whatever in the purple clouds. By infinitesimal degrees the dark cloud line merged upward into the golden red haze of the afterglow of sunset. A shadow lengthened from under the western wall across the valley. As straight and rigid as steel rose the delicate, spear-pointed silver spruces; the aspen leaves, by nature pendant and quivering, hung, limp and heavy, no slender, leaning blade of grass moved. A gentle splashing of water came from the ravine. Then from out of the west [came] the low, dull, and rumbling roll of thunder. (Source: *RIDERS OF THE PURPLE SAGE* by Zane Grey)

WEATHER: STORM: Venters looked out upon the beautiful valley—beautiful now as never before—mystic in its transparent, luminous gloom—weird in the quivering, golden haze of lightning. (Source: *RIDERS OF THE PURPLE SAGE* by Zane Grey)

WEATHER: STORM: When he reached the summit, the sky had become overcast with heavy white and black clouds, darkening the day. (Source: *SUNSET PASS* by Zane Grey)

WEATHER: STORM: Wild thunderstorms sparked lightning bolts that arced across the skies and spit out hail the size of a nickel. (Source: Author)

Weather - Sunrise (6)

WEATHER: SUNRISE: ... the morning sun burst wondrously through a grand arch into this valley, in a golden, slanting shaft. (Source: *RIDERS OF THE PURPLE SAGE* by Zane Grey)

WEATHER: SUNRISE: The glorious sunlight filled the valley with purple fire. (Source: *RIDERS OF THE PURPLE SAGE* by Zane Grey)

WEATHER: SUNRISE: The rosy sunrise found them on their way, headed toward the purple horizon. (Source: *WEST OF THE PECOS* by Zane Grey)

WEATHER: SUNRISE: The sun was crossing the gap far down the river and the Rio Pecos appeared a path of glory. (Source: *WEST OF THE PECOS* by Zane Grey)

WEATHER: SUNRISE: They were stirring long before the red burst of sun glorified the eastern wall. (Source: *WEST OF THE PECOS* by Zane Grey)

WEATHER: SUNRISE: Venters turned out of the gorge and suddenly paused stock still, astounded at the scene before him. The curve of the great stone bridge had caught the sunrise, and through the magnificent arch burst a glorious stream of gold that shone with a long slant down into the center of Surprise Valley. Only through the arch did any sunlight pass, so that all the rest of the valley lay still asleep, dark green, mysterious, shadowy, merging its level into walls as misty and soft as morning clouds. (Source: *RIDERS OF THE PURPLE SAGE* by Zane Grey)

Weather – Sunset (19)

WEATHER: SUNSET: After sunset, sky and cloud and valley were illumined by a golden ethereal light. (Source: *WEST OF THE PECOS* by Zane Grey)

WEATHER: SUNSET: It was the moment when the last ruddy rays of the sunset brightened momentarily before yielding to twilight. (Source: *RIDERS OF THE PURPLE SAGE* by Zane Grey)

WEATHER: SUNSET: Late in the afternoon, the ruddy sun split its last flame on the ragged notch of the western wall. (Source: *RIDERS OF THE PURPLE SAGE* by Zane Grey)

WEATHER: SUNSET: Slumbering, fading purple fire burned [as the sun set] over the undulating sage ridges. Long streaks and bars and shafts and spears fringed the far western slope. Drifting golden veils mingled with low, purple shadows. Colors and shades changed in slow, wondrous transformation. (Source: *RIDERS OF THE PURPLE SAGE* by Zane Grey)

WEATHER: SUNSET: Sunset came, bringing with the end of her labor a patient calmness and power to wait that had not been here earlier in the day. (Source: *RIDERS OF THE PURPLE SAGE* by Zane Grey)

WEATHER: SUNSET: The brook was a ruddy streak of sunset fire. The group lined up on the rim to watch the sunset. And just at that moment a flare of gold deepened on the bold face of wall across the river, to reflect its wondrous warmth back into the canyon. Low down the purple veils appeared to intensify and show caverns and gilded foliage through their magic transparency. From the cracked and cragged rim of the opposite canyon wall down over the seamed face and the green-choked crevices shone the mystic light, down the grassy, boulder-strewn slope to the second wall, and then sheer down this cracked and creviced form to the shining foliage, and the gold-fired flags and rushes that fringed the blazing brook. (Source: *WEST OF THE PECOS* by Zane Grey)

WEATHER: SUNSET: The first indication that time was flying appeared to be a darkening of the light. The sun had gone behind the western wall, and the day three-fourths spent. (Source: *WEST OF THE PECOS* by Zane Grey)

WEATHER: SUNSET: The last gleam of the afterglow faded off the river. Shadowy rifts of blackness marked the brakes of the river, in their successive and disappearing notches. Night fell upon the lonely land. A low murmur of running water soared upward. The air grew chilly. Wind rustled the brush. And a crescent moon peeped over the dark bold canyon rim. The river flowed on, melancholy and austere, true to its task, unmindful of the little lives and loves of men. (Source: *WEST OF THE PECOS* by Zane Grey)

WEATHER: SUNSET: The last rays of the setting sun sent golden bars though the leaves [of the trees]. (Source: *RIDERS OF THE PURPLE SAGE* by Zane Grey)

WEATHER: SUNSET: The pale afterglow in the west darkened with the merging of twilight into night. The sage now spread out, black and gloomy. One dim star glimmered in the southwest sky. (Source: *RIDERS OF THE PURPLE SAGE* by Zane Grey)

WEATHER: SUNSET: The sun came out dully red before setting and the barren world grew ruddy. Hen it faded under a steely twilight and black night. No stars showed. The black hills stood up against a dark sky. (Source: *WEST OF THE PECOS* by Zane Grey)

WEATHER: SUNSET: The sun set and the fire and the colors [of the canyon] changed to darkening gray. (Source: *WEST OF THE PECOS* by Zane Grey)

WEATHER: SUNSET: The sun set behind the high canyon rim, and a cool shade darkened the [canyon] walls. (Source: *RIDERS OF THE PURPLE SAGE* by Zane Grey)

WEATHER: SUNSET: The sun was setting behind him, far up over those rolling ranges, and it cast long rays of gold down across this canyon, to paint the gliding river and the huge, many-stepped wall of rock above. That wall appeared higher than any in view on this side of the river. It frowned forbiddingly, notwithstanding its front of glancing sunset hues. (Source: *WEST OF THE PECOS* by Zane Grey)

WEATHER: SUNSET: The sun was setting in the notch [of the pass], with broken clouds above, pearl and mauve and opal, with hearts of rose and edges of saffron [and] intense blue far above. (Source: *SUNSET PASS* by Zane Grey)

WEATHER: SUNSET: The sun was setting in wondrous hues. (Source: *WEST OF THE PECOS* by Zane Grey)

WEATHER: SUNSET: The wind died away; the red sun topped the far distant western rise of slope; the long, creeping, purple shadows lengthened. The rims of the canyon gleamed crimson, and the deep clefts appeared to belch forth blue smoke. Silence enfolded the scene. (Source: *RIDERS OF THE PURPLE SAGE* by Zane Grey)

WEATHER: SUNSET: Twilight was fast falling. (Source: *RIDERS OF THE PURPLE SAGE* by Zane Grey)

WEATHER: SUNSET: The sunset had changed its gold for red, so that the eastern walls [of the canyon] took on a rosy flush, while those nearer him deepened their purple. In between, shafts of light slanted down across the canyon, rendering it ethereally lovely—a garden of fertile beauty lost in all that wilderness of gloomy, dismal, barren land. (Source: *WEST OF THE PECOS* by Zane Grey)

WEATHER: SUNSET: The wind died away; the red sun topped the far distant western rise of slope; the long, creeping, purple shadows lengthened. The rims of the canyon gleamed crimson, and the deep clefts appeared to belch forth blue smoke. Silence enfolded the scene. (Source: *RIDERS OF THE PURPLE SAGE* by Zane Grey)

WEATHER: SUNSET: There was little sunset color, owing to heavy clouds. Thunder rumbled off in the hills, and as dusk fell quickly, sheets of pale lightning flared along the horizon. (Source: *SUNSET PASS* by Zane Grey)

WEATHER: SUNSET: There were fewer clouds and these hung round the distant peaks, as if anchored to the steep higher slopes. Pearl gray and sliver sheen and shell pink filled the great gap of sky. The curtains and shafts of color light created exquisite beauty, rarer, more delicate, quickly evanescent and soon gone. (Source: *SUNSET PASS* by Zane Grey)

WEATHER: SUNSET: While he ate, the sun set beyond a dip in the rim of the curved [canyon] wall. As the morning sun burst wondrously through a grand arch into this valley, in a golden, slanting shaft, the evening sun, at the moment of setting, shone through a gap of cliffs, sending down a broad, red burst to brighten the oval [canyon] with a blaze of fire. To him, both sunrise and sunset were unreal. (Source: *RIDERS OF THE PURPLE SAGE* by Zane Grey)

Weather - Sunshine (4)

WEATHER: SUNSHINE: The hot June sun pleasantly burned through his shirt sleeves; the dust tasted sweet; the wind, coming in puffs, brought the fragrant odors of the desert, spiced by a hint of sage; the hills slumbered in blue haze. (Source: *SUNSET PASS* by Zane Grey)

WEATHER: SUNSHINE: The sun hung low, directly in the center of the great V-shaped gap which appeared to split the very heart of the mountain range. And the gold was growing vivid. (Source: *WEST OF THE PECOS* by Zane Grey)

WEATHER: SUNSHINE: The sun lost its heat and wore down to the western horizon, where it changed from white to gold and rested like a huge ball about to roll on its golden shadows down the slope. (Source: *RIDERS OF THE PURPLE SAGE* by Zane Grey)

WEATHER: SUNSHINE: The sun sank. There was instant shading of brightness about him, and he saw a kind of cold purple bloom creep ahead of him to cross the canyon, to mount the opposite slope and chase and darken and bury the last golden flare of sunlight. (Source: *RIDERS OF THE PURPLE SAGE* by Zane Grey)

Weather – Twilight (6)

WEATHER: TWILIGHT: The sky was now turning from gray to blue, stars had begun to lighten the earlier blackness, and from the wide, flat sweep before him blew a cool wind, fragrant with the breath of sage. (Source: *RIDERS OF THE PURPLE SAGE* by Zane Grey)

WEATHER: TWILIGHT: Twilight began to creep out of the canyon. (Source: *WEST OF THE PECOS* by Zane Grey)

WEATHER: TWILIGHT: Twilight fell, and dusk and night. The night was interminably long. The blackness of her room seemed blacker for the sad, entering gray of morning light. (Source: *RIDERS OF THE PURPLE SAGE* by Zane Grey)

WEATHER: TWILIGHT: Twilight had already fallen in he gorge. It brightened to waning shadow in the wider ascent. He showed her Balancing Rock, of which he had often told her, and explained its sinister leaning over the outlet. Shuddering, she looked down the long, pale incline with its closed-in toppling walls. (Source: *RIDERS OF THE PURPLE SAGE* by Zane Grey)

WEATHER: TWILIGHT: Twilight had gathered under the [canyon] walls. Gradually the trees and caves and objects low down turned black, and this blackness moved up the walls till night enfolded the pass, while day still lingered above. (Source: *RIDERS OF THE PURPLE SAGE* by Zane Grey)

WEATHER: TWILIGHT: Twilight was stealing over the land when he hauled up beside the willows where Lambeth was hobbling the horses. (Source: *WEST OF THE PECOS* by Zane Grey)

Weather - Wind (10)

WEATHER: WIND: "When the wind blows a gale in the caves, it makes what the rustlers call Oldring's Knell. They believe it bodes his death. I think he believes so, too. It's not like any sound on earth. It's beginning." (Source: *RIDERS OF THE PURPLE SAGE* by Zane Grey)

WEATHER: WIND: ... the undulating surface of forest, like a rippling lake ... he heard the flutter of aspen leaves. (Source: *RIDERS OF THE PURPLE SAGE* by Zane Grey)

WEATHER: WIND: A cool wind blew across the oval [canyon], waving the tips of oaks, and, while the [sun]light lasted, fluttering the aspen leaves into millions of facets of red, an sweeping the graceful spruces.. (Source: *RIDERS OF THE PURPLE SAGE* by Zane Grey)

WEATHER: WIND: Always it [the wind] brought softly to him strange sweet tidings of far-off things. It blew from a place that was old and whispered of youth. It blew down the grooves of time. It brought a story of the passing hours. It breathed low of fighting men and praying women. It sang clearly the songs of love. That ever was the burden on its tidings,—youth in the shady woods—waders through the wet meadows—boy and girl at the hedgerow stile—bathers in the booming surf—sweet, idle hours on grassy, windy hills—long strolls down moonlit lanes—everywhere in far-off lands, fingers locked and bursting hearts and longing lips—from all the world tidings of unquenchable love. (Source: *RIDERS OF THE PURPLE SAGE* by Zane Grey)

WEATHER: WIND: As he mused, the west wind softly blew in his face. It seemed to soothe his passion. That west wind was fresh, cool, fragrant, and it carried sweet, strange burden of far off things—tidings of life in other climes—of sunshine asleep on other walls—of other places where reigned peace. It carried, too, sad truth of humble hearts and mystery of promise and hope unquenchable. (Source: *RIDERS OF THE PURPLE SAGE* by Zane Grey)

WEATHER: WIND: from high up in the carved crevices of the arch, floated down the low, strange wail of wind—a knell, indeed, for all that had gone. (Source: *RIDERS OF THE PURPLE SAGE* by Zane Grey)

WEATHER: WIND: The wind was strong in his face. It carried more than heat, and as he gained his objective point on the ridge, he both smelled and saw dust in the air. (Source: *SUNSET PASS* by Zane Grey)

WEATHER: WIND: The wind, blowing heavy, steady blast into his face, sickened him with enduring, sweet odor, and filled his ears with a hollow, rushing roar. (Source: *RIDERS OF THE PURPLE SAGE* by Zane Grey)

WEATHER: WIND: the wind, coming in putts, brought the fragrant odors of the desert, spiced by a hint of sage; the hills slumbered in blue haze. (Source: *SUNSET PASS* by Zane Grey)

WEATHER: WIND: While the west wind blew—its tidings, filling his heart full, teaching a man's part—the days passed, the purple clouds changed to white, and the storms went over for that summer. (Source: *RIDERS OF THE PURPLE SAGE* by Zane Grey)

(end Weather section)

SUMMARY

Zane Grey is one of the most descriptive writers that I found. His works are a good read for anyone interested in mental images of a story.

When I started out studying the creations of authors I enjoyed reading and considered good writers. I sought out all the best and most successful writers. Then I associated with other book readers to hear what books they found good reads. The common link between all of these was the visual images that the best writers created in the minds of readers who eagerly devoured the words that they found. Comments like, "I couldn't put it down!" gave me a clue that the author was likely very descriptive in telling their story. It turns out that these authors sold the most books and made the most income. Among the factors that make a book "a keeper" are content and descriptions of the people, places, and things that are sown together to make the book a top seller.

So who were the most descriptive writers found during this intense study? As of this writing I found these authors the best (and most popular):

Author Book Number of Descriptions Found

Zane Grey *Riders of the Purple Sage* 728

Nora Roberts *Heaven and Earth* 389

Nora Roberts *Jewels of the Sun* 287

Zane Grey *West of the Pecos* 262

John Steinbeck *The Winter of Our Discontent* 253

John Steinbeck *The Wayward Bus* 250

Bethany Campbell *Heartland* 221

John Steinbeck *The Grapes of Wrath* 204

Catherine Coulter *Reckoning* 201

Zane Grey *Sunset Pass* 197

Tom Clancy/Martin Greenberg *Power Plays Politika* 175

Charlotte Lamb *Circle of Fate* 172
Alstair MacLean *The Guns of Navarone* 172
Nora Roberts *Inheritance* 167
Jim Bishop *The Day Christ Died* 153
Tom Clancy *Patriot Games* 148
Jessica Steele *Beyond Her Control* 129
Catherine Coulter *Vortex* 124
Alstair MacLean *The Secret Ways* 111
Pearl S. Buck *The Living Reed* 98
Tom Clancy *Red Storm Rising* 92
Robert Louis Stevenson *Treasure Island* 80
Iris Johansen *Final Target* 63
Allen Chapman *The Radio Boys at Mountain Pass* 51
Dean R. Koontz *Strangers* 37
J.D. Robb *Devoted in Death* 36
C.S. Forester *The Sky and the Forest* 34

The average count is 179, so any book containing more than this number can be considered a better source of descriptive expressions.

I still have other books that I want to read and digest. But the authors listed above are the writers and their works that you may want to consider reading.

My team and I will continue to look for and capture terms, phrases, and expressions that stimulate the right side of your brain so creative writing can flourish. Adopt, adapt, and write your own content. Give yourself permission to be creative. You'll be glad you did.

You are the critical link to creating a better society. You can train your mind to become more creative. Try expressive writing by recording your deepest thoughts in short sessions. Conduct learning exercises by mentally creating the best description you can of things you see. Looking at the world outside, imagine how you can describe scenes so vividly that they help your mind see what you saw. As a side benefit, through this process you'll relieve stress and boost your own health. And you'll create some of the finest teaching sessions that will surprise even you.

You have an awesome responsibility and you need the best tools available to help you succeed. This book is one of those valuable tools. It was created after years of research and dedicated effort. It's been designed to stimulate the mind and make learning interesting and enjoyable.

Seek successful authors who write content in the same genre as your interest. Here are genre and authors to consider:

Action thrillers - Alstair MacLean

Adventure fiction - Alstair MacLean, Robert Louis Stevenson

Adventure stories for kids - Allen Chapman (Edward Stratemeyer)

Crime fiction - C.S. Forester, Iris Johansen

Espionage - Tom Clancy

Exotic settings - Alstair MacLean

Fantasy - Dean R. Koontz

Futuristic science fiction - J.D. Robb

Gothic romance - Dean R. Koontz

Historical adventure - Robert Louis Stevenson

Historical romance - Robert Louis Stevenson, Catherine Coulter, Barbara Cartland

Horror fiction - Dean R. Koontz

Hot macho action - Alstair MacLean

Military adventure - Tom Clancy

Multigenerational epics - John Steinbeck

Mystery - Dean R. Koontz

Natural history - John Steinbeck

Naval warfare - C.S. Forester

Novels about common people during Great Depression - John Steinbeck

Police procedurals, crime solutions - J.D. Robb

Political issues- Pearl S. Buck

Racial equality- Pearl S. Buck

Romance fiction - Iris Johansen, Catherine Coulter, Nora Roberts

Romantic suspense - Nora Roberts

Romantic suspense thrillers - Catherine Coulter

Satire - Dean R. Koontz

Science fiction - Dean R. Koontz

Social issues - John Steinbeck, Pearl S. Buck

Suspense fiction - Iris Johansen

Suspense thrillers - Dean R. Koontz

Travelogues - John Steinbeck

Wartime commando sagas - Alstair MacLean

Western adventure – Zane Grey

Women's rights- Pearl S. Buck

You have an awesome opportunity with descriptive writing and you need the best tools available to help you succeed. This book is one of those valuable tools. It was created after much research and dedicated effort. It's been designed to stimulate your mind and make your output more interesting, more profitable and more enjoyable.

This book is the perfect counter to AI-generated text. Your mind can be far more creative than an AI algorithm.

Just remember: DON'T PLAGARIZE. ADOPT AND ADAPT; Do your own work! Keep our profession professional!

Plan of Action

Here's what you can do about all of this.

1. Read the works of the best and most successful authors.
2. Read the descriptive expressions books that we're creating.
3. Study their descriptive expressions to learn how they use words to convey their message.

4. Let the writing style of these authors bubble up to the surface. Recognize and use what you find.
5. Note how they express their strategies for success.
6. Then adopt the style of your choice and create your own form of descriptive writing.

As you do so, you will become far more successful an author (or speaker) than you ever imagined. Go for it! A descriptive and profitable future lies ahead. Good writing!

ABOUT ROBERT BRENNER

Robert Brenner is an engineer, consultant, college professor, and teacher with extensive experience in research and information publishing.

A retired Navy mustang (enlisted then officer) with 11 submarine deployments under his belt, he holds a bachelor's degree in electrical engineering (BSEE) from the University of New Mexico, a master's degree in electrical engineering (MSEE) from the Naval Postgraduate School, and a master's degree in systems management (MSEE) from the University of Southern California.

He was designated a Very High Speed Integrated Circuit (VHSIC) microelectronics pioneer by the DOD and served in defense R&D before dedicating his energies to researching and writing books full time.

His whole world changed when he attended a three-day seminar on right brain thinking developed by Buckminster Fuller, the father of the geodesic dome. Ideas began to pour out of his mind. Shortly after the experience, he formed several companies and began writing in earnest. He proposed a series of computer troubleshooting books to Howard W. Sams and was soon in a seven-book contract. When the company was bought out, he began writing and publishing his own books, focusing on technology, the supernatural, and creative writing.

He began researching descriptive language 10 years ago when he made a commitment to improve his writing style. He collected all the words, phrases, and expressions he could find in an earnest effort to make his content come alive for himself and for other writers. He identified and studied the most successful authors including John Steinbeck, Jack London, Nora Roberts, Pearl S. Buck, C.S. Forrester, Tom Clancy, Dean Koontz, J.D. Robb, Alstair Maclean, C.S. Lewis,

Catherine Coulter and Iris Johansen, and then he created tools to help other authors achieve writing that amazes even them.

He has been a guest speaker at national conferences and symposiums and is the author of over 60 books including *Descriptive Language for Writers and Speakers, The Descriptive Expressions of Nora Roberts, Power Up! The Smart Guide to Home Solar Power, Going Solar: A Homeowner's Experience,; Solar Case Study: 5.0 kW Home Power Generator, Supernatural & Strange Happenings in the Bible, Bartering Basics* and *Bigfoot Encounters in Michigan's Thumb.*

He also wrote over 275 articles on business and computer applications. And he taught at the high school, community college, university, and graduate school levels. A futurist, he enjoys the challenge of research and is currently sharing his knowledge with professionals and home owners worldwide.

The author can be reached by email at rcbwrites@gmail.com

OTHER BOOKS BY ROBERT C. BRENNER

Bartering Basics: How to Trade for Food, Products, and Services

Bigfoot Encounters in Michigan's Thumb

Descriptive Language: A Guide to Creating Visual Images for Your Writing and Speaking

Descriptive Language for Writers and Speakers

Michigan Bigfoot Encounters (Upper Peninsula)

Pricing Tables - (9 national regions, multiple editions)

Pricing Tactics

Pricing Web Services

Power Up! The Smart Guide to Home Solar Power

Small Business Guide to Pricing

Solar Case Study: 5.0 kW Home Power Generator

Solar Case Study: 6.4 kW Home Power Generator

Solar Case Study: 7.4 kW Home Power Generator

Solar Power: How to Construct (and Use) the 45W Harbor Freight Solar Kit

Special Report: Scoping Services

Special Report: Software Services

Special Report: Virtual Services

Supernatural and Strange Happenings in the Bible

Supernatural and Strange Happenings in the Family

Survive a Power Outage: Emergency Lighting

The Descriptive Expressions of Nora Roberts

The Descriptive Expressions of John Steinbeck

Writer's Guide to Descriptive Language

COMING BOOKS

The Descriptive Expressions of Catherine Coulter

The Descriptive Expressions of Tom Clancy

Thank you for reading this book. If you enjoyed it, please take a moment to leave a review at your favorite retailer or library.

Don't miss out!

Visit the website below and you can sign up to receive emails whenever BrennerBooks publishes a new book. There's no charge and no obligation.

https://books2read.com/r/B-A-QUMKB-ESJNH

BOOKS 2 READ

Connecting independent readers to independent writers.

Also by BrennerBooks

Solar Case Study: 5.0 kW Home Power Generator
Solar Case Study: 6.4 kW Home Power Generator
Solar Case Study: 7.4 kW Home Power Generator
Survive a Power Outage: Emergency Lighting
Solar Power: How to Construct (and Use) the 45W Harbor Freight Solar Kit
Supernatural and Strange Happenings in the Family
Supernatural and Strange Happenings in the Bible: An Engineer's Study of Scripture
Descriptive Language: A Guide for Writers and Speakers: Volume 2 Places
The Descriptive Expressions of Zane Grey
Metaphors of Like: Second Edition

Watch for more at www.brennerbooks.com.

www.ingramcontent.com/pod-product-compliance
Lightning Source LLC
Chambersburg PA
CBHW022349280326
41935CB00007B/126

* 9 7 8 1 9 3 0 1 9 9 6 9 9 *